UNDERSTANDING
AMERICAN HISTORY
THROUGH FICTION

UNDERSTANDING AMERICAN HISTORY THROUGH FICTION
Volume I

Warren A. Beck

California State University-Fullerton

Myles L. Clowers

San Diego City College

McGraw-Hill Book Company

New York St Louis San Francisco Düsseldorf
Johannesburg Kuala Lumpur London Mexico Montreal New Delhi Panama
Paris São Paulo Singapore Sydney Tokyo Toronto

Library of Congress Cataloging in Publication Data

Beck, Warren A   comp.
  Understanding American history through fiction.

  1. American literature.   2.   United States—
History—Literary collections.   I.   Clowers, Myles L.,
joint comp.   II.   Title.
PS509.U52B4   813'.03   74-11266
ISBN 0-07-004217-9 (v. 1)
ISBN 0-07-004218-7 (v. 2)

UNDERSTANDING
AMERICAN HISTORY
THROUGH FICTION
Volume I

1234567890DODO7987654

This book was set in Times Roman by Compucomp Corporation.
The editors were Robert P. Rainier and Michael Weber;
the cover was designed by Anne Canevari Green;
the production supervisor was Leroy A. Young.
R. R. Donnelley & Sons Company was printer and binder.

Contents

Preface

In their constant effort to interpret the past, historians have used every possible tool from documents to computers to carbon dating. Among the oldest tools they have used are works of creative literature. From the time man first spun tales of valor around the campfire in his cave, creative stories have been indispensable in capturing the spirit of an age. Whether such writing was a Homeric saga glorifying the deeds of heroic Greeks, a song of the troubadors of the Middle Ages, a Shakespearean historical drama, or a novel of the American Revolution, creative literature has aided historians in their efforts to recapture the mood and spirit of times far removed from their own.

America's heritage has been especially enriched by numerous outstanding works of historical fiction. No historian has aroused the popular imagination or excited the public's interest in the Revolutionary era as has Kenneth Roberts. Abraham Lincoln acknowledged the importance of *Uncle Tom's Cabin* when he greeted its author, Harriet Beecher Stowe, with the comment, "So this is the little lady that caused the war." More Americans have learned the story of the South during the years of the Civil War and Reconstruction from Margaret Mitchell's *Gone with the Wind* than from all of the learned volumes on this period. Upton Sinclair's *The Jungle,* by triggering the passage of the Meat Inspection Act of 1906, played a key role in the movement for federal regulation of many facets of American life. For better or worse, Americans have learned of their past and have been influenced in their understanding of that past by historical fiction.

Historians have, of course, not entirely overlooked the value of fiction in classroom reading. With the availability of paperbooks a novel or two is often assigned as required reading in the hope that it will stimulate the interest of students in the subject matter as a whole. But in teaching the basic American history course it is obviously impossible to find one or even several novels which will adequately introduce beginning students to the extensive treasure of fiction available.

In the present work the authors attempt to meet this problem by providing students with a sampling of the way fiction writers have treated important epochs in American history. The selections are intended to supplement basic text materials and to arouse the students' interest so that they will do further reading. Of course, America's past is so varied and complex that not all subjects can be treated fully. Size limitations have also dictated the brevity of the selections. But the most important periods are thoroughly treated. Special attention has been paid to often neglected areas, such as the parts played by women and ethnic minorities in American history. Above all, social history is stressed in an effort to introduce students to the way people of yesteryear lived. From the hundreds of novels, poems, and short stories consulted in the preparation of this anthology, the authors have selected works of such famous writers as Lewis, Fitzgerald, Steinbeck, and Michener, as well as those of many obscure authors.

To the members of the historical profession who may feel that supplemental books of readings like this one are "sugarcoating" the pill of learning, the authors would like to stress that accuracy in his subject matter is as important to the writer of historical fiction as it is to the author of a scholarly monograph. And if students can be encouraged to read because the selections are entertaining instead of dull and prosaic, the learning process is advanced. In an age in which students are often motivated mainly by visual material, an introduction to the wonders of the historical past by a sampling of fiction may be a worthwhile innovation.

The authors have had a great deal of help and advice in this project. They would like to thank Donald Estes, Cathy Jones, Celia Violet, and Rex Painter of San Diego City College; Professors B. Carmon Hardy, Arthur Hansen, Jackson Putnam, and Edward H. Parker of California State University-Fullerton; and Kent M. Beck of the University of California-Irvine.

Warren A. Beck
Myles L. Clowers

UNDERSTANDING AMERICAN HISTORY THROUGH FICTION

Chapter 1

The Colonial Experience

Reading 1

The Forest and the Fort

Hervey Allen

The colonial era of American history (1607–1763) was the story of Europeans carving a new civilization out of a wilderness. The "forest primeval" was frightening to the first colonists, and they soon realized that they had to destroy the wonders of nature in order to survive. As their numbers grew along the coast, they constantly pressed westward into the wilderness. The "first" Americans, or Indians as they were misnamed by Christopher Columbus, initially welcomed the white intruders and even helped them survive in the new land. The natives quickly recognized, however, that the destruction of the forest and the arrival of the settlers meant the end of their traditional way of life. The following selection tells of the process by which the new American civilization was born.

In the beginning was the forest. God made it and no man knew the end of it. It was not new. It was old; ancient as the hills it covered. Those who first entered it saw it had been there since the beginning of habitable time. There were rivers in it and distant mountains; birds, beasts, and the mysterious villages of red men. The trees were vast, round, and countless; columns of the roof of heaven. The place beneath was endlessly aisled. There were green glades where the deer fed and looked at the buffalo; trails that went back into the animal time. There were valleys where the clouds lay and no man came there; caves where the wolves mated; peaks where the panther screamed.

But the forest itself was silent. It slept and dreamed of something in a perpetual grey-green shadow in the summer. The lightning flashed at evening and the thunder echo rolled. In the fall the leaves fell and the stars looked down through a roof of sticks. The snow sifted and glittered. Winds heavy with the silver breath of winter smoked on the mountains. The trees burgeoned. Red flashed into the green flame of spring. The grey-green shadow brooded in the forest again, gestating sunlight.

Birds, those free spirits of the weather, were the only beings who saw the spectacle entire. As the earth rocked, every spring and autumn their blood burned. They rose, trillions of them, feathered nations with innumerable tongues and various languages, and took to the air. Their nests and their love songs followed the tilting ecliptic like a paean of time. They also sang the praises of the Almighty One with innocent, unthinking hearts. High in cold atmospheres, they beheld the grandeur and beauty of His thought.

Northward a necklace of great lakes glittered across the breast of the continent. Eastward the tabled plains of the Atlantic flashed lonely to the unbroken water rim. Not a sail gleamed. Only the steam clouds over the warm river in the ocean cliffed towering into heaven. The moon rose out of them at the full and looked at the sun setting beyond the Appalachians into a sea of western grass. Between lay the forest, green, gladed, unbroken, beautiful; riding the still waves of the long mountains, stretching from ice blink to palms.

The fingers of innumerable days trailed across the roof of the forest, while spring and autumn ran up and down it countless thousands of times. The stars shifted in their houses. Eastward over the waters the wings of gulls wheeled; gleamed and vanished; vanished and gleamed—prophetically. Until in the fullness of time something whiter glinted there; held the sunlight steadily; discovered the tracery of sails. Man-made thunder saluted the land.

Then harbours reflected the lights of ships' lanterns; the windows of gabled houses gleamed orange in the dusk. Broad plumes of smoke arose from capes and along the estuaries by day. Fire and steel axes ate the forest away, thinning it westward. Field patches and road scars began to show among the trees. The haze of wood smoke gathered over towns.

Generation after generation the ships kept coming. From one century into another the white man increased his town bases behind him. The tentacles and network of roads began reaching out for the hills. Vainly the silent stone-tipped arrows flitted from the forest at twilight. The flash and roar of musketry replied. Manitou and Jehovah wrestled in the valleys together—and the tasseled corn-god lost. Death like a mist out of lethal nowhere fell upon the red man until he vanished. The forefathers he left behind him slept in quiet mounds beside the east-running rivers. Only tobacco smoke lingered like a memorial incense scenting the breeze.

Beyond the cloudy rampart of the mountains the Indian gathered his surviving tribes. In the years numbered 1700 he and the forest stood at bay together. And for a while the forest prevailed. In the quarrel between the two houses of the Great White Fathers lay the Indian's chief hope of continuing to exist. Now on one side, now on the other his hatchet rose and fell. What he fought for was to preserve the forest beyond the Alleghenies. If the trees and the game went, if the white man came there, the Indian must go, too.

He knew that. His great men and prophets arose by the secret council fire and said so. The wampum strings of alliance flitted from tribe to tribe. Many laid hands upon them and promised never to let go. Meanwhile, with sonorous oratory, he smoked the peace pipe or exchanged the war belt with the French or English—always on the side of the trees.

And for a while, for a long time, the forest stood there. It stemmed the onrush of the colonists of Europe. The frontier ceased to flow westward majestically. It blundered against the barrier of the trees, the tribes, and the mountains. It recoiled. The inflow of its peoples pooled like the trickle of waters rising slowly behind a dam head; fanned out northward; flowed notably south.

Beyond the mountains lay the Valleys of Eden. But to go there was to slip one's finger out of the handclasp of mankind. To go there was to go lonely; to defy the forest, the Indians, and the lawful king. To go there was to move westward without the baggage or the impediments of the past. It was to drop everything, except God, language itself, and the memory of simple numbers. It was to begin all over again, to become a something new and unique in time.

But that was the fascination of it. That was the lure. That was at once the refuge, the opportunity, and the goal.

The American did not begin by overthrowing society, by reorganizing an old civilization. He left all that completely behind him. He disinherited himself. He reinvented and reincarnated society. For the first time in memorized history man was free to act entirely on his own responsibility. He was back in the forest again. He had nothing but himself, the animals, and the trees to contend with. There liberty was not a dream and an idea to die for; it was a state of nature to be successfully lived in. In the Valleys of Eden, west of the Alleghenies, that was where and how new America began. The seeds of it were scattered in lonely cabins, lost apparently in an ocean of trees.

Out of them genesis.

Reading 2

Blessed Is the Land

Louis Zara

The American Indians have fascinated and perplexed observers from colonial times to the present. Two theses early emerged: one maintained that the civilizations of the red and white men were incompatible and that the sooner the Indian was eliminated the better, thus giving rise to the idea that "the only good Indian was a dead one"; the other thesis advanced the idea that the Indian was the epitome of the "noble savage," that is, the "first" American had lived in a state of purity and natural innocence until he was spoiled by the corrupting influence of the white man. In the following selection a Jewish colonial trader analyzes the cultural clash between the two races and anticipates the triumph of the white man.

Two things I learned: First, far from being stolid and impassive, as white men consider all peoples whose skins are darker than their own, the Indians can be as gay and wild as children, or as sober and grim as old men—like us. Second, the notion that the red men are descendants from our Ten Lost Tribes of Israel, whom Shalmaneser banished, is ridiculous. Indeed, it is an affront to our people, although so sainted a man as Rabbi Menasseh ben Israel believes it. No Jews, however long oppressed and far transported, could have become so corrupted as to fail to retain the least memory of Torah, or the most elemental concepts of law. How could the Hebrew language change so completely? How could circumcision, the Sabbath, the Shema, the Temple, the dietary regulations and the priestly ordinances be forgotten entirely? Could the Ten Lost Tribes, having been driven from Canaan, retain no mark or trace of their own, or of their Assyrian captors' speech, garb or costumes? Only tallow-faced scholars who see life by candlelight could be taken in by such harum-scarum theories.

The Indians have no calendar, no sensible alphabet or system of writing, except in signs, no recorded lore, and no learned people to guide them from generation to generation. No one can ever convince Ashur Levy that the Ten Jewish Tribes could have become so degraded.

I do not mean that the red Indians are unworthy. The Iroquois Nations are said to be well organized for war, and the nations deep in the southern lands between the English and the Spanish territories are known to be skilled in certain crafts. However, unless the redmen adopt our white ways and confederate against us, they are doomed. Their proficiency with bow and arrow is remarkable, although few are as swift of foot or as sure of aim as Kieft and Steinmuts boasted for them. They are already forgetting how to make fire by rubbing two sticks together; they rely on our flint and steel and, more and more, on muskets and ball, on thread instead of sinews, on our needles, our blankets and on our metal utensils, instead of on their clay potteries and baskets. Their medicine, in some ways as effective as alchemy, is magic; although they have an uncanny knowledge of the healing properties of roots and plants. Yet, the white diseases, especially the smallpox and the measles, have wiped out more villages than all our Indian-haters and land-grabbers. Caspar Steinmuts told me that, in the Massachusetts Bay Colony, the English preachers believe that smallpox is God's way of ridding the land of the savages and clearing it for the more worthy Christians.

How can one explain the redmen? I cannot guess what it is with them unless they are late creations and still in the dawnlight of their civilization. I am loath to call any people "savages" who stand in the image of God. They know nothing of the arts of iron. Even in making leather, they do not tan the hides; they merely cure them with deerbrains, which leaves the material supple yet inferior to ours.

It was much the same in Brazil. There, the Indians had the manioc, or cassava plant, which furnished ready food in every season. It was not half as much trouble as maize, which must be planted and tilled and hoed and raised carefully, then shucked and ground into meal. On the other hand, how did "savages" ever discover that the manioc plant, violently poisonous in the raw, could be treated simply to make an edible flour? I should like to hear what d'Acosta and David Israel have to say on that subject.

These Indians lead a hard life. They live in bark-covered houses that are hung with skins and mats, and are poorly heated by fires on a central hearth. The smoke rises to a hole in the roof. In the winter, with the wind blowing, the huts fill with smoke and all eyes, especially of the old, are irritated, and the lids smart and become sore. As for cuisine, these people have no sauces. They cook to eat and eat to live. When there is meat or maize, everyone eats. They know no condiments. Even salt is scarce and must be brought in from the licks where the deer go, or purchased from white traders.

When young, the redmen have admirable bodies. I have never seen males so handsome; their skins are hairless all over, with little fuzz even in the usual crannies. It is sad to see such men grow heavy with age; they never become as corpulent as our Dutch.

The maidens are shy and charming, the dames big-bosomed and strong as oxen. In each family, one old woman rules informally. However, in war or peace councils, only the men deliberate, and the wisest crone is excluded. All ceremonials relating to the crops, the seasons or battle, are the province of the men.

The Indians are said to prize continence more than we do. Is this because of their lack of natural heat? Their apparatus, as far as I can determine, is as well formed as ours. Yet they are no strangers to such white pastimes as fornication and adultery, especially when some of the braves go off on hunting parties and others stay behind. They provided us with every hospitality within their means so I may say that their women are no less ardent and willing than ours.

In the business of trading, they are pitiful novices. They have never heard of *"Caveat emptor!"* so anyone may cheat them. Once their hard needs are satisfied, they trade by caprice. They will buy anything; everything excites them. If a shiny trinket catches a brave's eye, he may give away pelts to a value of ten guilders. For a cheap bauble, he may surrender his most precious furs. They understand that white men esteem beavers and muskrats, so they are wary in trading these, but are careless with the other skins. Barsimson and I were generous, to insure good relations on future journeys. Of course, we dared not trade too high lest our profits shrink.

What did we carry for "Indian goods?" Ear-bobs and bells, gilded chains, hair trinkets, combs, mirrors, silver arm-bands, badges, spoons, awls, knives, daggers, thimbles, ladles, axes, fishhooks, beads, needles and thread and woollen cloth. On our next journey, we may take brass pots, copper kettles and iron hoes. If I were counsel to the Indian nations, I would urge that each tribe bargain through a single agent. Only if they establish their own trading factors will they ever get equitable returns for their furs.

That brings me to the land. The vast, ever-expanding land, so broad no horizons confine it, thrills me to the marrow. It is so rich, so fertile, veined with deep rivers and blanketed with grasses and timbers, that no one could make a mistake buying any acreages. In the Old World, no Jew was permitted to own land. How will it be here? Not since the Dispersion have we had such an opportunity to become rooted like other peoples.

Yet the purchase of land from the tribes is a sham. They do not possess real property as we do; the concept of boundaries and benchmarks is beyond them. Each tribe knows roughly the length and breadth of its fief or duchy, for it may not encroach upon its neighbors without risking or inviting, war. Within such limits, security means absolute freedom to hunt, fish, trap, till and roam. They assume that these liberties and privileges are theirs forever.

Selling land is, therefore, not a serious step in their eyes. They enjoy rituals, so they are beguiled by the grand powwows which our officials stage. They smoke, grunt, talk a little, stretch their arms from one horizon to the other and solemnly make their totem marks on our documents. Then they wait for the liquor to seal the ceremony. Only later do they awaken to the fact that their crosses on our parchments have deprived them of their birthrights.

I should not feel so forlorn if all were equally free to buy the land. The Christian nations, by virtue of having planted their flags, or of having driven out the weaker Christian nations, hold title. The governments charter companies, like our Dutch West India Company, to develop and exploit vast grants, and these companies go through the elaborate abracadabra to "buy" the land from the tribes. It is from the Company that a settler receives title to his parcel. I might not object to the legal hoodwinking if it favored us, too. Someday, I shall own land; I do not know how.

In fairness to New Netherland, I do not see how the gulf between the redman's thinking and ours can be bridged. To yield before their immemorial rights would mean, in effect, to erect a stockade across every beach and channel on this coast, and to evict ourselves from the continent.

Besides, the tribes observe no ethics in treating with each other. When it suits them, they invade their neighbors' hunting grounds. At the slightest offense, they attack, sometimes declaring a state of war, more often striking by surprise. For war, as with the Christian kingdoms, is their chief means of testing personal courage and endurance. To acquit one's self honorably in combat is the goal of life. Whoever perishes in battle is transported forthwith to a "Happy Hunting Ground," a more specific description of Heaven than either Christians or Jews can promise. At the close of each war, they make a ritual of "burying the hatchet."

Reading 3

To Have and to Hold

Mary Johnston

The first colony in Virginia was established as a commercial venture by the London Company. It was thought that gold would quickly be found and that the settlers could make a quick fortune and return home. These hopes were soon dispelled, and tobacco, not gold, became the economic basis for the colony. This meant that the temporary venture became permanent. The practically all-male Virginia colony was placed on a firmer foundation in 1620 when ninety young women arrived. Certified as "pure and spotless," they were put up for auction at 120 pounds of tobacco a head. The arrival of the maids in Virginia did more for raising the morale of the colony and created greater excitement than did the creation in 1619 of the House of Burgesses, the first popularly elected legislative body in America. The lusty bachelors did "willinglie and lovinglie receive the newcomes," and once homes were established, the English in Virginia were there to stay.

"I have ridden to-day from Jamestown," he went on. "I was the only man, i' faith, that cared to leave its gates; and I met the world—the bachelor world —flocking to them. Not a mile of the way but I encountered Tom, Dick, and Harry, dressed in their Sunday bravery and making full tilt for the city. And the boats upon the river! I have seen the Thames less crowded."

"There was more passing than usual," I said; "but I was busy in the fields, and did not attend. What's the lodestar?"

From *To Have and to Hold* by Mary Johnston. Published in 1900.

"The star that draws us all,—some to ruin, some to bliss ineffable,—woman."

"Humph! The maids have come, then?"

He nodded. "There's a goodly ship down there, with a goodly lading."

"*Videlicet,* some fourscore waiting damsels and milkmaids, warranted honest by my Lord Warwick," I muttered.

"This business hath been of Edwyn Sandys' management, as you very well know," he rejoined, with some heat. "His word is good: therefore I hold them chaste. That they are fair I can testify, having seen them leave the ship."

"Fair and chaste," I said, "but meanly born."

"I grant you that," he answered. "But after all, what of it? Beggars must not be choosers. The land is new and must be peopled, nor will those who come after us look too curiously into the lineage of those to whom a nation owes its birth. What we in these plantations need is a loosening of the bonds which tie us to home, to England, and a tightening of those which bind us to this land in which we have cast our lot. We put our hand to the plough, but we turn our heads and look to our Egypt and its fleshpots. 'Tis children and wife—be that wife princess or peasant—that make home of a desert, that bind a man with chains of gold to the country where they abide. Wherefore, when at midday I met good Master Wickham rowing down from Henricus to Jamestown, to offer his aid to Master Bucke in his press of business to-morrow, I gave the good man Godspeed, and thought his a fruitful errand and one pleasing to the Lord."

"Amen," I yawned. "I love the land, and call it home. My withers are unwrung."

He rose to his feet, and began to pace the greensward before the door. My eyes followed his trim figure, richly though sombrely clad, then fell with a sudden dissatisfaction upon my own stained and frayed apparel.

"Ralph," he said presently, coming to a stand before me, "have you ever an hundred and twenty pounds of tobacco in hand? If not, I"—

"I have the weed," I replied. "What then?"

"Then at dawn drop down with the tide to the city, and secure for thyself one of these same errant damsels."

I stared at him, and then broke into laughter, in which, after a space and unwillingly, he himself joined. When at length I wiped the water from my eyes it was quite dark, the whippoorwills had begun to call, and Rolfe must needs hasten on. I went with him down to the gate.

"Take my advice,—it is that of your friend," he said, as he swung himself into the saddle. He gathered up the reins and struck spurs into his horse, then turned to call back to me: "Sleep upon my words, Ralph, and the next time I come I look to see a farthingale behind thee!"

"Thou art as like to see one upon me," I answered.

Nevertheless, when he had gone, and I climbed the bank and reentered the house, it was with a strange pang at the cheerlessness of my hearth, and an angry and unreasoning impatience at the lack of welcoming face or voice. In God's name, who was there to welcome me? None but my hounds, and the flying squirrel I had caught and tamed. Groping my way to the corner, I took from my store two torches, lit them, and stuck them into the holes pierced in the mantel shelf; then stood beneath the clear flame, and looked with a sudden sick distaste upon the disorder which the light betrayed. The fire was dead, and ashes and embers were scattered upon the hearth; fragments of my last meal littered the table, and upon the unwashed floor lay the bones I had thrown my dogs. Dirt and confusion reigned; only upon my armor, my sword and gun, my hunting knife and dagger, there was no spot or stain. I turned to gaze upon them where they hung against the wall, and in my soul I hated the piping times of peace, and longed for the camp fire and the call to arms.

With an impatient sigh, I swept the litter from the table, and, taking from the shelf that held my meagre library a bundle of Master Shakespeare's plays (gathered for me by Rolfe when he was last in London), I began to read; but my thoughts wandered, and the tale seemed dull and oft told.

·   ·   ·

A cheer arose from the crowd, followed by a crashing peal of the bells and a louder roll of the drum. The doors of the houses around and to right and left of the square swung open, and the company which had been quartered overnight upon the citizens began to emerge. By twos and threes, some with hurried steps and downcast eyes, others more slowly and with free glances at the staring men, they gathered to the centre of the square, where, in surplice and band, there awaited them godly Master Bucke and Master Wickham of Henricus. I stared with the rest, though I did not add my voice to theirs.

Before the arrival of yesterday's ship there had been in this natural Eden (leaving the savages out of the reckoning) several thousand Adams, and but some threescore Eves. And for the most part, the Eves were either portly and bustling or withered and shrewish housewives, of age and experience to defy the serpent. These were different. Ninety slender figures decked in all the bravery they could assume; ninety comely faces, pink and white, or clear brown with the rich blood showing through; ninety pair of eyes, laughing and alluring, or downcast with long fringes sweeping rounded cheeks; ninety pair of ripe red lips,—the crowd shouted itself hoarse and would not be restrained, brushing aside like straws the staves of the marshal and his men, and surging in upon the line of adventurous damsels. I saw young men, panting, seize hand or arm and strive to pull toward them some reluctant fair; others snatched kisses, or fell on their knees and began speeches out of Euphues; others commenced an inventory of their possessions,—acres, tobacco, servants, household plenishing. All was hubbub, protestation, frightened cries, and hysterical laughter. The officers ran to and fro, threatening and commanding; Master Pory alternately cried "Shame!" and laughed his loudest; and I plucked away a jackanapes of sixteen who had his hand upon a girl's ruff, and shook him until the breath was well-nigh out of him. The clamor did but increase.

"Way for the Governor!" cried the marshal. "Shame on you, my masters! Way for his Honor and the worshipful Council!"

The three wooden steps leading down from the door of the Governor's house suddenly blossomed into crimson and gold, as his Honor with the attendant Councilors emerged from the hall and stood staring at the mob below.

The Governor's honest moon face was quite pale with passion. "What a devil is this?" he cried wrathfully. "Did you never see a woman before? Where's the marshal? I'll imprison the last one of you for rioters!"

Reading 4

The Rogue and the Witch

John Newton

Belief in witchcraft was both genuine and widespread in the colonies, although it was more extensive in New England than in any other area. The first execution for practicing witchery took place in Boston in 1638, and scattered accusations of witchcraft were made throughout New England. The pinnacle of hysteria was reached in Salem, Massachusetts between May and September 1692. A special court was created to try witches and some 20 persons were executed and another 150 imprisoned before the madness stopped. The following selection tells how a young cleric not only challenges the definition of witchcraft by the eminent Increase Mather but also attributes the hysteria to natural rather that supernatural causes.

One morning, early in the new year, Mather sent for his associate. John found his superior writing a treatise of profound learning to be called *Illustrious Providences,* which recorded the wonder-working of God in the New England colonies. There were "Remarkable Preservations in Time of Peril." There were "Philosophical Meditations" under thunder and lightning, magnetism, and other strange natural phenomena and, more than all, there was to be a discussion of "Demons, Possessed Persons, and Witchcraft." For some time Mather had been gathering stories of the strange performances of people supposed to be in league with the devil. John discovered, too, that Mather was being spurred to action by his son Cotton, who was violently antagonistic to those who were under suspicion of being witches, and in youthful zeal urged the adoption of most drastic measures to punish all those who were supposed to be in collusion with Satanic powers. Increase Mather outlined his proposed work to John very completely and minutely. It seemed to John that he had been called to listen in order to approve his colleague's conclusions, rather than to discuss the subject matter. Then the learned doctor abruptly stayed his presentation, as if he perceived that his listener was not in accord with him and, looking across at him, he said, "You are not a disbeliever in witchcraft, John Henniker?"

From the beginning of the interview, John realized that at some point in their conversation he would have to declare his own position. Even if Elder Mather did not force him to do it, it must be done for his own integrity. Not that John's thought was in advance of his age, but he had learned to see things through the eyes of Glory Upshall and that meant through the eyes of the oppressed. Did he believe in witchcraft? He was inclined to evade the question by asking in return, "What do you mean by witchcraft?" but instead, he met the issue boldly.

"The Scriptures so teach, sir," he began.

Increase Mather was about to express his agreement but John raised his voice and continued, "But if your question means that this disturbance of our colony is witchcraft, my conscience tells me that these cases which you call witchcraft are merely delusions."

His voice was strong and sure. "This strange insanity feeds on suspicion and the evil passions which lurk in idle minds," he said clearly.

Mather looked at him aghast. "Your boldness astounds me, Elder Henniker. You affront my learning."

"Those are not my intentions, Elder Mather," John answered quietly. "I have great respect for your authority and for the wisdom which has gained you that authority. But," he continued, "I must be true to my conscience, and to my beliefs as I determine them."

Mather's face whitened with rage and incredulity. "I summoned you so that we could co-operate in calling a convocation of ministers to pray that the people may be led aright in this matter." He cleared his throat. "Also," he said slowly and deliberately, "to adopt measures by which we can defy these devices of the devil!" His voice rose in accusing tones. He tossed a paper to John, who read it slowly with a sinking feeling in his heart.

The paper was a letter which Increase Mather intended to circulate to ministers, organizing them to collect facts concerning witchcraft and other strange delusions, which, when collected, would form a part of his treatise on *Illustrious Providences.*

John raised sad eyes to face Mather as he finished the letter. "I cannot co-operate in this manner," he said softly.

"You mean you would oppose me?" asked Mather.

"If holding true to my own beliefs is opposing you, Increase, I am opposing you," John said.

"You actually do not believe in witchcraft?" Mather spoke with a break in his voice.

"I do not believe that the affliction of the colony is one of witchcraft," John replied.

"You question my learning? My learning—the learning of one who has helped to bring you to your present position of influence!"

"Does a difference of opinion mean that I have no respect for your learning?" John asked, realizing, perhaps for the first time, the blindness of Increase Mather's position.

Increase rose from his chair and, controlling his anger with difficulty, he pointed his finger at John. "Young man," he said, "you saw that comet which appeared among the stars. The warning piece of heaven has gone off!" He leaned forward and spoke sharply, "You may leave this room, Elder Henniker."

John rose to his feet and faced him across the table. "Sir, I came here at your request. I answered your questions without equivocation and with honesty. I propose now to state my position before I leave." Deliberately and with an enforced outward composure he continued: "The town of Boston and the Bay Colony are passing through a period of commercial stagnation. Sickness, also, has become epidemic among us. Many of our people are strangers in a strange land; they are lonely and homesick. Fears harass their minds and intense religious feelings prevail. The time is ripe for a plague of delirium and superstition. Chance, or something else, has set fire to these inflammable materials. Local prejudices, grudges, and personal differences have fanned the flames, and what we now witness is not an outbreak of witchery, not a league of men with evil spirits as you suppose, but a delusion, which can be tragic in its results." His words gathered momentum and impressiveness as he went on. "This bewildered, stricken people will find only further incitement in such a book as you contemplate. To recount the stories of the performances of persons supposed to be in league with the devil can only add fuel to the fire already burning. We need sanity, assurance, confidence, faith and courage. The poor accused persons, prejudged, condemned before being brought to court, need justice and the mercy that seasons it."

John relaxed and lowered his voice. "Perhaps I have spoken as a young man should not speak to his elder but I have spoken, sir, as my conscience directs me and if I have transgressed, I ask your pardon."

Chapter 2

The Path to
Independence

Reading 5

Gilman of Redford

William Davis

The Boston Tea Party precipitated a series of events which eventually cul-
minated in the American Revolution. On the night of December 16, 1773,
342 chests of tea belonging to the East India Company were dumped into
Boston harbor. The patriots, poorly disguised as "Indians," steamed toward
the waterfront crying, "Boston harbor: a teapot tonight!" British efforts to
punish the Bostonians for this action united the colonial resistance that
shortly led to war. The following is a description of the "tea party."

From November twenty-ninth to that eternally memorable December six-
teenth, if any man in Boston was idle that man was not Roger Gilman. The
Dartmouth had quietly dropped anchor at the Castle, but the young secretary
of the Committee of Correspondence had knocked at Warren's door before
Captain Hall could greet Quaker Rotch, his owner, upon Long Wharf; and
that Monday morning Boston had been splotched with placards from North
Battery to the Neck.

> "Friends! Brethren! Countrymen! The worst of plagues, the detested *tea,* is now
> arrived in this harbor. The hour of destruction or manly opposition to the machi-
> nations of tyranny now stare you in the face."

Therefore let the friends of freedom rally that morning at Faneuil Hall.
—Fiercely emphatic words? Yes—and penned around midnight for the eager
printers, by men who knew that multitudes can never be stirred by the mincing
terms which please philosophers.

Again therefore a crowded hall and swarms standing in the streets. Samuel Adams again talking his homely Bostonese. Adjournment again to the
ampler Old South. A close packed meeting house. Samuel Adams speaking to
the motion, "*It is the firm resolve of this body that the tea shall not only be sent
back, but that no duty shall be paid thereon.*"

. . .

No other town meeting in all New England had ever been like unto this.
Seven thousand were standing outside about the meeting house. Inside the

From *Gilman of Redford* by William Davis. Published in 1927.

standing room was packed, yet there was no scuffling nor elbowing to force admission. Winter though it was, the windows had been flung wide, and snatches of the oratory were passed from mouth to mouth to the edges of the crowd; and the shout rippled out to the snowy Common when the question was stated "whether it be the determination of this body to abide by its former resolution with regard to not suffering the tea to be landed?"

Who can recall most of that spontaneous eloquence, cautioning or exhilarating, which wrought more perchance for the world than many stately apostrophes by Greek or Roman? But never could I, nor any other, forget the solemn warning of young Josiah Quincy when the thoughtless too soon began clamoring "A vote! A vote!"

Forth he stood, slim and gallant, with that hectic flush kindling his cheeks which told that never would he be suffered to do battle for the America he loved, and often did I recall his words when the conflict thickened and the heavens rained blood:

"Shouts and hosannas will not terminate the trials of this day, nor popular resolves, harangues and acclamations vanquish our foes. Let us consider the issues before we advance to those measures which must bring on the most trying and terrible struggle this country ever saw."

So the hot heads were stilled, but Dr. Young, Samuel Adams and others spoke gravely to the half-Tory profferers of faint counsels; "Now the hand is at the plough there must be no looking back."

Half past four. The short winter day was ending. A keen wind whistling down the alleys was turning the slush to ice, when the chairman rose to put the question, "Shall the tea be landed?" Then like a broadside echoing along vast crags, from the church, from all the standing thousands without came back the "NO!" Next followed shouts "Adjourn!" but adjourn we did not. Our Rubicon was not yet crossed.

Poor Rotch, fearful for his ship and his skin had driven to Milton to lay one last plea before Hutchinson for that pass which might avert the crisis. He would be back at six, and till six we waited, dinnerless and almost in the dark —and Boston waited with us.

It is written that Hutchinson took his stand with none of his great royalist friends around him: no Auchmuty, no Flucker, no Admiral Montagu. The most loyal of them would have urged him to yield, and give London its last chance for deliberation. Wise, learned and devout was counted Thomas Hutchinson but by that blunder upon that December afternoon he struck his name from among the reconcilers of the English race, and graved it among the non-worthies of America.

It was six when the noise outside the meeting-house told that a chaise, driven furiously, was coming down Marlborough Street. The crows were calling "Room for the owner!" and at a nod from Warren I went with Paul Revere and escorted Rotch through the jammed aisles and up to the foot of the pulpit.

The luckless merchant's stock and wig were all awry. In the light of the few candles which had been set near the pulpit he peered forth, scared and cold, at the dim sea of faces gazing upon him from out the great gloomy body of the building. Never there was a less impressive orator, nor one less anxious to blurt out his message. But deliver it he presently did, others taking his halting words and flinging them far and wide.

Rotch had offered to send back the tea if Hutchinson would give him a pass to clear the guns of the Castle and the warships. His Excellency had coughed and palavered, then at last doggedly repeated his refusal; "To grant a pass to a vessel which I knew had not been cleared at the custom house would be a direct countenancing of the violation of the acts of trade"—So closed the interview.

When Rotch and his interveners had finished, a long low roar came out of the darkness; then reckless voices were raised "A mob! a mob!" Yet in a great quietness the final question was formally put to him, "Whether he, Rotch, would send back his vessel with the tea in her, under the present circumstances." The man's hesitation was pitiful, but at last he got out his answer; "He could not possibly comply, as he apprehended a compliance would prove his ruin" and if lawfully summoned he must perforce land the tea for his own safety.

The church, I repeat, was nearly in darkness. Only around the great pulpit was a little circle of candlelight. There were dim gray panels where once had been the windows. Suddenly now into that candlelight emerged the form of Samuel Adams; under the dim tapers his face shone deathly pale, but there was the wonted ring to his tones as he shook back his long hair, then flung his voice out into the darkness; *"This meeting can do nothing more to save the country!"*

From the back galleries and windows, high above the muttering and growling of the crowd there pealed a yell, piercing to spine and marrow like the howl of the Iroquois; at which summons I charged for a friendly window and leaped forth into the night.

. . . It was in a carpenter's shop near the church, where we smeared our faces with paint, stuck tall feathers in our hair and bundled ourselves with blankets. I remember how a tall, gawky boy, Jo Lovering, held the candles while we put on our thin disguise, then brought to each one of us a dependable hatchet.

It had been agreed in the Committee that the names of those asked to join should not be told even to their comrades. It might well be a hanging matter, —everybody knew it. Each man approached had been told to count the cost.

Under those blankets there was many a laced and ruffled coat, but many, too, only of solid linsey and fustian, for a hard bit of stevedoring lay ahead, and the work could not fail through lack of Yankee muscle. Revere, I soon recognized, grinning behind paint worthy of a medicine man, but the leader was the tested and iron-handed Lendall Pitts, relied upon the hold down the boisterous and see that all things were done decently and in order.

There were only about a score of us when we stepped forth in our blankets into the dark street. The lamps had been lit at the crossways, and a few lanterns escorted us over the dirty ice and snow. It was becoming a keen, crisp night. The streets were still full of people, and as we passed along, a short silent column, one heard the word running on ahead of us, "Here come the Mohawks! Here come the Mohawks!" As we advanced others began falling in behind, usually very poorly disguised. Some were mere lads ready for a lark, but more were square-shouldered determined men who knew their business. We marched quietly in a loose military formation, down Water Street and then cut past Battery March and along the water front. The spars of the shipping and the tall black wharf-houses loomed up like spectres out of the darkness. As we passed dwellings there was a flinging up of windows, and against the candle-lit rooms we saw the figures of leaning, wondering girls. But there was no wild shouting, no tumult. By Fort Hill indeed some enthusiast in the attendant crowd struck up an impromptu song:

"Rally, Mohawks, bring out your axes,
And tell King George we'll pay no taxes
　　On his foreign tea.
His threats are vain, and vain to think
To force our girls and wives to drink
　　His vile Bohea!"

No one, however, in that grim, set column caught up the refrain. Stolidly we tramped along the water front, with a great scuffling of feet behind us.

Out at their anchorages we could see the rows of lights from the men-of-war, but not a sound drifted from them. Montagu was snug ashore drinking wine with a rich Tory; he had given no orders. His Excellency was warming his slippers in Milton. We came down upon Griffin's Wharf; and as we approached a line of men with muskets stood before us, then Pitts near the head of our column muttered some password and the armed files opened like magic. It was the militia guard over the teaships, its chilly vigil ended. I thought I caught Henry Knox's tall form in the darkness, but said nothing. The wharf was almost deserted; the crews had been paid off, and only the ship's keepers and the officers were aboard. It was low tide and the three Indiamen, with a few lights from the windows in their high stern cabins, were resting aground in absolute quiet, with their spars dimly canted to one side.

There they were, the *Dartmouth,* the *Eleanor,* and the brig *Beaver.* We tramped out onto the wharf, our heavy feet making the old timbers rattle like musketry, but that was the only noise. During the march the word had been passed quietly down the line how the band was to divide. I followed Lendall Pitts' party, and after we crossed the gangplank of the *Dartmouth* and trampled her deck, rioters and worse now before the law, we drew together and in relief from our long silence gave once again our piercing warwhoop, bringing a frightened second mate instantly out of the stern cabin. "Keys to the hatches, candles, matches—and be quick!" Pitts was ordering, giving the fellow no chance to parley, and in a minute we had the keys and the lights. The *Eleanor* and the *Beaver* we knew were likewise in good hands.

It was awkward work for some of us, but there were at least a few in our band who displayed a marvelous knowledge of where the tea was stowed and how to get it out. We took turns at the block and tackle hoisting the heavy chests from the hold. Once on the deck our axes smashed the boxwood, and the noise of the chopping must have gone far along the water front. When sufficiently shattered the chests were deliberately flung over the bulwarks. If some struck upon the bare flats a hundred excited boys, sternly restrained from entering the ships, were proud to speed the good cause by floundering into the cold mud and completing the destruction.

After our single warwhoop there was no shouting, and the throngs of people who piled out upon Wheelwright's, Gray's and other wharfs, or scrambled upon roofs or even the masts or rigging of near-by shipping, kept also a marvelous silence. It was stiff, hard work, never giving us a minute for moralizing. Once we hoisted and almost demolished a case of innocent goods—it cost us some trouble to put it back. Once we detected a fellow (a late volunteer) cramming some tea into his pockets. Everybody knows how we dropped him incontinently into shallow water. He hit on his side, had all his wind knocked out of him, and only by a mercy got safe to the spiling.

The moon came out at last, and the wind blew very chill, but we were warm from the work. It had seemed a trifling task when we talked of it; but never had I imagined it could take so long to break out all that quantity of tea. "Enough," vowed the man beside me, "to steep all Cape Cod Bay!" At last after three hours of unremitting hoisting and chopping the pulleys rattled for the last time. "All out!" shouted Pitts. "All over!" shouted back a companion spirit, probably Revere. And the men at the other two vessels had likewise completed their tasks.

Without another order we walked back across the gangplank, and ten minutes later the *Dartmouth* was as silent as we had found her, not a spar, not a rope the worse, only perchance some splintered case boards and Indian sacking and a certain scattered blackness upon her decks to tell that the good ship belonged henceforth to history.

We reached the head of the wharf and again formed in a little column. The men-of-war had stirred not; no alarm gun had boomed from the Castle. Hours later we knew that all the royalists about Boston were only too glad to have the fearful tension end without recourse to bloodshed. The next move was London's, and London was three thousand miles away. "All things," John Adams could write the next morning, "were conducted with great order, decency and with perfect submission to government."—To which government?

The strain being over, and we all being very human, some of the younger of us began now to yell again and to flourish our axes. It was growing late, but not too late *that* night for the lights still to be burning in every Boston window. Somebody produced a fife and began to shrill the Liberty Song. Our hundreds of loyal attendants caught it up, as we trailed back through the town toward the Green Dragon where it was agreed that our cohorts should disband. Of course what befell when we passed the Coffin house has become an old story; for Admiral mMontagu himself leaned from the rich old Tory's window, and called down on us as we passed, "Well, boys, you've had a fine evening for your Indian caper. But mind, you've got to pay the fiddler."

Reading 6

Enough Good Men

Charles Mercer

Chaffing under the restrictive mercantilist laws of Great Britain, the colonial merchants were in the vanguard of the resistance to the Crown. The limitations placed on colonial business by the Navigation laws passed in the preceding century did not become objectionable until the British began to enforce them vigorously after 1763. To the merchant, then, the desire for liberty meant opposition to business restraints; but for others, it meant something else, as this selection demonstrates.

From *Enough Good Men* by Charles Mercer. Published in 1960 by G. P. Putnam's Sons. Reprinted by permission of publisher.

He knew what he was and where he stood in his times. He was for "liberty" as opposed to "tyranny." Yet what did "liberty" mean, for instance, to a man like Timothy Murdoch? It meant freedom to pursue his goal of accumulating wealth without the tax and trade restrictions of established government. This was the "liberty" bandied by merchants, planters, land speculators and manufacturers. Opposed to it was the "liberty" conceived by English merchants, speculators and manufacturers to pursue their goal of wealth without restrictions from the selfish, tyrannical colonists.

"It's a *mercantile* situation," he said once to Joseph Reed.

Reed, fingering his high brow and staring at him gravely, replied, "These are *mercantile* times, Alex. And I, for one, am glad. Business ameliorates everything. Business, as opposed to the mob, is conservative and brings about change slowly. Without it there is no stability. The Greeks would have been happier if business had been a strong force in their time. They overthrew their tyrants and then, much worse, enthroned the mob of the ecclesia. The Romans, lacking the influence of business, abandoned a republic for a military dictatorship that eventually led to a terrible rule of personal despotism. And think how rashly our ancestors acted in a religious fervor that might better have been directed into the less sanguinary channels of trade and commerce. They decapitated a Stuart and enthroned a Long Parliament so immeasurably more despotic that they were forced to revolt again. The head of a Cromwell for the head of a Stuart—and then another Stuart to the throne."

Perhaps business did ameliorate everything. Nevertheless, there was widespread abasement of "freedom" here. The word should not be so widely bandied in a time when you could buy a Negro slave for thirty pounds on Front Street, when for twenty pounds you could buy the services of a hapless white child until he reached his majority. And was there any philosophically defensible justice in the fact that ninety per cent of the taxable population of Philadelphia was disenfranchised by a suffrage qualification of fifty pounds personalty or a fifty-acre freehold? Those people's notions of "liberty" were quite different from that of Timothy Murdoch.

Such thoughts could not be expressed in most of the homes Alex visited or he would have been socially ostracized for what he actually was: a radical. Few knew that he and Reed were ardent Sons of Liberty. If it were widely known in this conservative city, their practice would dwindle instead of growing. Business again, he'd tell himself wryly when he felt hypocritical because he disguised his radicalism.

Reading 7

Oliver Wiswell

Kenneth Roberts

The Battle of Bunker Hill (June 17, 1775) was the first set battle between British regulars and American militia. It also illustrated two different military concepts. The British were used to the formal style of European warfare, in which musket volleys were fired from close range as preparation for a bayonet assault. In direct contrast, the American forces employed the tactics they had learned from the Indians, which stressed concealment and accurate shooting from a distance. The following highlights the differing military strategies.

The rest of that morning was a sort of hazy hot dream. Not until noon did we hear the rattle of drums in near-by Hanover Street and the shuffling of marching regiments moving down toward the wharves from their camp on the Common. There was something about that hurried recurrent slapping of thick-soled shoes on a hard road that made my hands perspire and dried my tongue to the consistency of leather; that filled me with the same trembling, half-sick eagerness I had felt as a boy, when I crawled on hands and knees through underbrush to shoot my first moose.

We waited and waited, after that, for something to happen. George Leonard came in to share our windows with us. We talked and talked, wondering what would be the outcome of that long argument at British headquarters.

Two o'clock passed. Then there was a swelling of voices on all the housetops; an agitated sound made more significant by a thousand tense movements, quick changes of groupings and the flickering of gesturing arms and hands among the watchers.

A line of boats, packed with men, crept out from our side of the river and began to move slowly across the glassy strip of water that lay between them and those rising meadows of Charlestown where not long ago the peaceful cattle grazed.

In spite of the blazing heat of the cloudless day, the men in the boats wore uniforms of scarlet cloth, bound to them by heavy white crossed belts, and on their backs were strapped knapsacks that couldn't have weighed less than eighty pounds. All of us in my room, barring Mrs. Byles, knew the wrenching labor of carrying a dead doe out of the woods. Every one of those scarlet-clad soldiers carried the equivalent of a doe on his back—so majestically arithmetical was the trained British military mind on this vital occasion.

The shape of Charlestown peninsula, as we saw it from our upper windows on Sudbury Street, was that of an enormous muskrat, half submerged, and swimming to the right. Farthest to the right was the low swelling of the muskrat's head; a little behind was the higher swelling of its shoulders; still farther back was the largest swelling of all: that of its rump. Protruding from the rump, long and flat on the water, like a muskrat's tail, was Charlestown Neck.

As I've said, the low fortifications thrown up by the rebels were on the middle of the three swellings; and across the floating tail that in reality was Charlestown Neck, more and more rebels coming for the fight still were moving. Those distant tiny figures, like a choppy and eccentric stream, irregularly flowed up over the rump of the muskrat, then down upon his back, and, ascending again, were lost among the walls of fresh earth upon the muskrat's shoulder.

My eyeballs smarted from tensely watching the line of rowboats that seemed to crawl in a deadly lethargy, slower and slower and smaller and smaller as they grew more distant, until they seemed only toy boats almost standing still, with red-painted toy soldiers motionless in them.

My ears ached from the banging of the guns; but within our room there wasn't a sound except the heavy breathing of George Leonard, the tapping of Mrs. Byles' cane and the spasmodic sound of Buell's wrenching hiccups.

Now the world we lived in seemed to be half breathless silence and half thunder; for as the lengthening line of boats moved obliquely across the glassy waterway toward the head of the giant swimming muskrat, the booming from the frigates and from Copp's Hill was violent, but between the individual shots from the great guns, we were conscious of profound silence: all the town around us was completely still. Not a sound came up to us from the streets, and the thousands gathered upon the housetops were voiceless, and stood or sat or leaned without motion, as if posed in some vast tableau.

What we most wanted to know was whether those slowly moving boats would circle the nose of the swimming muskrat and pass along its far side to the narrow tail.

Buell stood, almost leaning upon me; and in the interval between two cannon shots, I felt inordinately irritated at the muted jerky hiccupings that racked him. They seemed a disturbance, an intentional intrusion upon the drama, like coughing in a playhouse.

"Damn you, stop that," I almost said to him.

He seemed to feel something of this himself. "Excuse me," he said. "Can't appear to help it. Well, no matter. Look, there ain't a sail been shaken out on those frigates! I guess there ain't no question what that means."

Leonard turned on him, "Of course there is! They got a fair wind, haven't they? Why wouldn't it be good strategy to lie where they are till the last possible moment: then get under way in a hurry, move around to the Neck and bottle 'em up before they know what's happened to 'em? Why wouldn't it?"

I had a momentary faint hope that he was right: that perhaps those boatloads of soldiers would keep on around the muskrat's nose and that the frigates would soon set off to support them.

But he wasn't right. He was wrong; for the line of boats went straight to the beach at the base of the muskrat's head, and those red-coated figures flowed out along the sand like a widening pool of blood.

"There you are," Buell said. "Gage and Howe outranked Clinton and Burgoyne and Percy, so Gage and Howe won the argument. Gage and Howe told 'em Americans can't shoot, of course, and always run every time anyone fires a cannon at 'em, and turn pale and faint whenever they see a bayonet!" Again he made a hissing sound and turned from the window to sit on the bed, where I heard him opening another bottle of wine.

No sooner were the boats empty than they turned and rowed back to our side of the river, coming fast unburdened; and through the next hour we sat and watched an endless ferrying of scarlet infantrymen to the Charlestown shore; watched those who had been landed form into companies and regiments on the lower slopes of that lowest of Charlestown's three hills.

My father sighed shiveringly. "It can't be possible; they can't be going to attack that hill in front! They *can't* be!"

George Leonard spoke under his breath, "Never! Howe's a soldier. Gage —Clinton—Burgoyne—why, they couldn't do such a thing!"

Buell was close behind me again, smelling of wine and noisier inside. "They can too!" he said. "They can march right up the front of that hill, the way British gentlemen always do—until somebody learns 'em better."

"Never," George Leonard repeated huskily.

Mrs. Byles and Doctor Miller looked angrily at Buell, and I was angry at him myself for daring to speak what I feared was the truth.

"There's just a chance," my father said, "that they might be going to march around the peninsula, half on one side and half on the other, and join forces at the Neck."

Buell hiccuped. "Why should they march, when they can row around in boats? They'd be throwing men away if they *marched* around. Why, they'd lose five or six hundred! But if they *rowed* around, they probably wouldn't lose one. Not a damned one!" He looked earnestly at the bottle in his hand. "I doubt if I ever learn to be a drinker! Try, though!"

Not until that hot afternoon was at its hottest did the rowboats deposit the last load of soldiers on the beach. By then, on the top of the low muskrat head, the troops were drawn up in two long lines. Those two lines ran all the way across the head of the muskrat, as two scarlet hair ribbons might have spanned a girl's head from ear to ear.

There was no doubt now as to how those scarlet lines were going to attack; and in my room there was no more talk among us.

The two long lines moved down from the muskrat's head to his neck and began their ascent of the shoulder, which was the middle hill topped by the walls of brown earthworks. They moved with such smoothness, such precision in keeping their formation, that it was hard to believe they were composed of embattled human beings; and, as they surged upward upon the rising meadows, red coats and white breeches bright above the grass, they brought me the illusion that I beheld not men, but the stripes of a vastly wide red, white and green pennant, flung far across the face of the hill.

The moment that this wide pennant began to rise upward upon the hill, the gunfire from the frigates and from Boston ceased abruptly.

I found myself sweating as I had never sweated before, and I'd known what it was to sweat; for I'd swung a scythe on my father's farm in August; but never until now had I sweated until I shivered.

The long pennant of scarlet and white rose steadily: rose and rose until it seemed to us a man might have tossed a stone from it into the breastworks on the hilltop.

Then, as if the advancing scarlet lines had touched a trigger and released countless little mines, fleecy puffs of white smoke jetted from them with symmetrical regularity. The smoke was thick and white against the green hill: the men might have thrown expanding balls of cotton into the air, all at the same time.

To those in my room, the sound of this British volley firing came slow and long delayed—then we heard it: a muted pattering like the muffled popping of corn in a full popper.

But from the brown rectangle toward which the scarlet lines advanced, no white puff arose. The walls of earth were smokeless and still.

George Leonard got up suddenly. His chair fell over with a clatter. "Fire! For God's sake, fire—if you're ever going to!"

As if that had been a signal, the whole front of the breastworks on the hill spouted smoke.

On the instant the long scarlet pennant seemed struck by a sudden sharp wind. It shivered and fluttered; it undulated, thinned and thickened.

For a long moment it thus thickened, thinned and fluttered. Faint wisps of smoke rose from it, as though hot irons touched it lightly. Then its likeness to a pennant vanished.

The scarlet lines bent, broke and crumbled. Their edges flaked off and became scarlet human figures which fluttered leaf-like down the hill, dropping away from what seemed a long heap of scarlet leaves, a queer bright shadow of the original scarlet line—as if that line in disappearing, had left its empty shell, red, upon the ground.

"Look!" Leonard whispered. "Look at the long piles! All those men in the grass—they're shot! One volley did for damn near half of 'em!"

He dropped the glass on the floor; fumbled for it stiffly. I picked it up and looked through it at the hilltop. It brought the twisted scarlet shadow close.

It wasn't a shadow, but soldiers in tangled heaps that writhed and heaved. Single figures reared up gropingly from the heaps and then sank back. I thought of the sounds that must be coming from those men, and at that thought my insides quaked; I thanked God we couldn't hear them.

I tried to ask whether anyone else wanted the glass, but my voice just croaked indistinguishably. Leonard awkwardly took the glass from me.

Nobody spoke. The scarlet shadow stayed where it was, but the moving scarlet figures went swiftly down the hill to the bottom; and there, like scarlet quicksilver, they gathered in blobs that expanded, contracted, swirled, thinned and gradually flowed again into scarlet lines that lay along the center of the little valley—lines shorter than those that had first moved with such smooth precision toward the silent earthworks.

Wisps of smoke were rising now from houses at the foot of the hill, and the guns on the frigates boomed wrathfully. The smoke from the houses thickened and spread, bellied out, billowed up into a dark cloud streaked with grays and yellows—a cloud that, constantly rising, drifted off to the eastward before the hot breeze from the west. It towered upward and hung against the sky in dark swags and folds, a half-drawn dusky curtain behind the bright green hill with its silent crown of entrenchments just above the scarlet shadow.

George Leonard looked at his palm. It was wet. He rubbed it against his thigh. "Charlestown's afire," he said. "Don't you want the glass, Seaton?"

My father shook his head.

Leonard took up the glass, got down on his knees and rested it on the window ledge.

He made a hissing sound. "They're going up again."

Buell hiccuped. "What's strange about that? Didn't they do it wrong the first time? They got to keep on doing it wrong, even if it kills every damned one of 'em!" His voice became politely formal. "I trust they have their packs on?"

"Yes," Leonard whispered.

"That's nice," Buell said. "Those packs weigh a hundred pounds, and if they took 'em off, they wouldn't be fighting the hard way. Those British generals wouldn't want 'em to win the easy way! Oh my, no!"

Mrs. Byles leaned heavily on her stick. "If they've got packs on," she said, "they've probably got 'em on for a good reason! General Gage and General Howe——"

Buell stopped her. "Excuse me, ma'am. I wish you'd go to bed so I can speak my mind! They ain't got a good reason for anything, ma'am. When they marched men to Concord and back, thirty-five miles, on the coldest night in April, they didn't let 'em have food or over-coats! And now, on the hottest day of the year, with only half a mile to go, they give 'em hundred-pound packs full of food and equipment for a week, and expect 'em to run up hill! Reason be God-damned, excusing me, Mrs. Byles!"

Reading 8

The Guns of Burgoyne

Bruce Lancaster

One of the decisive battles of the Revolution resulted from the attempt of British General John Burgoyne to cut the colonies in two. Marching down from Canada via Lake Champlain and the Hudson River with German mercenaries, Canadians, American Loyalists, and Indian allies, Burgoyne planned to link up with Lord Howe's forces at Albany. But before reaching Albany, Burgoyne and his army of 7,000 were defeated at Saratoga (October 1777) and surrendered to the Americans. It was this victory that made it possible for the United States to obtain the aid from France which proved to be the significant factor in the outcome of the war. In the following selection Ahrens, a German artillery officer, analyzes the weaknesses of the British army in the American wilderness and attempts to inform Burgoyne of them. In addition, he discusses the difficulty that the British had with their Indian allies—when the British attempted to train them, the Indians often deserted.

The General slapped the table. "You found it so, too? Amazing! What a contrast! British regiments which have fought all over Europe, camping in the heart of a world fresh from the hands of its Maker." A red arm swept in a great flourish to indicate the unspoiled immensity and Ahrens again had the impression that he was a public, an audience for the big man in scarlet and white. "The lake flows untroubled and unheeding past our—our pigmy rumblings.

From *The Guns of Burgoyne* by Bruce Lancaster. Published in 1939. Reprinted by permission of Jessie Payne Lancaster.

Its calm surface mirrors His Majesty's colors with the same unconcern that it will later mirror the flaming crimson and gold of the oaks and the maples, blushing under the sharp-fingered touch of autumn!" He threw back his fine head and stared past Ahrens as though listening to fluttering applause.

"Exactly, sir." Ahrens nodded. "The contrast, wherever you look. I saw a platoon of the 21st—your oldest regiment, I believe—halt to allow a file of Indians, painted red and black, to trot by."

"Gad, sir!" Burgoyne shook his head. *"You* see it. But I tried to show it all to Lady Acland. Red skins mingle with red coats. The pavements of London rub elbows with the trackless forest. Rifle and tomahawk, field-piece and arrow, old regiments and old tribes, all crowded about this—this Elysian body of water. Pointed it all out to her. What did she say?" His voice rose to a mincing treble. " 'Oh, General, how nasty the Indians smell!' " He buried his head in his hands, a thwarted artist. "Never mind. One day, Lieutenant, I'll put it all on paper, all on paper. Another child of my fancy to keep these company." He tapped a thick volume on whose cover Ahrens read: *"Dramatic Works of J. Burgoyne, Esq.,"* over the name of a distinguished West End publisher.

Ahrens nodded respectfully. Then he asked: "What brings the Indians to camp? There seemed so many of them."

Burgoyne's eyes widened. "What brings them? My dear sir, don't you know they're our allies? The eyes of the army, sir! They so screened our advance down the lake that to this day the Scotch-Yankee St. Clair doesn't know just where or how many we are! In-valuable!"

"And later—they will be employed against white men?"

"To be sure to be sure. Most necessary. In a primitive world, natural man must lead the civilized—up to a certain point, of course."

"But the stories we hear in Europe? Scalping, torturing, killing of women and children?"

Gentleman Johnny's jovial face clouded. "There it is, there it is," he said, half to himself. "What will happen when we push south into the rebel country?" Then aloud he said: "La Corne St. Luc, savage old man of Auvergne, keeps shouting: 'Il faut brutalizer les affaires—il faut les brutalizer!' " He shook his head. Then he brightened. "But I'm sure I can hold them in check." He dove into a mass of papers, selected a couple of sheets. "Listen to this. My address at the Bouquet River last week, my address to the tribes. They tell me it produced an excellent effect."

He cleared his throat, squared his elbows. "I begin by welcoming them —but that wouldn't interest you. Here we are—I flatter them, then admonish them. Let me see—where are we?" He frowned at the sheets while Ahrens' imagination supplied the rustling of a curtain, the flare of footlights.

"Yes, yes. Here it is. 'Persuaded by your magnanimity of character joined to your principles of affection to the King' and so on 'I enjoin your most serious attention to the rules which I hereby proclaim for your invariable observation during the campaign.' At this point, Lieutenant, there were loud cries of 'Etow! Etow!' Like our crying 'Hear, hear!'—a sound which I may say I have often heard during my speeches in Parliament." Then he grinned boyishly. "You know, I felt like an older fellow explaining house-rules to a group of new boys. First day of the new term. Then here are the rules. Pitched it in strong to them, I did.

" 'I positively forbid bloodshed when you are not opposed in arms. Aged men, women, children and prisoners must be held sacred from the knife or hatchet, even in time of actual conflict. Base, lurking assassins, incendiaries, ravagers, plunderers of the country, to whatever army they may belong, shall be treated with less reserve, but the latitude must be given you by order, and *I* must be the judge of the occasion.' " He raised his eyes, grinning. "Here again they cried 'Etow! Etow!' Then one of their chiefs replied and swore obedience on behalf of the tribes. Or so the interpreters told me. So I shook hands with the old chief and shouted 'Etow!' Really! Just like that! 'Etow!' Should have heard 'em yell! Then I had rum served and they staged a war-dance. Gad, Ahrens! What a sight! Hundreds, thousands of the red beggars. Painted red and black and blue and yellow! Some of them stark naked, leaping and crouching! One of 'em—ho-ho-ho-ho! Never saw such a thing. One of 'em, stripped naked he was, but to preserve decencies, he'd tied a dead blackbird about his privities! Ridiculous! Magnificent! And the others—some wore helmets made of buffalo heads, horns and all. And our men standing about in a great circle. Should have seen it, really. Bearskin caps, brass helmets, red coats, blue coats, with the mass of savages whooping and tossing in the center. And the falls roaring beyond and the pines high over everything! It was—Come in, Charteris. Something for me?"

Charteris, languor gone, stepped quickly through the door. "Word from General Fraser, sir. Runner reports that he has pushed down. Indians are in contact with the forts. Light infantry will be, in an hour or so. Some gun fire but no damage."

"Contact?" Burgoyne sprang from his chair. "We'll move the main body down the lake at sunrise tomorrow. Land above the forts. Send out the orders to all units, Charteris. At once!" Rapidly he ran over the prearranged schedule of attack, his flamboyancy, his foppishness completely gone. He was hard, keen, competent. "See that they all understand. Translations are here. Ahrens, you'd better take 'em to Riedesel. He'll issue 'em to his commanders. And here's a set for you in English in case there's any question. Lord, I hope Breymann and Baum will forget their eternal squabbling!"

"Then I'll stay with the Baron?" asked Ahrens.

"No, no. Report back to me. Wait, though. I've written a general order for the whole army. You can put it into German for me later. Read it to all units tonight. Listen to this, Charteris."

He selected a small sheet of paper from his table, then faced his two officers, hand thrust in the front of his waistcoat, head thrown back.

"The army embarks tomorrow to approach the enemy. We are to contend for the King and the Constitution of Great Britain, to vindicate Law and to relieve the oppressed—a cause in which His Majesty's troops and those of the Princes, his allies, will feel equal excitement." He fixed Ahrens with his magnetic eye. "The services required of this particular expedition are critical and conspicuous. During our progress occasions may occur in which, nor difficulty, nor labor, nor life are to be regarded." His voice swelled to a rising crash. *"This army must not retreat!"*

Ahrens felt himself carried away by the sweep and swing of Burgoyne's delivery. Even Charteris murmured: "Bravo, General! That will fetch 'em!"

Burgoyne smiled calmly. "Short, soldierly and stirring! By gad, I don't believe you can better it! And the peroration—'This army must not retreat!' Thuds out like drum-beats. We'll sweep the rebels out of their forts and down the Hudson. Untrained rabble, gentlemen, cannot stand before His Majesty's fighting regiments. We'll be in Albany in a fortnight! Sooner! Join hands there with Howe and the rebellion is as good as over. Now off with you!"

"What the devil?" Ahrens looked back over his shoulder as he walked with Charteris from the wide door of the barracks, sun dappled under the pines. Two men were nearing the entrance. The foremost was short, bull-necked and with extraordinarily long arms and thick shoulders which strained at a white coat, almost effeminately laced and braided. But it was his companion who drew the exclamation from Ahrens and even widened the bored eyes of the Englishman.

Six feet four inches in height, naked except for a breech-clout and long Indian leggings, the second man seemed to float rather than walk over the soft carpet of pine-needles. From his shaven head a stiff scalp-lock of pure white jutted up, an eagle feather bound into it. A long white beard fanned out over his muscular chest. His eyes were fierce, blue, staring, his nose a beak, his mouth a steel trap, his whole face like some savage pagan god from the earliest dawn of history, a face of terror, yet of strange beauty.

Charteris rubbed his square chin, eyes narrowed. "God's teeth! If you'd told me of it, I'd have given you the lie. Look at the tomahawk and scalping-knife at his belt!"

"But who is he?" asked Ahrens.

"Take a long look, young fellow." There was almost awe in Charteris' voice. "Heard of him, now I see him. That is, that *must* be, La Corne St. Luc.

The other, the fop in the white coat is Langlade. Don't be misled by the coat. They are the most famous Indian leaders in America. Both Frenchmen. Langlade sprang the trap that did for my father's old friend, Braddock. But St. Luc! Old Auvergne family. Speaks the primest court French and every known Indian dialect. Can out-run, out-fight, out-think, out-last any Indian on the continent. Going on seventy. Knight of St. Louis. Fought against us in the Seven Years' War. Tried to go back to France after the peace. Shipwrecked. Both sons drowned before his eyes. Led the survivors through fifteen hundred miles of wilderness in the dead of winter. Never heard of pity or mercy. Scalps women and children like any savage. If he takes a strong captive he'll give him a knife, and, unarmed, fight him to the death. The Indians worship him. Has a nice taste in wines and silks, too. Dashed glad he came over to us."

Ahrens' eyes followed the Auvergnat through the gaping entrance. "Women and *children*! A chevalier de St. Louis! And with *us*! What do you think of it, Major? The Indians with us, I mean?"

"Indians? Haven't enough. Bring in ten thousand! Give old St. Luc a free hand!"

"But look here, Major. We aren't fighting savages; we're fighting Europeans, or people who used to be. You'd give that man a free hand against them?"

Charteris gave a wry smile. "Never heard of a tender heart being part of the equipment of a good soldier. These people are rebels, and that's all there is to it. They've asked for it. Give it to 'em. Never forget this, young man. In war your enemy is always a filthy scoundrel. The next turn of the wheel, of course, may make him your ally, in which case you endow him with virtues to which the gods themselves never aspired. But while he's your enemy, you'll never thrash him unless you feel in your heart that he's a son of a bitch. For the duration of the war, of course."

Ahrens shrugged his shoulders. "I suppose you're right. After all, what are we here for? To end the rebellion. Have to do it as best we may. We must accept the Indians, I suppose. Matter of getting accustomed to things."

They crossed a wide clearing where hundreds of red-coated men were going through embarkation drill, the ground being staked off in oblongs the size and shape of bateaux. Ahrens eyed them keenly. "Thought all your light infantry was ahead with Fraser. What are these fellows?"

Charteris shaded his eyes. "Light infantry? Oh, I see what you mean. Skull-caps and short jackets? They are just ordinary infantry. Usually wear tail coats and cocked hats. No new uniforms in over a year. Someone forgot. Cut up the tails for patches. Hats wore out. Trimmed down the cocks, tacked brass plates on front like the L.I."

"Better than tails or cocked hats for this sort of country, I'd say, with its undergrowth, brambles and so on."

Charteris shook his head. "Not regulation. Should be in tails. We'll give them new coats in Albany."

"When do you think that will be, Major? The General said a fortnight. Sounds too soon to me."

"Never predict on professional subjects. Tell you a few things, though. In addition to too much artillery, we've too much baggage, too few horses. When Burgoyne got to Quebec, he found Carlton had done nothing about carts or animals. Gentleman Johnny didn't do much either. Too busy with—well, you'll see her. Need double the number of beasts we have, treble. Seen our wagons? A few heavy ones, from England and the Continent. The rest, little two-wheeled carts pieced together here in Canada. Green wood. Tell me they fell to pieces by the hundred on the march down from Chambly. And we've got fifty miles of wild country before we reach Fort Edward at the headwaters of the Hudson. Need cavalry, too. What have we got? Two or three hundred Brunswick dragoons and never a sign of a troop-horse. Laughing-stock of the army, plunging along in their great boots and spurs."

"You paint a cheerful picture," said Ahrens grimly.

"That's not all. Bad feeling. St. Luc frothed at the General's speech to the Indians. If he walks off, they'll go trooping after him. We look down on the Brunswickers and Hessians. They don't like us. *Our* fellows get along after a fashion, but on your side Breymann and Baum are at each other's throat half the time. Hard to keep their swords in their scabbards. Albany in a fortnight? The way needs smoothing."

"But there's another side of the picture," said Ahrens. "We've got, by all accounts, a first-rate commander."

"Agreed. And the men worship him."

"Also, you've some of the finest regiments in the British Army here along the lake. Ours aren't far behind. The General tells me we've Canadian rangers and Tories as well as Indians for irregular troops."

"Yes, yes. There's that," said Charteris abstractedly.

Ahrens laughed. "Wouldn't the General fume if when we reached Albany we found Howe sitting waiting for us?"

There was a dry cough. "Look here. I imparted treasonable matter to you in Hanau about the plan of campaign. I'm going farther now. When we get to the Hudson and start down toward Albany, don't get eye-strain looking for Howe's bayonets coming north. Can't tell you more than that, and keep it to yourself. Now—follow that path to the left. Take you to Riedesel. He holds court in a marquee to be nearer his troops. My respects to the Baroness. Put her in command and we'll be in New York in a fortnight, not Albany."

.   .   .

"Can't learn. When we pushed out toward Ticonderoga, I guided a detail of light infantry. They wanted to reconnoiter the Yankee outposts. The officer in charge marched the men through waist-high scrub in parade formation. I could almost hear the rebels licking their lips. Dropped five of the men. Did that officer learn a lesson? No, sir! That was the way British infantry always advanced, he said. Said he wouldn't have *his* men wriggling on their bellies like Indians. Must have comforted the five men to know that they were winged when in perfect formation. There may be wild riding ahead of us and I didn't want to squire anyone like that over *this* road."

Reading 9

Oliver Wiswell

Kenneth Roberts

The American Revolution was not only a revolt against the mother country but a civil war as well. Perhaps a third of the colonists were loyal to the Crown, and in Georgia and South Carolina, the Tories, as they were called, constituted a majority of the population. Although 50,000 Americans, at one time or another, actively fought for the Crown, British officials seldom appreciated them or heeded their advice. In this selection Oliver Wiswell, an American Loyalist who fought for the British in the South, expresses the resentment that many Tories felt toward the British war effort.

To see Sir Henry Clinton I went through the same routine that every officer must follow in order to reach the presence of a general—officer of the day, adjutant general's office, the general's secretary, one of the general's aides; and finally, after long waiting, the general himself, a little paler, a little puffier, a little more sunken-eyed than when I'd seen him in November.

When I was finally admitted, and stood to attention before him, he looked up at me with condescending amusement. "Bless me," he said, "the young historian turned soldier! You've been gone long enough, Captain, to have found out everthing you were sent to get and a deal more." I have no doubt he thought of the look he gave me as quizzical.

"Yes, sir," I said, "I've learned a lot, most of it unpleasant." I took Lord Rawdon's letter from my pocket. "I was told to give you this, sir."

Clinton looked at it front and back. "Well," he said, "you *did* cover ground in your travels!"

He detached the seal from the letter, opened it, ran his eye hastily over the contents, and added, "Ah Yes! I had the bulk of this news a week ago. Rawdon speaks well of you and Lieutenant Buell, Captain; very well indeed. He also mentions certain opinions you formed in your travels through the south."

I suddenly knew that I couldn't convince Clinton by word of mouth. The mere fact that I had an American accent would put the black seal of unreality on everything I told him.

"Sir," I said desperately, "it's a long story. I've made notes for the report I'll make to Mr. Thompson, and I won't be long writing it."

"Come, come, Captain," Clinton said. "You didn't feel obliged to write a report for Lord Rawdon, did you?"

"No, sir," I said, "but that was because I knew he wouldn't—that is, I'd talked to Colonel Cruger and I think the colonel had perhaps explained some of my findings——"

Clinton folded the letter and stared at me. "You can make your written report, Captain," he said, "but I'd like an idea of your findings right now. What do you propose to say in that report?"

"I'm going to say, sir," I said, "that in spite of the magnificent marches made by British and Loyalist troops in South Carolina, in spite of the brilliant battles which they've won, in spite of having gained complete control over the southern states within the year, every gain has been thrown away because the victorious army stubbornly refused to understand Americans."

"Indeed," Clinton said.

"That's my firm belief, sir. Stanch Loyalists throughout the back country in both North and South Carolina have been badly treated because of being Low Church. British officers will not understand that Low Churchmen needn't be rebels. They say the rebel movement in New England was Low Church, so the same thing must be true in the Carolinas. It isn't true, but British officers won't believe it isn't."

"That's making a mountain out of a molehill," Clinton said.

"The Loyalists don't think so, sir," I said. "You've lost the active support of thousands of southern Loyalists on that one account. You've lost thousands more through promising help to Loyalists in various sections; then withholding the help, withdrawing your army and leaving the Loyalists to their fate. They no longer dare trust you! What's more, so many things have gone wrong under British leadership that they think nothing can go right, ever."

"Come, come, Captain," Clinton said, "you don't believe in such schoolboy ideas!"

"I do indeed believe them, sir. For seven years I've seen things go wrong in this war. For seven years British armies haven't followed up their victories, British ministers have refused to believe what they were told, British fleets have delayed too long, the wrong men have been put in high positions, Loyalists have been treated cavalierly by the very men who should be most grateful to them.

"The day of miracles is over, sir; and there'll never be a sudden end to all these blunders. They'll continue; and if those officers in South Carolina are right—as Buell and I think they are—one more mistake at this time will be fatal."

"Just what do you mean by that?" Clinton asked.

I'd gone too far to turn back. "Well, sir," I said, "Cornwallis is taking post at York, so that fleet and army can work together. They say in the south that if Washington marches his army down into Virginia and catches Cornwallis on that badly defended little point at York, it'll never get away except by swimming."

Clinton laughed heartily. "What daydreams you find in an army! Don't your friends in the south know Washington has his eye on New York?"

"They know some people hold to that, sir," I said, "but they think differently. They think that when Washington has word from Lafayette about the situation at York, he'll leave New York and move his army down into Virginia. They say Lafayette can wrap Washington around his little finger; and Lafayette's staying right where he is, watching every move Cornwallis makes. They say Lafayette'll coax him down."

Clinton looked at me incredulously. "Am I to gather, Captain, that you plan to recommend to Mr. Thompson that we give up the campaign in the south?"

"I think I must, sir. You'll never get back the territory you've lost; never! And the longer you continue to occupy cities on the coast, the more violent the feeling'll be against the Loyalists and against the English. You're only promoting civil war by occupying any part of the south; and I think I can show you, sir, that the best interests of England and America will be served by an immediate cessation of fighting."

I knew the look in Clinton's eye. I'd seen it before in Howe's eye, and again and again in Eden's. "Poor fool!" the look said. "Poor, simple, misguided, gullible, American fool!"

I knew he'd speak soothingly to me, as to a child or a hopeless idiot; and he did.

"That's all very interesting, Captain, and you must write it out at once. Write it out by all means, and I'll see it reaches the proper authorities."

"Sir," I said desperately, "this report ought to be made in person. Mr.

Thompson sent me to make it; and unless I can tell Mr. Thompson in person what's going on——"

"Write your report and bring it to me," Clinton said sharply. "You hold a commission in the King's American Dragoons, and Colonel Thompson would be the first to uphold me in assigning you and Lieutenant Buell to that duty. Since he's colonel of the regiment. I think he must be planning to come here in person to take command. If I'm right, Captain, you can readily see how useless it would be for you to suggest a cessation of hostilities to him or his immediate superiors."

"But they don't know conditions," I persisted. "The English people ought to be told what a useless, stupid war they're fighting! If I can only see Mr. Thompson——"

General Clinton struck a bell sharply, and an officer popped in. "I'm ready for you now, Major," Clinton said. "Captain Wiswell's just leaving. Hurry up with that report, Captain Wiswell. We need every available man for the defense of this city."

Chapter 3

The Building of the Nation

Reading 10

Those Who Loved

Irving Stone

One of the most remarkable couples in the nation's history was Abigail and John Adams. During his long and distinguished public career, Adams was an important Revolutionary leader, a diplomat in Europe, the nation's first Vice President, and its second President. In all of the uncertainties of this difficult era, Abigail supported her husband with wise counsel which often determined his course of action. Although she had little formal education herself, Mrs. Adams, as her letters show, was an intelligent, perceptive, and charming woman. During the time when the Constitution was still a piece of paper, the critical task was to convert its words into an effective government. The burden of that task fell upon the nation's first leaders, one of whom was John Adams.

There were fifty at dinner: the Governor's Council, the heads of the departments, Boston's leading selectmen, a variety of old friends including Francis Dana, now associate justice of the Massachusetts Supreme Court, Elbridge Gerry. Their ladies were gowned in silks and chambray gauzes. So many toasts were drunk to the returning Adamses that Abigail feared she might grow tipsy. She tried to catch John's eye as he talked excitedly to the men around him. Was this sumptuous banquet and resplendent official welcome a tribute for past services or an initiation dinner?

They had arrived home at a particularly auspicious moment. Before departing from London they had known of only three states which had ratified the Constitution: Delaware first, then Pennsylvania and New Jersey. News of the ratification by Georgia, Connecticut and Massachusetts had not reached them. Now they learned that Maryland had ratified in April and South Carolina in May. Only one more vote was needed for the federal government to come into being. The word in Boston was that their neighboring state, New Hampshire, was certain to sign in a matter of days, that Virginia too was poised to sign and that New York could come in within weeks. John Adams had reached home in June 1788, when the nation he had worked so long and heroically to create was about to be born.

"And that," Abigail decided in her mind, "is what I am celebrating at this reception."

The following day John was received in the Representatives' Hall of the State House by the General Court. Both Houses of the legislature assembled to pay him honor. A permanent chair had been assigned for his use "whenever he may please to attend the debates." The Acting Speaker of the House read a paper announcing that John Adams had been elected a representative to the Congress for a one-year term.

Back in the Hancock great parlor they found Charley and Tommy. Abigail was determined to gather both her little boys into her arms and cover them with kisses. But at the threshold she saw two young men garbed in spotless white shirts and gray smallclothes, their hair worn long and full over their heads. She stared, transfixed. Charley was now eighteen and a junior at Harvard College. His face, a replica of his sister Nab's, handsome and aristocratic, wore a warm and mischievous grin. Tommy, at fifteen and a half, was shorter, more compact; his face had the same plain open expression she remembered.

The moment for embraces passed. The boys approached their parents tentatively, bowed, shook hands, murmured their pleasure at seeing their mama and papa again. Johnny, they said, was well and would be in Boston as soon as he could find transportation from Newburyport, where he was apprenticed to Theophilus Parsons, a leading lawyer. They all seemed subdued here in the governor's house. Charley whispered:

"We can't wait till we all meet at home, Ma."

That evening when they had retired to their chamber and were resting on the handsome damask sofa, Abigail read from the report in the day's issue of the *Massachusetts Centinel*:

" 'Every countenance wore the expressions of joy—and everyone testified that approbation of the eminent services his Excellency has rendered his country, in a manner becoming freemen, federalists, and men alive to the sensations of gratitude.' "

"Most handsome," John murmured. His cheeks had been flushed since the first cannonading from the Castle. "I know that a man should not be rewarded for doing his plain duty, but I must say in all honesty that I enjoy it."

"Do I reship my furniture to New York?" she teased.

"Assuredly not."

"Might you find the Senate more tempting?"

"That has been proposed to me by friends. I think not. The Senate will be a smaller body but it is still part of the legislature. I have served many years in legislature."

The following morning Francis Dana came to call. He had been ill and looked poorly.

"As an old friend, may I presume to make a suggestion?" he asked.

"Of course."

"Then I would urge you to repair to New York immediately. The Congress committee which will set up the apparatus of government will be appointed at the beginning of July. You must become a leader of those discussions. You have been out of the country for ten years now. Though we know you in New England, the rest of the country knows you less well. In this way you will become known to all and put yourself into position for the highest offices in the new government."

"You are not suggesting that I can be elected President?" John asked in mock seriousness.

"George Washington will be President. The people want it. They credit him with winning the war. As President of the convention his was the most ameliorating voice. Without him I doubt me we could have secured ratification. He is a genius in his ability to persuade people of divergent points of view to work together harmoniously. The idea of a federal union is acceptable to people who fear federation only because they know that General Washington will become our President."

A silence followed his outburst. Dana continued after a moment.

"But you see where this places you, John?"

That night as they lay in the four-poster in the spacious guest room, Abigail propped her head inquisitively on one elbow.

"When New Hampshire ratifies, how will our national elections commence?"

"We're not certain yet. For the House and Senate it's simple: each state legislature selects its two senators. The representatives will be elected by popular vote in each state: one representative for every thirty thousand of the population. That means over one million men may vote for their representatives in Congress. . . . "

"You never did accede to my request to remember the ladies," she murmured.

He blushed. "Even though women do not have the vote they will live in a republic where the laws of free men will protect them. . . . "

"Yes, John. . . . What about the President and Vice President?"

"The Constitution says each state shall appoint, in such manner as the legislature may direct, a number of electors equal to the whole number of senators and representatives to which the state may be entitled in the Congress. These electors will vote for the President and Vice President. The federal government can commence shortly after all the ballots are counted at the seat of the government."

"Which will be?"

"The Lord alone knows! From what I gather, sentiment is evenly divided between New York and Philadelphia. There will be anguished bloodletting before that issue is decided."

"Who nominates the candidates for the presidency and vice presidency? How much bloodletting will there be before that issue is decided?"

He jumped out of bed, began to pace the bedroom floor in his ankle-length linen nightgown, hands gripped tightly behind his back. She noticed how far his hairline had receded, how the oval bald spot gleamed in the lamplight.

"There are no nominating methods prescribed. Groups of men who want to advance a candidate will meet informally and chart procedures. So will the government leaders in each state. They will work to have those electors selected who will vote for their favorites. Individuals or groups will be free to advertise their choices in the newpapers. Sodalities will arise in each state to persuade their neighbors. I won't know until it's over and study the results as a historian just how the process will work. All I know at this point is that the Massachusetts General Court will choose two electors at large, then they will select eight more names from a list of twenty-four sent up from our eight congressional districts. These ten men, all of them outside of government, will meet in the Massachusetts Senate Chamber and by majority vote select men for the President and Vice President."

She did not consider it discreet to ask if he also knew who their final choices would be.

Reading 11

Tale of Valor

Vardis Fisher

The purchase of the vast Louisiana Territory placed a great strain on the Constitution. Some individuals even plotted secession as a result of it. Partially to appease his opponents and partially to learn something of the nation's greatest real estate bargain, President Jefferson sent his secretary, Meriwether Lewis, to explore the vast area. With William Clark sharing the command, the expedition (1803–1806) journeyed into the unknown. Their instructions from the President and some of the problems they expected to encounter are treated in the following selection.

From *Tale of Valor* by Vardis Fisher. Published in 1958. Reprinted by permission of Opal Laurel Holmes, Publisher.

It was a simple problem. It was stated in a few words, which he had memorized, in the long letter of instructions which President Jefferson had sent him.
Those words said:

> As it is impossible for us to foresee in what manner you will be received by those
> people, whether with hospitality or hostility, so is it impossible to prescribe the
> exact degree of perseverance with which you are to pursue your journey, we value
> too much the lives of citizens to offer them to probably destruction. your numbers
> will be sufficient to secure you against the unauthorised opposition of individuals,
> or of small parties: but if a superior force, authorised or not authorised, by a
> nation, should be arrayed against your further passage, & inflexibly determined
> to arrest it, you must decline it's further pursuit, and return.

There the problem was, in plain words! From all that he and Clark had
learned, a superior force, egged on by the British, would be arrayed against
them. The President's orders in that case said explicitly that the party should
turn back! What were he and Clark to do? They were not the kind of men who
ever turned back. On the other hand, they were Army men, under Army
discipline and rules, and under the explicit orders of their commander-in-chief,
the President.

Captain Meriwether Lewis, Indian fighter, explorer, former secretary to
his ruddy, freckled-faced Albemarle neighbor and now his trusted adventurer-
in-discovery, chewed bark and searched his mind for a way out. He tried to
stand all the facts up so that he could see them. There were these: that Thomas
Jefferson's dream of a great United States now filled a continent; that for
twenty long years, as Minister to France, as Secretary of State, as Vice-
President, he had tried with every resource at his command to get the western
part of the continent explored and claimed for the United States before the
British or French or Spanish could explore and claim it; and that in his
Monticello home he had agonized in prayer over what he was doing, saying
to Lewis, "I have no right, I have no right, but I must, I must! God grant that
I am not making waste paper of the Constitution! But if Louisiana can be
bought I must buy it, even though I make ten thousand enemies for every
friend! And you, my friend, must explore it!"

But not with too much perseverance! Well, that set up another group of
facts. Jefferson had said to him, "My friend, you and your men may never
come back"—and he had looked at him clearly as an expendable man. But he
had also said, "If you all perish it will be my political ruin. The Federalists
will never stop crowing. For they say I expect to find a mountain of solid salt
out there, with an eagle of salt sitting on top of it!" He had said, in effect, "Go
on—and on, even if you all perish, even if I am ruined!" But he had said, in

effect, "The death of you and your party would be a major disaster—so use the utmost prudence in the degree of risk you take." *Which* had he meant? Lewis knew that he had meant both. His dream of a great United States that would be a world power was such a mighty beating force in him that he was willing to sacrifice anything to attain it. At the same time, his reluctance to spend even one man to win half a continent held him back and plunged him into a struggle with himself that Lewis had understood very well.

For it was his own struggle, now. When the men were enlisted for the Corps they had been told that they would go on a journey fraught with great dangers. They had not been told that they were headed for a vast unknown and the Pacific Ocean. They had not been tested in battle. They might not look with any enthusiasm to the founding of a greater nation upon their blood and bones. . . .

In the letter of instructions the President had also said, "To provide on the accident of your death . . . you are hereby authorised . . . to name the person . . . who shall succeed to the command on your decease. . . ." That was another matter that tormented him. If he fell, Will Clark would succeed him, and no better man could be found, he believed, in the whole wide world. When Jefferson called him to Washington and asked him to lead an exploring party, he had told him to choose an assistant who was a frontiersman, with thorough knowledge of the woods and the wilderness; who was bold and resourceful and a practical fighting man; who could endure great strain and hardship without complaint; and who, preferably, had some scientific skills. Lewis's mind turned to two friends, but he had sent the first invitation to Will, outlining the task and asking him to "participate with me in its fatigues, its dangers and its honors, believe me there is no man on earth with whom I should feel equally pleased in sharing them as with yourself."

Clark had replied at once: "This is an immense undertaking fraited with numerous difficulties, but my friend I can assure you that no man lives with whom I would prefer to undertake and share the Difficulties of such a trip than yourself."

But what if Will Clark also fell under Indian guns? Sergeant Nathaniel Pryor, perhaps—a lean, hard loose-jointed man who seemed to have the respect of all the men. The trouble was that though they had recruited their handful of men from hundreds who had wanted to go, they did not yet know them—and here were the Sioux, lusting for battle! It would take a hard winter, and possibly some fighting, to show what kind of men the captains had.

He looked down at his dog, who had pointed his ears forward and was growling. Lewis had no doubt that Sioux Indians were observing him while he walked. There might be a hundred of them, with their black fierce eyes fixed on him now. This whole country roundabout smelled of Indians—as some areas smelled of beaver or muskrat, some of bear or deer. It smelled of danger, and he liked that, for he had made the deliberate pursuit of danger his way of life. On up the river were other savage nations, the traders said—the Arikaras and Minnetarees; and beyond them, somewhere in that unknown which no white man had ever entered, were the Blackfeet, the most ferocious of all. These redskins, it was said, made fiendish and diabolical torture of captives their favorite amusement, the women being even more savage than the men. And beyond them, what? Jefferson had said, "You'll surely encounter many Indian tribes who have never laid eyes on a white man. They may all try to kill you." And again his gaze had said, as clear as day, that Lewis was expendable and he was deeply sorry about it.

Jefferson had said, "But what else can I do, except send an exploring party?" For he had known for a long time what the British were up to: having lost their colonies in ignominious defeat, and then developed for them such hatred that no American in England was treated with anything but contempt, they were now determined to colonize as much of this continent as they could. What they could not seize they would let the Spanish or French have, rather than the Americans. With what venom the parents had turned on their children!

Knowing all this, Jefferson had written to George Rogers Clark: "They pretend it is only to promote knowledge I am afraid they have thoughts of colonising. . . . Some of us have been talking here in a feeble way of making the attempt to search that country but I doubt whether we have enough of that kind of spirit to raise the money. How would you like to lead such a party?"

General Clark had declined, for reasons unknown to the man chewing green bark and turning an inner ear to the rumblings in his stomach. Talking in a feeble way! It had not been in a feeble way that the President had talked to his secretary. He had said, We must have all that country for the United States. *We simply must!* He had read about it everything he could find, and night after night in a big room lined with books he had talked to Lewis about it, saying that there might be untold wealth out there in minerals, lands, forests, as there certainly was in pelts.

What an elated man he had been when the whole of Louisiana had fallen into his lap! He had sent ministers to Paris hoping to buy New Orleans for two million dollars, and right out of the blue Napoleon's minister had asked them what they would give for *all* of Louisiana. How large was *all* of it? Jefferson had wondered aloud when talking after midnight with his secretary, or wandering with him in the grounds, their two tall ungainly forms looking to the servants as if at any minute they might topple over. Did it rightfully include a part of Canada? Did it include what was known as California? "The Constitution gives me no right to buy land but we must have it, all of it. . . ."

We must have it, Lewis thought, chewing bark. He knew that the whole matter possibly rested upon his judgment and Clark's. For if they did not push through to the ocean and claim it—if they perished or in defeat turned back, Jefferson's enemies would never allow another party to go, never, and the whole enormous wealth of it would lie there for the British to take. Yes, good Lord, he was aware that the whole matter rested in his hands, now, right here in Sioux land!

"... *you must decline it's further pursuit* . . ." That was an order from the commander-in-chief. If only he knew whether he had meant it, or had merely put the words down in a moment of compassion! Perhaps he should go back and ask Captain Clark what he thought. He was not Captain Clark, really, and what a pity it was! Jefferson had intended that he would be, but the thickheaded brass of the War Department had denied the commission. Sensing his chagrin and hurt, Lewis had said to him, "Between us it will make no difference: you're to be absolutely equal with me in all things. We mustn't let the men know. You'll be Captain Clark to me and Captain Clark to them." When before their men the two captains always addressed one another by title and often when together alone.

Returning to the keelboat and going to his friend, who still stood watch, looking toward the east bank, Lewis said, "Captain Clark, the woods over there smell like solid Sioux. I expect maybe a hundred of them were watching me."

"At least that many," Clark said. He nodded his head to the northeast, where clouds of smoke lay low above the autumn woods. "Signal fires. They're calling them in to hold a big powwow."

Lewis grinned faintly and said, "We should have brought the Hill of Devils with us." A month earlier the captains had been shown a conical hill, in which, the Indians said, lived a multitude of devils. These fiends, only eighteen inches high, had huge heads and the sharpest arrows on earth, which they shot into anyone who approached their home. Indians had been seen running away as filled with arrows as a porcupine with quills.

Sensing that his friend was in no mood for levity, Lewis said, "Will, there's one thing I can't make up my mind about. In his orders to us the President said that if we meet a superior force we must decline battle and turn back."

Clark looked at Lewis, his face showing astonishment. "You never told me that."

"I never thought of it, I guess."

"Why would he imagine we wouldn't meet superior forces, or that we'd turn back if we did? We might meet superior forces a dozen times before we reach the ocean. As for turning back, I'd never heard of that."

Lewis felt a warm glow inside. This was his kind of man, the kind who never turned back. But he said, "You and I didn't undertake this enterprise to turn back but there are two things that worry me. One is that the President told me that if we are all killed his political life would be ruined. The other —"

Clark interrupted. "His political life would be ruined? If we're all killed —"

"Yes, we'll be ruined too," Lewis said, his eyes full of mischief. "But what he meant, my friend, is this, that if he's ruined politically there would never be another exploring party. Then the British would gobble it all up."

"I expect that's right," Clark said.

"The other thing is, do we have a right to sacrifice all our men? I mean it's all right for you and me. Our lives belong to us. But at what odds are we going to risk our men?"

William Clark was looking at him, looking straight into his eyes. It was not that he doubted for a moment the courage, or the valor, of this man who had fought with him in one Indian war after another. He knew that they didn't come any bolder than Merne Lewis, or any more reckless—and it was because the man was so reckless that he looked at him now, wondering what change had come on him, or if the President had given him secret instructions. Then he thought he knew what it was.

He said, "From the start I've figured we're all expendable men. I'm sure the President looked at it that way. We certainly don't want to take foolish risks. On the other hand, we set out for the ocean and that's our goal. As for our men, every one of them was told that his life would be in great danger on this journey and that he might not come back."

"That's true," Lewis said. "Still, some of them are so young."

Clark had turned back to the signal fires. He now looked again into Lewis's eyes and said, "You told me the President left the matter to our judgment."

"He said he couldn't prescribe the degree of perseverance. He also said he valued too much the lives of citizens to offer them to probable destruction. And he said without qualification that we are to turn back if we meet a superior force—and by that I expect he meant such a force as all the Sioux warriors, if they should come against us. Believe me, Will, I've been out there in the woods all this time thinking about it. I want to obey orders, and I know you do. We also want to win this great unknown land for the United States. Maybe it's a bigger gamble than we yet realize, but I would say here and now that no matter what comes we'll go on. We'll go on as long as there is one to follow."

William Clark put out a hand and said, "That settles it."

That settled it. Neither captain ever spoke of the matter again.

Reading 12

Letter of Marque

Andrew Hepburn

During the bitter struggle between France and England (1794–1815), American trade prospered. But as each of the rivals tried to keep the neutral countries, especially America, from trading with the other, both repeatedly interfered with neutral shipping. The most important grievance that the United States had was with Britain over the impressment of seamen. Whenever it had a shortage of men, the British navy stopped American ships and seized American seamen. By 1812 an estimated 5,000 sailors were believed to have been impressed into the Royal Navy. The British justified the practice on the grounds that British deserters could obtain American citizenship illegally and then sign on with American merchantmen at high wages. To the young nation this practice was extremely galling. The following selection tells how impressment was done.

Stockton made no reply. Because none of his men had ever been impressed, Captain Williams would not believe it could happen to him. One thing was sure; if the frigate did want men, there was nothing the *Caroline* could do about it. The mate looked at the guns and wondered grimly what would happen if they were to resist the frigate's demands on them. Four-pounders were good enough to scare off marauding Arab dhows or Chinese pirates, but they were hardly the size or weight to impress a man-of-war.

Captain Williams snapped shut his long glass. "There!" he exclaimed. "As I thought. The boat is leaving the *Diomede* with the same number of men she had before."

"I hope you are right, sir."

"I know I am right. Heave the ship to, Mr. Stockton, and we will wait for her."

Every man in the ship was on deck to watch the frigate, but Stockton was too sick at heart to order them back to work. They would be lucky if no more than a quarter of them were seamen in the Royal Navy by nightfall.

The *Caroline* was brought around and hove to with her head to the southward, and Stockton looked across at the frigate. The boat had just returned and the big ship instead of hoisting her out, took her under tow with her crew on board, and stood down for the *Caroline*. She sailed by, close astern,

From Andrew Hepburn, *Letter of Marque*. Reprinted by permission of Little, Brown and Company.

and Stockton caught a glimpse of the red coats of the marines through her open ports and a cluster of blue uniforms aft, with indistinguishable faces above the rail, looking down on them. The frigate dropped the boat and went on for a quarter of a mile, where she was again hove to.

The boat, her varnish work flashing in the sun, came alongside, her crew peaked their oars smartly, and the midshipman in charge of her bawled angrily for a ladder. At Stockton's nod, the boatswain flung the Jacob's ladder over the rail and the midshipman climbed aboard, followed by ten bluejackets armed with cutlasses and pistols.

Captain Williams was at the rail to meet him.

"Good morning, sir," he said cheerfully. "I am Captain Williams. If you will come below, I will show you my papers."

The little midshipman, who was about fifteen years of age, looked him insolently up and down.

"I have no desire to see your papers. It's your men I want. Line them up against the rail."

A moment of stunned silence fell over the ship. Captain Williams was thunderstruck. Then his face grew red with anger.

"Rudeness will get you nowhere, young man. My men are American born, every one of them."

"That is what all you Yanks say," the little midshipman said perkily. His voice sharpened. "Line 'em up or I'll take every one of them."

The captain's face was now purple with his bottled rage but he had no choice. While he fumed, silent and helpless, the men were lined up with their backs to the rail, their faces angry and sullen. The midshipman strutted down the line, looking them over like so many cattle. In spite of his fury, Stockton had to acknowledge that the boy was no fool. Unerringly he picked out nine of the ship's best seamen and ordered them to step forward.

"These men are Britons," he said cockily. "You don't breed 'em like this in America."

A low angry sound broke from the seamen that was so threatening that the bluejackets, hands on their cutlasses, closed in around the midshipman and the men he had selected.

Stockton looked at Captain Williams, but though he was still flushed with the heat of his anger, he remained unmoving, helpless in the face of this disaster. There was nothing to be hoped for from him. Stockton moved forward to face the little midshipman.

"Please consider what you would do to us by taking these men," he said, trying to speak with restraint. "You have chosen a quarter of our crew and we are bound to the northwest coast and China. We won't even be able to man our guns."

"Get aft and hold your tongue!"

Stockton had held himself in thus far, but to be addressed in this manner by a little squirt ten years his junior was more than his self-control could stand.

"Who do you think you're talking to, you little jackanapes!" he roared.

The midshipman flung aroung. "Into the boat with him!"

"No, you don't, by God!" Stockton exploded, swinging at him.

The little midshipman's voice rose to a scream. "Wicks! Jones! Seize that man!"

It seemed to Stockton that the bluejackets swarmed over him in one mass of flailing arms and legs He had not come up the long road from the forecastle without learning how to take care of himself and he fought more furiously than he had ever done in his life. Later he could dimly remember giving a sweet blow under one red ear that had knocked a huge bluejacket across the deck, and a punch in the stomach that had doubled up another. After that, they piled on top of him and he couldn't sort out the details. With ten against one, the fight was of short duration, but when they had secured him, he got a faint solace, even at the moment of his defeat, from seeing that there wasn't one of his captors who wasn't marked by his fists.

The bluejackets passed him down into the boat and lashed him to the thwart. While he was still laboring for breath, he heard scuffling and swearing from the deck above and other men were pushed down into the boat. Last of all, Macy was lowered and put on the bottom boards, where he lay still and white.

Stockton swore under his breath and tugged at his lashings.

"He's not hurt bad, sir," said one of the men from behind him. "It's me, Nelson."

"What happened to him then?"

"He's just knocked out, sir. He put up an awful scrap after you did. But they hit him on the head with a pistol butt, the dirty bastards."

"Silence, you bloody Yanks!" growled one of the boat's crew.

"So now they admit we're Yankees," Nelson said. "Changed their tune."

"Quiet, Nelson," Stockton ordered. There was no sense in starting a row in the boat.

"Yes, sir. But if I get my hands around that whore's son's throat—" At another low-voiced command from Stockton he subsided, muttering.

Eventually, the little midshipman came down the ladder and the boat was shoved off. Not a head appeared above the rail of the *Caroline* as they pulled away.

The British frigate looked large and menacing as they approached her.

She lifted her black sides with the yellow wales slowly to the long swell until her green cooper sheathing was exposed, wet and glistening, spotted with barnacles and brown weed. Her gun deck ports were closed, but the carronades on her spar deck were run out and manned. Stockton could see the faces of her crews looking down at them through the open ports.

As the boat came alongside, her crew peaked their oars and laid them in, Stockton's lashings were cast off, and he climbed with the others up the boarding cleats on the frigate's side. When he reached the deck he marched aft before anyone could stop him, conscious of many eyes following him, to where a group of officers were standing at the foot of the mizzenmast. They stared at him, struck speechless by his audacity in approaching the sacred quarterdeck with blood on his cheek and his jacket torn halfway up the back.

"Gentlemen," he said politely, "can you please direct me to your commanding officer?"

They gazed at him without answering, and one of them laughed. Then a tall beefy lieutenant turned to him.

"Sir Robert is below," he said, "and cannot be disturbed. If you will go forward, my man—"

"Sir, this is a matter of some urgency. I am the chief mate of that American ship, and my men have been forcibly—"

"Get for'ard, I say!" roared the lieutenant, his eyes blazing.

Stockton, his face set, stayed where he was.

"I insist—" he said doggedly, but he got no farther. He was grabbed from behind by a couple of marines who turned him around and propelled him forward. The other men from the *Caroline* were lined up against the rail by the entry port, except for Macy, who lay stretched out on the deck, still unconscious. The little midshipman was writing their names in a book.

"Take that one down to the cable tier and secure him," he snapped to the marines.

Stockton was taken below to the gun deck and thence down a steep ladder into the darkness. He could tell easily enough were he was. A damp musty stench greeted his nostrils as they descended, and when one of the marines struck a spark from his flint and steel and lighted a lantern hanging from a hook in the deck beam, he could see the massive anchor cable coiled in tiers to the deckhead, leaving a space about ten feet wide, extending the width of the ship. At intervals, staples were driven into the bulkheads, to which chains and leg-irons were fastened. One of the marines snapped a leg-iron around Stockton's ankle, the other blew out the light, and they both climbed up the ladder.

For some minutes Stockton stood where he was, waiting until his eyes should become accustomed to the dim light from the hatchway. Above the noise of the crew going about their work and the creaking of the ship, he could hear the scurrying of rats somewhere in the cable.

He explored the space as far as his leg chain would allow and fingered the staple by which it was fastened to the bulkhead. There was certainly no hope of escape in that quarter.

He sat down on the deck and for a moment was overcome by the swiftness with which all his plans had been overthrown. He was still angry at the high-handed manner in which he and his men had been handled, but now his anger was also partly directed toward himself. He blamed himself bitterly for allowing his temper to master him. Had he restrained himself, Captain Williams would still have two mates. Gone now was his chance for an early command. He and the other men might well be kept in the Royal Navy for years. By that time, younger men than he would have commands, and he would probably be lucky to get a mate's berth in a small ship.

Reading 13

Magnificent Destiny

Paul Wellman

In the War of 1812 the United States suffered a succession of defeats on land and gained its only real successes on water. The Battle of New Orleans on January 8, 1815, was the most spectacular land victory of the war for the Americans, even though it was fought after the Treaty of Ghent had been signed, ending the war. The battle lasted less than half an hour, but the British suffered more than 2,000 casualties (280 killed), while the Americans sustained only 71 casualties (13 killed). Because of his leadership at New Orleans, Andrew Jackson became a national hero and was started on the road to the Presidency. This sketch describes the course of the battle and Jackson's role in it.

That night of January 6, in the very dawn of the new year of 1815, Major General Sir Edward Pakenham entertained as his guest a gray-haired, weather-beaten man, in his headquarters at the Villeré house, which stood some distance behind the British camp beside the Mississippi River. The garb of the visitor, donned for the muddy journey through the swamps from Lake Borgne, singularly differed from his usual splendid uniform of blue, white, and gold.

Vice-Admiral Sir Alexander Cochrane, commander of the British fleet, as hard-bitten a sea dog as the King's Navy boasted, already had made the eastern seaboard of America feel his wrath. Now he was in serious, even angry conversation with Pakenham, his host.

"With respect, sir," the general was saying, "the position occupied by the enemy is very strong."

"For British troops to carry? I'm astonished to hear such words from you, Sir Edward," retorted the admiral.

"My demonstration in force, the twenty-seventh of last month, revealed that the Americans are very cunningly entrenched, with some artillery, and a ship on the river for enfilading fire——"

"Mud ramparts!" interrupted Cochrane testily. "And behind them a chaw-bacon rabble!"

Pakenham slowly reddened at the sneering tone.

"What in God's name do you propose to do?" insisted the admiral.

"The position our force occupies here was injudiciously chosen," said the general. "Mind, I do not criticize Keane, who selected it. He was, as you know, attacked that very night and had tuck-and-go of it. Say what you will of them, the Americans have shown themselves nimble at night fighting, and have harassed us continuously. I have a casualty list of over three hundred——"

"Who spoke of night fighting?" broke in Cochrane.

"I referred, sir, only to *their* attacks. As for ourselves, we should be better off at almost any other point but this. I have even considered a withdrawal and new landing——"

"In the face of those miserable Dirty Shirts?" The admiral's scorn was open. "Why, your army, sir, should blast them off the face of the earth!"

"It might take more doing than you surmise, sir."

Cochrane gave Pakenham a bitter, even contemptuous look.

"If you are unwilling to take the risk, Sir Edward," he said, "perhaps I can bring over a few stout lads from my ship's crews to take that rampart of mud." And then he added, sneeringly, "Your soldiers might then make themselves useful bringing up the baggage."

Pakenham leaped angrily to his feet. Nobody had ever in his life accused him of cowardice, and this slur, undeserved as it was, made him furious. Had not Cochrane outranked him, there might have been a glass of wine in the face.

When he spoke, his voice shook with passion. "Sir Alexander," he said, "my soldiers need nobody to defend their courage, and this very closely touches my personal honor. We will assault that position—tomorrow. Or at the very latest, the day following!"

Andrew Jackson had hardly slept at all, and he had been awake continuously since three o'clock that morning of January 8. It was Sunday and in New Orleans the faithful were attending early mass.

Daylight had come at last, but a fog hung over the field, and from his lookout in the Macarte house he could make out nothing of the enemy. Nevertheless, he had been aware throughout the night of the sound of sledge hammers from the direction of the British lines—new artillery batteries being emplaced, very probably.

Just an hour ago a disturbing report had come from Commodore Patterson that men were crossing the river in boats at a point below where the *Louisiana* lay. That might mean a flank attack on the newly built "Kentucky Bastion," over on the far side of the Mississippi.

Those Kentuckians! He had looked forward most hopefully to their coming, but when they arrived two days before they were almost unarmed.

"I can't believe it!" he exclaimed in bitter disappointment when this was first reported to him. "I never, in my whole life, saw a Kentuckian without a pack of cards and a bottle of whiskey and a gun!"

But it was true. Of the twenty-three hundred men in the contingent, only seven hundred carried firearms. The others were enlisted militia who looked to the government to supply them with weapons—and the government, with its customary dilatoriness, had failed to do so.

Jackson expressed his opinion of the government and all politicians, in an eloquent, sardonic, searing, blasphemous condemnation such as only his tongue could fashion.

"I'll confront them with this!" he finished. "On my honor, I will! Some day I'll make those damned lily-livered, pusillanimous, time-serving, treasonable, cock-a-hoop sons of bitches in Washington sweat for this, or my name isn't Andrew Jackson!"

But after he thus expressed himself he tried his best to provide the weaponless with some kind of arms. Every gun that could be found in New Orleans was requisitioned—antique muskets, fowling pieces, even old Spanish *escopetas,* so far out of date that men had to be shown how to load and fire them. Yet not enough arms, even of this almost worthless sort, could be obtained to go around. It was enough to make a commander's head ache.

He sent the Kentuckians across the river to the bastion under the command of a brigadier general named David Morgan, and gave them some of Patterson's naval guns to support them. They were to guard against a flanking movement, and such a movement might now be in progress.

Yet he believed that the major blow of the British would be delivered directly at his front. Caught up in the unreasoning intensity of his dedication to the young nation he was defending, and filled also with the exaggerated passion for combat which was natural in him, he awaited the assault almost trembling with eagerness, or anxiety, or simple desperation. All the concentrated hopes and fears of the weeks were at last coming to an awful culmination.

Steps on the stairs. He had called a conference of his chief officers this morning for last-minute instructions in the plan he had prepared for the coming battle. He put down his excitement, and it was as if a vertigo had left him. When he turned to his staff, he was the cold, deadly-sure Jackson again.

He looked at their faces, one by one: Coffee's vast, granite countenance; the cold assurance of Carroll's eyes; Humbert, huge-mustachioed and a little drunk but an old soldier, ready; Villeré, young and just now subdued; Reid, handsome but very grave.

"Gentlemen," he said, "this may be the day the enemy has chosen for his grand assault." He repeated to them the message from Patterson. "If there is an attack on the Kentucky Bastion," he went on, "it will be no more than a diversion. Here—right here—will be the line where the British will smite with everything they have."

He paused. Nobody spoke. There was a slight shuffling of feet.

"I have given you your instructions," he resumed. "I repeat them once more."

Genius sometimes shatters military values and reassembles them in terms of the future. Jackson had thrown aside all military pedantry, and was preparing to fight as his own genius dictated.

He knew savage Indians at war, and how they often lay in wait for an unsuspecting enemy, hiding behind trees. Jackson, a product of the frontier, imagined nothing less than a gigantic ambuscade, in which a deadly force was to be hidden behind *an idea,* a sheer creative innovation much more decisive —if it worked—than any physical concealment and surprise.

"The rifle must be our hope," he said. "At one hundred yards, which is the battle range of the British musket, only forty per cent of hits can be expected from that weapon. But the American rifle will account for *fifty per cent at three hundred yards.* And at two hundred yards —twice the musket's battle range—our border marksman aims with certainty at an enemy's head or his heart. We have, therefore, the advantage of our riflemen. We must give the British every opportunity to accomplish their own defeat."

To General Humbert, who still thought in terms of war as it was taught him by Napoleon's armies, the novelty of the idea was difficult to accept at all, and especially as Jackson was proposing to put in into effect.

"But the rifles—even if they are as superior as you say, *mon Général*— hold only the left half of our front," he said.

"Very true," said Jackson. "But let me remind you of the enemy's reconnaissance in force a week ago. He came, remember, in two columns, the heaviest by the river. He will come that way again. His first demonstration was to feel us out and discover the weakness of our defense. He believes that two columns will seize us between them at a disadvantage. But his two columns, I promise you, will never act in unison. I will beat them one after another."

They listened with rapt attention, none lifting his voice.

"What did the British learn in their reconnaissance?" he continued. "The main discovery was that our greatest artillery strength is on our right, near the river, with the *Louisiana* to back it up. Continental battles have been decided by artillery fire—you well know, General Humbert, that Napoleon's concentration of guns has been his greatest tactical asset. Therefore, I firmly believe, the enemy will again advance a column along the river, much of the way protected from the *Louisiana's* enfilade by the levee. But this will be, gentlemen, more of a threat than the full assault. The column which attacks our left, near the woods, will this time be far heavier than the other, containing the best troops, the real assault."

He paused and looked them over, his eyes alight with his inspiration.

"And there," he finished, "is where my surprise awaits. I have purposely massed my rifles on that side, so thickly that they must fire by turns. Gentlemen, I confidently expect that we may see something new in war today."

A rocket suddenly soared upward through the fog into the clear air above, from the enemy position.

"I believe that is a signal of some kind," said Jackson.

Almost at once the men in the group could hear through the misty gloom a distant mutter of drums and the thin squealing of fifes.

"By God, gentlemen!" cried the General. "I think they intend to attack us under cover of the fog! Return to your units at once, and have your men stand to their posts! And may God help us this day!"

They needed no prompting. Leaving beside him only Major Reid, they clattered down the stairs to mount and ride to their respective sectors of the battle line.

Jackson stood staring, almost as if in a hypnotic trance, or as if he sought by sheer will power to see through the shrouding fog. It was the gravest moment his life had known.

However well he had laid his plans, they might be all nullified by the heavy mist. Hidden by it the British could approach within fifty feet of his rampart before they became clearly visible. The whole basis of his strategy—the far-killing power of his riflemen—would be lost. If the enemy, approaching within fifty yards, broke suddenly into view they might receive a single volley from his men, no more. Then their bayonets would be at the throats of his people.

It was a contingency he had feared but hoped prayerfully would not occur. Standing there, looking out from the gallery, his fists clenched so tightly shut that the nails cut the palms of his hands.

Presently he turned. He did not speak to Reid, but the aide followed him down the stairs and just behind him stepped out of the house.

The dense fog which hid everything was frosty. A heavy rime lay on the ground, and Jackson's breath was like steam before his face.

Painfully he stared through the white murk, listening to the sounds which told him of heavy concentrations of marching troops, now definitely coming nearer.

An actual feeling of nausea came over him. He had hit upon his improvisation, based on the shooting ability of his Tennessee hunters, which he hoped and believed would counterbalance the weight of the British battalions. To have the weather render his plan useless before the battle even started—it was too tragically disheartening!

Reid, glancing at his General's tense face, understood the turmoil going on within him. Then he noticed something that gave him a momentary thrill of hope.

"I believe, sir," he said, "there's a breath of air beginning to stir."

He pointed at a tree, green even in this midwinter season, and Jackson followed his gaze. A few leaves, sure enough, fluttered slightly.

"Pray God it does," said the General. And it *was* a prayer, a supplication to heaven from one who knew little of praying.

The stirring leaves began to dance, a cold whiff of air touched his cheek, and as he looked, the blanket of fog suddenly began to shred away.

Then, dimly at first, but growing clear as solid blocks of scarlet, the advancing British columns appeared.

Striking through the mist as it rolled apart and dissipated, the January sun shone on a field that looked as if it was of polished silver. A heavy frost had settled on the cane stubble, and the brilliant red tunics of the oncoming army contrasted vividly with the white earth underfoot.

"Just in time!" exclaimed Jackson. "Thank God, just in the nick of time!"

All indecision, all weakness left him. Something hot and alive seemed to flow back through his veins, sending its strength and vitality into his body.

"Major," he said to Reid, "send an order up and down the line. Every officer is to warn his men again, according to instructions given, making sure each soldier in his unit understands to which rank he is assigned, and at what commands he will take position on the fire step."

It had come. At last he was face to face with the dread British attack, fearsome because of the iron discipline and the natural courage of the British soldiers. He knew his only chance was to break the attack before it reached him. If those red columns ever came to his wretched mud rampart, their numbers and training could hardly fail to clear the works and make a butchery of the defenders.

. . .

Jackson mounted, settled himself in the saddle, struck in his spurs. The bay leaped forward, thudded across the yard, and rose under him to skim over the fence. As he rode he felt keen, alert, filled with savage anticipation.

In a moment he curbed the animal to a walk, and went slowly down the fieldworks, on the escarpment behind the trench, looking down at the long rank of his men already on the fire step of the rampart, their rifles lying on the parapet ready to be used. Below and behind them in the trench, out of the line of fire, stood two other ranks, each equaling the first, one behind the other, making a triple array.

This was the acid moment for his plan. At the word, which would be given by himself when he believed the enemy was in sufficiently good range for execution, the men on the fire step were to fire. But this would be no mere haphazard volley, such as was the custom of European troops. Each of his riflemen was to choose a picked target.

Having fired, the first rank would step down and reload, the second rank mounting the step to send their rifle bullets singing toward the British with the same careful aim. This rank would in turn be succeeded by the third rank, and by the time that rank had given its volley, the first would be reloaded and ready to take its place. If the thing worked as well as he hoped and planned, the stream of fire from his parapet would be almost continuous.

As he had predicted, the British were advancing in two rivers of red, with a glittering froth of bayonets, spiked with ensigns, flowing far back into the distance. Jackson tried to estimate their numbers. Ten thousand? He had fewer than four thousand, of whom a half only were riflemen. He could only hold a last-minute hope that they had been schooled well enough in the past few days to obey the simple commands on which everything depended.

With a rolling concussion the British artillery opened. Yes, they mounted new batteries during the night, Jackson told himself. Eight hundred yards, perhaps. Navy guns, by the sound.

A new barrage of Congreve rockets soared toward the rampart.

Jackson thought: They seem to have the range somewhat better.

A mighty explosion shook the ground.

Ammunition wagon, said his mind. Over to the right of headquarters. Direct hit by one of those damned rockets.

Slowly he continued to ride on the level ground behind the trench, where he and his horse were in full view of the enemy.

Just above his head a howling fiend passed, and an artillery horse fifty yards in the rear seemed suddenly to fly apart.

Reid, now mounted also, overtook him. "They're using red-hot shot," he said. "Some of the cotton bales in the rampart are burning."

Jackson's few guns began to respond to the enemy bombardment with belching roars. A choking, blinding cloud of smoke mounted.

"That's worse than the fog!" he cried impatiently. "Major, get back to the house. You can see better from the room above. When the enemy gets within four hundred yards, pass the word up and down for the artillery to cease fire."

"Yes, sir." Reid was almost shouting to make himself heard in the din. He hesitated. "Sir, with all respect, you're too exposed up here."

Jackson turned to him with the odd half-grin. "I've reached an age where my blood's not so hot that it tempts me to expose myself out of vanity," he said. "However, example is the greatest inspiration to men. I must not exempt myself from danger."

"Sir," said Reid, "the men have no doubt of your courage. By your leave, sir, they'd do much better if they weren't afraid *for* you."

Some logic to this. Jackson nodded, rode back to the house with his aide, and dismounted.

Across the frosted field the scarlet columns had appreciably narrowed their distance from the American works.

He descended to the wide bottom of the trench. Slowly he walked down it, speaking to his soldiers.

"Remember, boys, one rank at a time. Fire on the order, not before."

"Yes, sir, General."

"You bet, General."

The men's faces were serious. A few saluted awkwardly.

He passed on.

The big guns behind the rampart suddenly ceased fire and the breeze cleared away the powder smoke. The British artillery, however, continued to thunder in the center, between the two advancing columns.

Young Captain Jack Donelson, dark-eyed and thin-faced, judged the enemy's guns were concentrating on the American cannon, over toward the right. He understood there had been some losses over there, but nothing to shake the men.

The British were in rifle range now, he thought. Tense in the sharp frosty morning, he glanced up and down the trench at his own company of men, proud of his command. Then he mounted the fire step to watch the oncoming enemy.

The sight was impressive. British drums rolled, every man marched in step, every musket was at the same exact angle, every bayonet gleamed, whetted to a razor edge. All at once the column near the cypress woods, to the rattle of the drums, fanned out with well-drilled precision. By squads Donelson watched the red uniforms wheel to left and right, forming an extended front reaching from the trees out toward the ruins of the Chalmette house, a plantation home burned during the earlier fighting, about half a mile from the American parapet. For a moment the scarlet ranks stood stationary while more troops came up from behind, widening out, forming a second, even a third, front.

"When we goin' to shoot?" said a bearded Tennessean near Donelson. "I reckon I could hit a runnin' deer from here."

"Not until the order comes," said the captain.

He heard a hoarse voice cry. "Hooraw fer Ol' Hickory!" Then a cheer. The General was coming down the ditch, bareheaded, his face pale with determination, his eyes blazing. To Donelson he seemed at that minute a straight sword of fiery courage.

At the place where his nephew stood on the fire step, he halted and glanced up.

"How're you doing, Jack?" he asked with a twinkle. "Rather be home with Aunt Rachel?"

"Not by a million, sir!"

"We'll smash 'em!" said Jackson. And every man within hearing believed him absolutely.

The General climbed to the fire step beside his nephew.

"I was afraid the fog would hide them," he said. "Give our boys daylight to see their front sights, and they've got a target no real Tennessean can miss."

A sudden idea occurred to him. Frontier targets usually were cards with V-notches cut in them, rather than round bull's-eyes. The marksman aimed to strike the point of the V, and "Cutting the V" was an expression meaning perfect shot.

"Boys," he said, "I'm going to give you a V to shoot at! See those white crossbelts the redcoats wear. They make a V right above the cross-plate. Pass the word up and down the line to aim for the V—at the cross-plate that marks the point of the V. Tell 'em to cut the V!"

"Yes, *sir!*"

The homely thought appealed to every man of them. Jackson could hear his words, meaningful to the backwoods riflemen, caught and carried on in a ripple of phrases, the length of the rampart in either direction.

He descended from the fire step with his half smile on his face and walked back toward his headquarters.

Young Donelson waited, listening to the din of the British artillery, and he thought the order that would set all the rifles blazing would never come. The red ranks had resumed their advance, and it seemed irresistible, as if by its very momentum it would roll over any defense or obstacle.

Then he saw, far down the trench, the General lift his sword and bring it down. At once along the line came the command.

"Make ready!"

He echoed it to his company. And added, "Remember, men—by ranks, at the command!"

On the fire step hunting shirts crowded close to the rampart and brown Tennessee faces lay close to brown curly-maple rifle stocks. Flintlock hammers clicked back, and keen eyes squinted through sights on the long octagonal barrels.

"Remember," cautioned Donelson again, *"above* the cross-plates."

Far off to the right a thundering broadside burst from the *Louisiana* as she raked the British column near the river. An answering roar came from the enemy batteries.

Why doesn't that order come down? Donelson thought.

The long scarlet rank, marching smartly, bayoneted muskets stiffly at the carry, swept forward. Now the British artillery ceased fire for fear of injuring their own troops, and for a few moments a strange, chilling quiet seemed to hang over the field, in which the roar of drums and the shrilling of regimental fifes, and even voices of officers shouting orders, came suddenly clear and near.

"Look at them bastards dress their lines!" someone cried.

Far away, it seemed, a voice cried the signal.

"Aim your pieces!" shouted Donelson, and he heard the order echoed in each direction.

"Fire!"

With a tearing crash the parapet seemed to blaze a sheet of flame, followed instantly by a billow of smoke.

"Second rank!"

Already men were leaping up from the trench bottom to the fire step as the first rank descended to reload.

"Fire!"

Another flaming blast of death from the mud rampart.

The third rank replaced the second on the fire step.

"Fire!"

And now the first rank, rifles reloaded, was ready to keep up the furious pace.

"Fire!"

Jackson had waited with almost quivering anxiety to hear his first volley lash out. He watched as a second, a third, a fourth succeeded it almost without cessation. And by that time he knew that his innovation was working better than he had dreamed.

"We can keep it up forever!" he exulted. "Give 'em hell, boys! Give 'em hell!"

Through the acrid smoke haze he saw the British line suddenly grow ragged as it rolled forward with its dread precision. Gaps opened wide in it here and there, as if men had stepped aside from each other.

They had not stepped aside. The soldiers who had filled those gaps reddened the frosted field with their scarlet bodies.

Chapter 4

The Rise of the Common Man

Reading 14

Hunters of Kentucky

Samuel Woodworth

The election of Andrew Jackson to the Presidency in 1828 was interpreted as a victory for the "common man." Born under the most humble circumstances and orphaned at an early age, Jackson was the first "people's President," despite the fact that he was a wealthy Tennessean. During his bid for the Presidency, the "Hunters of Kentucky" was a popular campaign song that helped make Jackson a living legend. The song not only refers to "Old Hickory's" triumph at New Orleans but it also trumpets the prowess of the Kentucky riflemen who constituted the bulk of his forces there.

Ye gentlemen and ladies fair,
Who grace this famous city,
Just listen if you've time to spare,
While I rehearse a ditty.
And for an opportunity,
Conceive yourself quite lucky
For 'tis not often here you see
A hunter from Kentucky.

Chorus:
Oh, Kentucky! The Hunters of Kentucky!
Oh, Kentucky! The Hunters of Kentucky!

We are a hardy freeborn race,
Each man to fear a stranger,
Whate'er the game we join in chase,
Despising toil and danger,
And if a daring foe annoys,
Whate'er his strength and forces,
We'll show him that Kentucky boys
Are "Alligator Horses."

Now Jackson he was wide awake,
And wasn't scared at trifles,
For well he knew what aim we take
With our Kentucky rifles.
So he led us down to Cypress Swamp,
The ground was low and mucky,
There stood John Bull in martial pomp,

And here was Old Kentucky.

They found at last 'twas vain to fight,
Where lead was all their booty,
And so they wisely took a flight,
And left us all our beauty,
And now if danger e'er annoys,
Remember what our trade is,
Just send for us Kentucky boys,
And we'll protect you, ladies.

Reading 15

Canal Town

Samuel Hopkins Adams

National growth in the era following the War of 1812 was hampered by the high cost of transportation between the Eastern seaboard and the West. Canals were one solution to this problem, and the greatest canal was the Erie. When completed (1825), the $7 million project insured the commercial supremacy of New York City and speeded the settlement of the West. Its construction was an engineering miracle made possible only by overcoming the superstition and ignorance of people. The health problems encountered in the building of the canal and their solution are the subject of the following selection.

Natural seepage, it became only too evident, would not suffice to maintain a dependable depth in the new channel, even for the strictly localized traffic. Some of the small hill streams were now diverted. Together, the several sources brought the level to a point where shallow craft would float.

No engineer had considered the possible effects of pressure in the vicinity of the banks. Quicksands developed, resulting in leakage which ruined some adjacent farmlands. Squire Jerrold, whose project comprised the most porous part of the terrain, was plagued with threats of lawsuits. Within the village limits, breaks and faults in the geological structure caused cellars to fill and noisome pools to gather in depressions. The resourceful anopheles mosquito availed herself of these golden opportunities for egg-laying. Horace found a number of specimens, displaying their gauche and familiar attitude against inner walls. Having once suffered the discredit of the mistaken prophet, he was chary of playing Cassandra a second time. He waited.

Results were not long in showing themselves. On the third Sunday of a humid July spell, Dominie Strang, after preaching for less than two hours and with much still to expound, toppled across the pulpit in collapse. It might have been a signal, so prompt was the response from his flock. A dozen of them were down that evening. Other congregations fared no better. Within a fortnight, ten percent of the populace were alternately burning and shivering. It was an epidemic.

"Every house its own earthquake," quoth Carlisle Sneed between chattering teeth.

Palmyra had lived through onsets before and expected to survive this one. Happily it was a disabling, rather than a virulent type. But a new factor was present, an economic threat more disconcerting than any physical woes. The place was getting a bad name. The evil word, "unhealthy," was attaching to it. Wiseacres from the regions around surmised that the pestilent miasmas of the Montezuma Marshes had blown westward on prevalent winds and settled down upon the valley. While the affliction was at its height, flies reinforced the mosquitoes and contributed their quota of befoulment with the result of adding the gripes to the shakes. Palmyra was an unhappy town.

In this, its hour of travail, Rochester (now, in its expansion, having discarded the belittling "ville"), allegedly envious of its neighbor's prosperity, dealt it a foul blow. The *Rochester Telegraph* published a headline, "Palmyra Plague." The local organ came back with a red-hot editorial, stigmatizing Rochester as "a nest of scandal and an emporium of mud, disorder and outcasts." Palmyra it roundly declared to be "the fairest, the most enlightened, the most prosperous, the healthiest and lawfullest community between Hudson River and Lake Erie, and this statement we challenge malice successfully to confute."

Once hatched, the malignant phrase gained currency with the traveling public. Coach passengers manifested a tendency to avoid the local inns and bed down farther along the line. Custom at the Eagle fell off by a round quarter. New money ceased to flow into the village. Several projected businesses, including a chandlery and a storehouse, delayed construction. Worst of all, the danger loomed that the canal authorities might abandon their announced plan, upon which the village was capitalizing, to establish a local payoffice with all the consequent influx of ready money, and to make the two basins, soon to be enlarged to three, the chief loading port for the whole locality. And now possibly to lose this! With the warehouses already bursting their walls with waiting produce! What a blow to local pride and prosperity!

Attack of an unforeseen nature followed. Broadsides appeared in the various camps, cunningly worded to play upon the reputation of the valley for unhealthfulness. Work could be had under better and safer conditions in the Montezuma region. No fevers. No ague. Good wages. Good fare. Liberal liquor allowances. Generous prize offers. Work for one and all. Another bid issued from the vicinity of Lock Port where work was under way on the Western Section.

"Dig, Dry-shod and in Comfort," invited the contractors. "Why Risk your Health among the Miasmas?"

Squire Jerrold's men deserted, almost in a body. Genter Latham lost two sub-foremen and many of his best diggers. Not an employer in the stretch but suffered from the specious representations. The village trustees appealed to the Canal Commission. How was the work to be completed if these pirates were allowed to lure essential labor away with false promises? The Commission did nothing.

"Treason!" editorialized the *Canal Advocate* which had conscientiously rejected the proffered advertisements. "What kind of patriotism is thus displayed? These miscreants care nothing for our State's most glorious enterprise."

At a meeting of contractors and sub-contractors, the question of an increased wage-scale was mooted. Center Latham, the largest employer, vehemently opposed it.

"No digger is worth more than four shillings a day and damned few of 'em that much," was his dictum.

Nevertheless Squire Jerrold sent out a call for one hundred and fifty men at sixty cents a day, almost precipitating an open quarrel with Genter Latham. Lock Port raised its bid to seventy-five cents, and was followed by a like raise in the Montezuma area. Palmyra was threatened with paralysis. About this time, Editor-Pastor Strang, sorely afflicted in his bowels and with recurrent shakes to boot, retired from journalism, turning over his plant to a pair of energetic young men, Messrs. Grandin and Tucker, who immediately initiated a save-Palmyra campaign and set about organizing the citizenry.

Carlisle Sneed had been heard to say of Genter Latham that "no moskeeter with a fipsworth of sense in his noodle would risk breaking his beak on the old sharkskin." Nevertheless the great man looked yellow and seamed as he lumbered into Dr. Amlie's office. Horace reached for his thermometer, but the visitor waved him back.

"I ain't sick."

"You don't look well."

"You're nothing to brag of, yourself," retorted the other with a weak grin.

"I don't get much rest, these nights," admitted Horace, whose practice had increased beyond normal endurance.

"We're calling a town meeting tomorrow evening," said Mr. Latham.

"About time, too."

"That's as may be. Will you come with your microscope?"

"If the Board invites me."

"They'll invite you. And they'll listen to you this time."

"They'd better," gritted the medico. "I'll give them something to bite on."

The gathering, with the village trustees on the platform, had more than a touch of the grotesque. Nothing short of impending catastrophe could have dragged so many of the leading figures from their beds of pain and uncertainty. Chairman Levering, blinking out upon a sea of pallid faces, poised a tremulous gavel and, with a chittering jaw, proceeded to "c-c-call this m-m-m-m-m-meeting to orrrderrrrr." Simultaneously two trustees raced for the door with identical expressions of anguish and foreboding. Dr. Murchison in a front-row chair, bent over a stout cane, his skin of that unsightly hue termed "puke" except in the daintier prints which refined it to "puce." The old man, with a temperature which Horace Amlie expertly guessed to be at least 102, was game.

Horace, himself, was gaunt as a ferret from sleeplessness and overwork. Several times during the proceedings he was called upon to escort tremulous gentlemen to their distant goal. Palmyra's claim to be the healthiest settlement along the canal was not being well supported.

After a general discussion focusing on the dastardly threat to the town's growth and prosperity, Mr. Genter Latham (temperature 101½) moved that Dr. Horace Amlie be invited to express his ideas. The motion was seconded by Trustee Van Wie (twelve pounds underweight). Horace, who had fallen asleep on his bench from exhaustion, hauled himself to his feet and surveyed the assemblage with sore and uncompromising eyes.

"Well," said he, "how do you like it?"

A mutter of discontent answered him.

"You don't like it. Neither do I. You're getting just what you asked for."

Up rose the Honest Lawyer, shivering like a leaf. "Are you presuming to lay upon us the blame for a visitation of Heaven?" he challenged.

"It's a judgment of Heaven, I agree," said Horace. "But for what?"

"Our sins," said Deacon Dillard piously.

"Just so. Filth is a sin. And sickness is the judgment."

The Rev. Theron Strang, apologizing for a preliminary fit of active nausea, felt impelled to dissent mildly from this heterodoxy. Filth and flies were of Beelzebub, he admitted, but there was no Scriptural warrant for attributing disease to them, as his young friend implied. Dr. Murchison, for the medical faculty, concurred with the parson. Tenderly rubbing his distended abdomen, he repeated the time-honored theory of miasmatic poisoning. Horace stepped to the platform.

"Those of you who are queasy or incontinent had better leave," he warned. "I'm going to make you sick at your stomachs."

"Not me," announced Carlisle Sneed. "I got no stomach left to be sick at. I'm quitting." He tottered out followed by several other sufferers.

Horace extracted a covered fruit jar from his tail pockets and set it down on the table with a bang. It was half full of dark blobs, some of which appeared to be in a state of fermentation.

"Flies," he said. "Collected from local premises. Would anyone like to smell them?"

Mr. Van Wie volunteered, and was obliging enough to gag violently.

"Anyone else? Dr. Murchison? Mr. Upcraft?"

The Honest Lawyer shook his head. "What if they do stink?" said he contentiously. "So does a skunk. But a skunk's juice is healthy. It's good for a rheumy cold. Ain't that correct, Dr. Murchison?"

"A skunk," said Horace, "is a cleanly and respectable creature beside a fly. So is the dirtiest hog that ever wallowed in a swill-pile, or the foulest crow that ever scavenged in carrion. I'm going to tell you something about the flies that light on the food you eat."

With simple directness that brought out every point of disgust and nausea, he gave a five-minute character sketch of the local *muscae,* their breeding and feeding habits, their capacities as freighters of filth, and the human ailments which, in the opinion of enlightened science, they bore with them wherever they alighted. He then passed to the hardly more appetizing mosquito. When he sat down the hue of the faces below him was greener by several degrees. Maltster Vandowzer swallowed a brace of pills from the palm of his hand and broke the uncomfortable silence.

"Vell, vot do ve do? Vot doos de yong man vant?"

"An appropriation for quicklime."

"Vot you do vid it?"

"Lime every drain and cess in town. Scatter and lime such compost heaps as yours."

"Do you warrant that to cure our gripes and fevers?" asked Upcraft.

Horace was not thus easily trapped. "I'll warrant the dysentery will lessen," he replied. "Give me more money to treat the mosquito-breeding pools and I'd almost warrant the fevers."

"I maintain that there is sufficient evidence against the accused insects," insisted the always lawyerlike Honest Lawyer.

Horace had begun to tell them of the experiment at Shea's camp, when Deacon Dillard interposed the objection that they were dealing with conditions in the village, not out in the wild country where it might be quite different. He sat down, surrounded by the reek of mint juice which clung about all who worked in the minteries. It gave Horace an idea.

"Deacon, I've heard that you boast your workmen are the healthiest in town."

"It's true, too."

"Do you know why?"

"Because I pay 'em well, treat 'em well and feed 'em well."

"That's well known." Horace was not above currying favor by discreet and honest flattery. "But it isn't the whole story."

"What's your way of it, then?"

"Are you bothered with flies in your distillery?"

"No, siree!"

"Or mosquitoes?"

"Never see one of the dum things. The smell of the good mint keeps 'em away."

"There's your evidence, sir," said Horace, turning upon the Honest Lawyer. "The Dillard establishment stands near insect-breeding marshland. Nevertheless, no flies, no mosquitoes; hence, no fevers."

"*Post hoc, sed non propter hoc,*" growled Upcraft. "That ain't proof."

"It's flub-a-dub-dub," declared Murchison.

Chairman Levering joined the attack. "You say the canal breeds disease?"

"It does. The fevers have followed its course."

"Then you would do away with the canal, would you?"

"That's it," broke in Jed Parris. "Blow up the poxy Ditch and go back to honest teamin'."

Genter Latham was on his feet, his face aflame, his eyes brilliant with fever, but his mind under cool control.

"That's what it might come to, fellow citizens," he said with forceful quiet. "That, or as bad. If the present excavations are abandoned, if the canal is carried northward to the lake, east of us as the anti-Clintonian busybodies would have it, do you know what it means to Palmyra? Ruin!"

He sat down. An apprehensive murmur passed through his audience. That might all be so, somebody grumbled, but was it any reason for giving this young medical upstart the town's money to spend on bug-fights? The economy argument was stressed and backed by citations of householders' rights. Dr. Murchison heavily ridiculed the younger man's "fairy-tales with flies for hobgoblins." Chairman Levering's personal enmity for Horace inspired him to an attack upon the young doctor's professional ability.

On the other hand, what Squire Jerrold called the *"argumentum ad nauseam"* had made an impression. Deacon Dillard swung to Horace's support. Decker Jessup, O. Daggett, Silas Bewar and others of the smithy coterie were there to back up their fellow member. When, after sundry threats of personal violence had enlivened the proceedings, the question was put to general vote, the clean-up forces were found to have won decisively.

Horace went to work. In three days he made himself the best-hated man in Palmyra. With twenty-five dollars' worth of lime and a corps of volunteers, he invaded barns and outhouses, found offenses in the gardens of such respectables as the Leverings and the Evernghims, scattered Simon Vandowzer's maggot-breedery, and substituted the pungent tang of the chemical for the more familiar and homey odor of the hot-weather latrine. Lawyer Upcraft, scenting possible business among the new smells, tried to stir up some of his clients to suits for trespass. It came to nothing, because Genter Latham announced that he would bring the best legal talent of the state, at his own expense, to defend Dr. Amlie and his "limers."

At once the dysentery tapered off, presently dying out. But the fever was more obstinate. While new cases were fewer, the incidence was still above normal provided by the comparatively inconsiderable breeding places of the creeks, now supplemented by the canal pools. Both Latham and Jerrold warned Horace of the impracticability of obtaining a grant for draining these latter. Stoutly though he had spoken for it, the proponent of the mosquito theory realized that his case was neither proved nor proveable. If only he knew more about the mysterious "fomites." Read as he might, all procurable data —and these were pretty scanty and scattered—left him with a disturbing modicum of doubt at the back of his brain. If the fomites were, indeed, microscopical agencies of disease lurking on the person and in the clothing of the afflicted as well as inhabitating the unhealthful swamps and marshes, then it was only reasonable to believe that flying insects could and did transport them from place to place, from sick man to well man.

Unfortunately no microscopist had yet succeeded in identifying a fomite. If Horace could have produced a sketch of a horrendous crawler, bristling with horns, fangs and stingers, what a telling argument he would have had for the general public! Lacking such concrete evidence, he was prudently inclined to go slow after the initial clean-up. The taunt of "bugs on the brain" had hurt. He had a natural distaste for his growing reputation as a gratuitous busybody, a medical neversweat. Anyway, he had accomplished one good. Palmyra smelt sweeter than before.

Reading 16

The President's Lady

Irving Stone

Although he won a plurality of the popular votes, Andrew Jackson was
unable to obtain the Presidency in 1824. Four major candidates vied for the
Chief Executive position. Since no candidate received a majority of electoral
votes, the election went to the House of Representatives. Henry Clay, the
fourth-place candidate and thus constitutionally ineligible for consideration
by the House, apparently threw his support to John Quincy Adams in exchange for the Secretary of State position, which was regarded as the
stepping-stone to the Presidency. Jackson's supporters charged that a "corrupt bargain" had been made, and the issue destroyed the credibility of
Adams's Presidency. At the end of this selection Jackson promises that he
will be back—and he kept his word.

"I've just found a good reason to hope you are elected, Andrew. The rent at
the White House should be somewhat cheaper than it is here."

Andrew shook his head, smiling ironically.

"Not really. Mr. Monroe tells me he is going out poor and dissatisfied."

"And that's the office for which you, Mr. Adams, Mr. Crawford and Mr.
Clay are battling so furiously!"

"Maybe it's part of the genius of this form of government that men want
to serve in the highest offices, knowing that they will come out impoverished
and tender from the many beatings."

Their rooms were crowded with a host of neighbors from Tennessee,
officers from the Creek and British wars, the ever-growing clique of president-
makers and the many eastern friends Andrew had accumulated since his first
trip to the Congress in 1796. It wasn't until midafternoon of the second day
that she perceived their callers were men only. No woman had so much as left
her card at the Franklin House. Though there was a written invitation from
President and Mrs. Monroe to a reception at the White House, Washington
society, dominated by the wives of the higher officials, was pointedly staying
away. That evening when she went in to bid Emily good night she found her
niece in tears. At her feet she saw a newspaper which had obviously been
crumpled in high anger. She picked it up, smoothed out the page and saw that
it was the Raleigh *Register*. The offending article read:

I make a solemn appeal to the reflecting part of the community, and beg of them to ponder well before they place their tickets in the box, how they can justify it to themselves and posterity to place such a woman as Mrs. Jackson! at the head of the female society of the United States.

Emily sought refuge in her aunt's arms.

"Oh, Aunt Rachel, they're saying the most terrible things about us: that we are vulgar, ignorant and awkward frontierswomen without breeding or decorum. But they have never even met us!"

Rachel had never made any pretension about her education or culture. The imputations against her background she resented more for her parents' sake than for her own. She held Emily at arm's length.

"Wipe your eyes, child. This is all part of what your uncle would call 'the consequences of politics.' As for my lack of social polish, neither Mr. Madison nor Mr. Monroe seemed to notice it."

Late that afternoon they had their first callers: the wives of two senators. Rachel wore a dress of pale brown cambric finished at the bottom by two rows of "letting-in-lace," embroidered between with muslin leaves and touched off by an apron of cambric trimmed with two rows of quilted muslin. She had refused the elaborate hair styling with curls which Emily insisted was the newest thing, saying that she thought the height of her hair on top of her head made her face seem a little less round. She had tea served in her parlor. Her practiced eye perceived that it was curiosity that had helped overcome the ladies' prejudice. She thought, I'll not let them know what I see; but neither will I make a great effort. They must like us for what we are.

It did not prove to be a difficult task: at the end of an hour the women had become friends and were exchanging stories about the domestic problems in different parts of the country. Nor would they leave until Rachel had accepted their invitations to tea.

That, and Elizabeth Monroe's party for them at the White House, broke the ice; Emily was the happiest girl in the capital because there were invitations for each day. The December weather was springlike in its warmth; Rachel paid calls, and went with Andrew to dinner with friends, but they turned down the hundreds of invitations for the evenings to the theater, to parties and balls, content to remain in their hotel sitting room before the fire, smoking their pipes and receiving a few intimates. On Sunday mornings they went to the Presbyterian church to hear Mr. Baker preach, and one night a week they went to the Methodist church for Mr. Summerfield's prayer meeting.

On December 16, the results from the last state to vote, Louisiana, reached Washington. Andrew had the largest popular vote, 152,901; Mr. Adams came second with 114,023; Mr. Clay 47,217 and Mr. Crawford 46,979.

In the electoral votes by states Andrew had a decisive lead also: 99 to Adams's 84, with Crawford showing a surprising 41 to eliminate Mr. Clay from the race. Because no one candidate had achieved a majority the election would go into the House. Andrew's supporters were certain he would be selected: after all, the most people had wanted him, and the most states: he had the electoral votes of eleven states and needed only two more for a majority. With Mr. Clay out, the Kentucky legislature adopted a resolution recommending that their representative in the House support Mr. Jackson; the Missouri representative declared that since the people of his state wanted Clay first and Jackson second, he contemplated casting his vote for General Jackson; Ohio should be his, too, for he had received only a few votes less than Clay, with Mr. Adams running an unpopular third.

In January there were blizzards and snowstorms which brought Rachel down with a cold. The Senate was in session and Andrew attended faithfully each day. Old friends came in for dinner. Though Andrew refused to let them join politics with their food, they were nevertheless surrounded by intrigue: if he would make certain promises, commit himself as to whom he would name Secretary of State, the presidency could be his. There were rumors to the effect that Henry Clay had made such a bargain with John Quincy Adams, Mr. Clay to throw all of his influence and votes to Mr. Adams in return for Mr. Adams's appointment of Mr. Clay as Secretary of State. John Eaton was disturbed, but Andrew did not take it seriously.

"Mr. Adams is an honest man and a good man. He would not engage in a corrupt bargain. If he gets the majority of votes in the House, I will be content. He was my first choice, anyway."

They awakened on the morning of February 9, the day of decision, to find snow falling heavily. Andrew donned a greatcoat and boots and left the hotel in time to reach the Capitol by noon, so that he might participate in the senatorial count which would name John Calhoun as vice-president. When Rachel asked if he were intending to remain after the Senate adjourned and the House took its seat to vote for president, he replied that he did not think it proper for him to be in the House while the members were being polled.

He was back shortly after one o'clock, ordering dinner sent up to their room so they could avoid the milling crowds below in the tavern. The first course had just been set on their parlor table when Andy came in, the expression on his face clearer than any marked ballot: Mr. Adams had been elected on the first count! By prodigious efforts and brilliant maneuvering Henry Clay, singlehanded, had swung Kentucky, Ohio and Missouri behind Adams.

John Eaton stormed in, his face black with disappointment and chagrin, and proceeded to give Henry Clay a thorough castigation. Andrew heard him out, then said quietly:

"That's not altogether fair to Mr. Clay, John. He has a right to throw his influence to the man he thinks best for the job. You remember he once accused me, right on the floor of the House, of being a 'military chieftain who would overthrow the liberties of the people.' "

That evening they attended the last of President Monroe's regular Wednesday levees. Andrew congratulated Mr. Adams cordially. While riding back to the hotel in the Jackson carriage, John Eaton commented on how quiet the city was: no bonfires, no victory celebrations or cheering crowds.

"They wanted you, General," Eaton concluded morosely. "They feel cheated."

But nothing could shake Andrew's calm acceptance. For her own part, Rachel was content. On the whole it had been a decent election; the predictions that the Republic would fall into ruin because its Chief Executive was to be chosen by popular vote had failed to materialize; and so had her own fears of being pilloried by the opposition.

Back in their suite with a log fire crackling on the hearth, they had a hot toddy with Andy and Emily.

"How much longer do you think we will be in Washington, Uncle Andrew?" asked Andy anxiously. "I must be getting back to Nashville and starting my practice. I've got a bride to support, you know."

"Your uncle and I have a wedding present for you that will make things a little easier," said Rachel, knowing how disappointed the two youngsters had been at Andrew's defeat. "We are going to give you the Sanders plantation."

There were expressions of joy and much embracing before the young couple left for their rooms. Despite the fire, the room was chilly; Andrew wrapped a blanket about Rachel's legs, tucking it under her feet.

"Well, Rachel, my dear, I tried to make you First Lady of the land. You are not too disappointed, are you?"

She smiled inwardly, ran her fingers over the bony ridge of his face.

"Whatever disappointment I may feel is for you."

"Well, then, I'll be happy to get back to the Hermitage."

"For how long?" she asked softly. ". . . until the next election?"

His eyes met hers. They were stern.

"I will be fifty-eight in a month. Mr. Adams is certain to serve the regular two terms. Surely you don't think at the age of sixty-six . . .? This is *forever!*"

He used that word to me at home, thought Rachel, but this time he means it. Perhaps at long last he will be content to remain a gentleman planter.

Forever lasted five days. On February 14, President-elect Adams offered the post of Secretary of State to Henry Clay. All hell broke loose, in Washington and across the nation . . . and particularly in their two rooms in the Franklin House. People came and went continually, all passionately protesting against what now appeared to have been a swap of votes for office.

Every ounce of Andrew's calm and acceptance vanished. She knew from the sense of outrage that shook his long lean frame that nothing in his tumultuous career, always excepting the maraudings of the British, had ever made him so utterly determined to avenge a wrong. As he stood in the far corner of the room surrounded by his most ardent supporters, she heard him cry:

"So the Judas of the West has closed the contract and will receive the thirty pieces of silver? The end will be the same. Was there ever witnessed such a bare-faced corruption before?"

A dozen voices answered him at once.

"But surely Mr. Clay will know that the whole country is outraged?" "He can't be so stupid as to accept . . ."

"What, refuse his part of the booty?" Andrew's voice, as it penetrated to her, was shrill and cold. "But he must go before the Senate for confirmation. By the Eternal, gentlemen, I still have a vote there, and I pledge you my word that I shall unboosom myself. This barter of votes is sheer bribery, and if allowed to continue will destroy our form of government."

Three weeks later, in a slanting rainstorm, the family left the capital, all four riding in the carriage with the extra horses tied behind. Andrew was silent, his head on his chest, his eyes closed; he was still smarting from his defeat in the Senate where he had been able to garner only fourteen votes against the appointment of Mr. Clay. She had persuaded him that, as a matter of form, he should attend the inauguration. He had complained to her that Mr. Adams "had been escorted to the Capitol with the pomp and ceremony of guns and drums, which is not consistent with the character of the occasion." However he had been among the first to shake hands with Mr. Adams, and had administered the oath to Calhoun, the new Vice-President, in the Senate.

As the carriage passed the boundary of Washington City she felt him stiffen at her side. He turned in his seat, gazing long and hard at the capital. In his expression she saw the unshatterable resolve she had known so well during the years leading up to the Battle of New Orleans.

He brought his face around to hers.

"We'll be back."

Reading 17

The Gorgeous Hussy

Samuel Hopkins Adams

One of the more remarkable episodes of Jackson's Presidency was the "Eaton Malaria." The person of Margaret (Peggy) O'Neale Timberlake Eaton became a hot political issue that was used by Secretary of State Martin Van Buren to discredit Vice President John C. Calhoun so as to ensure Van Buren's position as Jackson's successor. Unintentionally, Mrs. Calhoun aided Van Buren's cause when she, as the capital's social leader, snubbed Peggy. Jackson's reaction to this snub led to the resignation of nearly his entire cabinet. The background of this affair is presented in the following selection.

Vice-President and Mrs. Calhoun joined the group. The latter was watching Peggy's gracious dominance of the function with soured eyes. "One would suppose her the President's lady and the central figure of the entertainment," she commented. "That hussy!" she added in a lowered voice.

"A hussy, perhaps. But a gorgeous hussy," said General Berrien, fingering his moustache with the air of a connoisseur of the sex.

"That gorgeous hussy," prophesied Mr. Calhoun gloomily, "will set us all out at the tail of the cart before all is said and done."

"I'll wager you are discussing the topic of the day, gentlemen of the Cabinet." The interposition came in the highpitched voice of Mrs. Bomfret Beall, who had approached on the arm of an escort.

"What topic is there, Madam, which had not already been exhausted in your interest?" said Van Buren, with that perfect courtesy of his which, nevertheless, left the lady a little uncertain as to a possible thorn in the posy.

"The Eaton malaria," she replied, and waited, perkily expectant.

"The Eaton malaria?" Berrien echoed the phrase, and burst into laughter. Van Buren frowned. Ingham, a rather slow brain, looked puzzled. Branch cackled aloud. "Oh, that's pretty!" he exclaimed. "Cruel clever of you, Madam."

"Oh, but it's not mine," she disclaimed. "Mr. Pishey Thompson, the fashionable English bookseller, deserves the credit. 'The Eaton malaria,' says he at a banquet at my house, 'has spread from the banks of the canal to the residence of the President.' Isn't it cute!"

The quip was, indeed, not without local wit, since malaria was known as "canal fever," and John H. Eaton was President of the Chesapeake Canal Company. "The Eaton malaria," she reiterated with relish. "Pray Heaven we be not all infected."

Aware of a quiet approach, she looked around and up into the faint, ironic smile of Randolph of Roanoke. "May I offer you my arm, Madam?" said the Virginian.

"I thank you, sir. But for what purpose?"

"To conduct you to the President, that you may repeat your pious warning for his behoof."

The lady, uttering a faint shriek, retired. With a bow to the group, the gaunt figure followed.

As he passed on, Branch said under his breath to Berrien: "They say he could have been the fair Peggy's lover if—well, if it were possible to him."

"I trust I was not meant to hear that remark, sir," said Van Buren severely. "This is all grave matter, gentlemen, and I may warn you, unsafe. The Secretary of War, while an amiable, is by no means a pacific, gentleman. But it is to your loyalty that I prefer to appeal. The President is like enough to have his hands full without the introduction of such petty and persistent annoyance as open discord among the ladies of his official family."

Little encouragement he got from the faces of his colleagues. They might fear John Eaton's fury or Andrew Jackson's denunciations, but what man wed to woman does not prefer the swift reprisals of external wrath to the slow poison of domestic resentment?

Little Van left the impromptu conference. Arrived upon the ballroom floor, he sought out and led forth the happy Peggy. From his place on the dais, the new President beheld the wife of his Secretary of War gallantly partnered by his dapper and elegant Secretary of State, one of the most sought-after and elusive swains in Washington. He chuckled privately. There was a bitter draught from a cassia-wood cup for the enemy to swallow!

. . .

To the social rancor which Peggy had aroused was now added a lively and determined political hostility. Washington Society was predominantly Southern. The Southerners honestly and obstinately believed in the right of the States to determine their own course even to the extent of secession, and Jackson's militant challenge on behalf of national unity and authority inspired them with more wrath than fear. Webster they regarded as the mouthpiece of the policy, but to the beautiful wife of the Secretary of War was ascribed the influence which had seduced the President of the United States, himself a Southerner, from his natural and logical allegiance. What wiles had been employed to accomplish the seduction was the subject of spicy and malevolent surmise.

These political lightnings for a time overbore the fires that played around the wife of Jackson's Secretary of War. Her position, if now secure through Presidential favor as semiofficial First Lady of the Administration, was still anomalous. The leaders of local Society refused her recognition. An important fraction of the diplomatic corps, led by Madam Huygens, withheld from her anything more than the coldest formality. The Cabinet deadlock stood. The President fumed and fulminated about "insults," "disloyalty," and "ingratitude." Secretaries Branch and Ingham and Attorney-General Berrien took their stand on a "no coercion" platform and could not be moved.

Slowly the conviction seeped down into general public consciousness that the Beautiful Bellona was more than a social portent; that she had become a formidable factor of government. The opinion, attributed to Vice-President Calhoun, that "Mrs. Eaton is, in fact, the President," gained whispered currency. The war broke out again with renewed virulence.

It began with a flank attack. At dinners the fashion was inaugurated of toasting that innocent exile from the Presidential Eden, Mrs. Emily Donelson. "To her example and unyielding propriety; marble is too fragile to inscribe them on!" toasted a public admirer. Mrs. Calhoun, who had withdrawn to the fastnesses of South Carolina to avoid contamination, Mrs. Branch and Mrs. Berrien were extolled as "the female phalanx that resisted the introduction of European court morals under General Jackson." Even the lively Mrs. Ingham was held up as a prop of virtue and a pattern of propriety, greatly to her gratification and somewhat to her surprise.

Peggy was content. In fact she was enjoying life hugely. To have the ordering of the President's House; to go to banquets at the British and Russian legations and sit on the right hand of the host; to be the playful, dutiful, and adored wife of the Secretary of War on the one hand and the close confidante and adviser of the President on the other; to be the object of Blair's flattering hostility, Amos Kendall's secret watchfulness, Ike Hill's grudging respect, as to a doughty foe; to be stared at wherever she went as "The American Pompadour" and often acclaimed for her unfaded beauty and her unfailing *bonhomie:* what more could life offer to a spirited and conquering belle of thirty— or a little bit more?

"We've lammed 'em into fits," declared Peggy to Anne, borrowing from the argot of politics to express her exultation over the foe.

"Don't be too perky," advised the shrewd printress. "They've got something in the pot yet for supper."

Up to this time, the newspapers either had ignored the Cabinet warfare, as mere female bickering ("catscratchery" one of them termed it), or had alluded to it in vague terms without using names. Suddenly the masked batteries of journalism burst into sound and fury, flame and smoke.

The *National Journal* led the way, with a direct prophecy of disruption if Mrs. Eaton were not dispossessed.

"It is proven that the families of the Secretaries of the Treasury and Navy and the Attorney-General refused to associate with her."

Other publications followed. There appeared upon the streets of the Capital, this screed:

General Jackson commands All
Mr. Van Buren contrives All
Mrs. Eaton rules All
Office-seekers approve of All
The tariff men want All
Trade and Commerce suffer All
The nullifiers threaten All
Fence men grasp All
The newest converts get All
Uncle Sam pays All
Honest men are obliged to bear All
If God had not pity on All
The D——I will take All.

"My wife's name in the public prints!" mourned the conservative and gentlemanly John Eaton. "My wife's reputation an inquest of political controversy!"

"What did you expect when you married me, my dear?" returned Peggy, unperturbed. "I told you that I was born to trouble as the sparks fly upward."

Anne Royall, working night and day, completed her drama, *The Cabinet, or Large Parties in Washington,* but no theatre, either in the Capital or in Baltimore, dared put it on. The subject was too perilous. She turned her talents to some lively broadsides dealing with Peggy's detractors. The Cabinet ladies squirmed as Georgetown Society had done aforetime under her lively pen. The Reverend Campbell preached another sermon, anonymous in reference, upon the stimulating text "Her feet take hold on hell." President Jackson was reported unofficially as stating that *his* foot would take hold upon a specified portion of the reverend gentleman's anatomy, were it not protected by the clerical cloth. Things were ripening for a very pretty explosion.

Secretary Eaton, constitutionally the most self-controlled of men, became morose. He fell to brooding. In vain did his wife strive to dissuade him.

"You men!" she scolded good-humoredly. "You always mess things up. Look at Uncle Andy. This is a woman's quarrel. Better leave it to me."

Instead, he rushed into print with a "Candid Statement" over which Peggy groaned, though she was too tactful a wife not to praise its style and purport to its author. Candor was not a monopoly of the Secretary of War, however. Other members of the Cabinet could and did employ it with stinging effect. Mr. Ingham intimated that there was sound, moral reason for the exclusion of Mrs. Eaton. Mr. Eaton challenged Mr. Ingham. Mr. Ingham took the ground that the challenge, being issued on a Sunday, was null and void. Mr. Eaton said that Mr. Ingham was a coward. Mr. Branch declined to answer certain provocative questions advanced by Mr. Eaton. Mr. Eaton announced his intention of pulling Mr. Branch's nose. Mr. Branch declared his readiness to defend that organ with his life. Mr. Berrien publicly stood by his colleagues for the sanctity of American womanhood. Mr. Eaton intimated that Mr. Berrien was no more bullet-proof than anyone else. Mr. Berrien, perceiving the force of this argument, organized a bodyguard for himself. General Jackson paced his sanctum waving his beribboned cane and vociferating that he'd cut off *all* their ears with a carving-knife if he weren't President of the United States, and be damned to it!

Meanwhile, Washington thrilled to the spectacle of the bellicose Secretary of War parading Pennsylvania Avenue with his apparel only too obviously distended by a pistol-butt, while the pacific Secretary of the Treasury went to and from his official duties by the most private alleys and secluded by-streets that he could find. Once, indeed, he complained bitterly to the President of a plot to assassinate him. Messrs. Berrien and Branch also were depleted in sleep and spirits from the expectation of persecution. All three suffered, in fact, from the jitters. The atmosphere of Washington had become too stimulating to their nerves. They were fair game for Peggy's *bon mot* which went the rounds of the town.

"General Jackson has surrendered to the Ladies," a newspaper had jeered. "The government has become a petticoat government."

To which Peggy retorted: "All that some of the Cabinet officials need is petticoats to make them perfect ladies, which is more than some of their wives will ever be."

Anne Royall rushed into the breach with a series of "Cabinet Portraits," which sold like hot cakes for five cents apiece. Secretary Ingham was "The Quivering Quaker." Secretary Branch appeared, in full naval uniform and an outrageously elongated nose with a protective fence around it, as "The Twittery Tar." Attorney-General Berrien was dubbed "The Black-Alley Barrister." Naturally, Mrs. Eaton was blamed for these effusions. Indeed, she was again spending many a spare hour at the little printing-shop. The controversy, however, reached a stage where it bored her.

"They talk and talk and talk and don't do anything," she complained to her friend.

"What do you want them to do?"

"Shoot," said Peggy, "I wish Bizarre were here."

"I wish I were a musicker," said Anne.

"Why?"

"I'd set all this to tunes and make a comickal opera of it," grinned the printress. "They couldn't keep *that* off the boards."

"Anne," said the other irrelevantly: "have you ever heard anything of Rowdy?"

"Horsey knows," put in that astute artisan, looking up from his job of distributing type. "He's travellin'. All over the world. Yurrup, Arrup, and Jerrup."

"Isn't he coming back?"

It was Anne who answered: "I doubt it. Unless you should be a widow. He'll never get over you, Peggy."

"Do you think so?" said the beauty softly. "Poor Rowdy!"

"*He'd* be shooting somebody," was Anne's opinion, "if he were here. Peggy, how long do you suppose this sort of thing can go on?"

"For Rowdy? Why, you just said, yourself—"

"No; *not* for Rowdy! For the Cabinet. For General Jackson. For the whole Administration."

Peggy yawned. "How can I tell? Forever, I expect."

"Parfy!" retorted the printress sardonically. "Do you think it's likely to re-elect Andrew Jackson?"

Peggy sat up. "I hadn't thought of that."

"Think of it, then." Anne did some thinking herself. Out of the process was evolved the question: "Peggy, who is the most sagacious man in Washington?"

Peggy folded her hands. "My husband," she answered primly.

"Sweet, ltttle, dutiful wife! But I'm in earnest."

"Oh! Well, Amos Kendall, perhaps."

"Not a bad guess. But I'll tell you a wiser one. Martin Van Buren."

"He's always been lovely to me," declared Peg, who was inclined to take personal views of political figures.

"Of course. He's too smart not to be. They don't call him the Wizard of Kinderhook for nothing."

"Then you don't think it's my fatal beauty that attracts him?" said Peggy, with mock wistfulness.

"Pooh! The Little Magician wants to be President. I'd like to know what he thinks of all this fuss."

"Ask him."

"Ask him, yourself. Any man will do more for a pretty woman than a plain one."

"Can you see the wife of the Secretary of War making a call on the Secretary of State? What would Duff Green's paper say?"

"He's sometimes at home in the Seven Buildings."

"Bachelor Chambers!" Peggy looked sweetly shocked. "Anne, I'm surprised at you."

"We'll both go. Shall we? I'll make an appointment."

"It might be fun," conceded the other.

Time ripened slowly in the patient and bland purposes of Martin Van Buren. He was delighted to receive the ladies, but he was in no haste to accommodate their polite curiosity. Before they had taken many sips of his elegantly served hospitality (Peggy's choice was coffee; Anne's, wine), they discovered in him a readier listener than talker on the politico-social imbroglio. Anne's most searching hints he parried as cleverly as her direct questions. Peggy was amused. She had always liked the dapper statesman who had been, in his tactful and unobtrusive way, one of her staunchest adherents. If she ever wanted it, she would confidently ask his advice; but this feinting and fencing of Anne's was no sound method with the Little Wizard. He was so much better at it, himself. Anyway, Peggy did not feel that she needed advice. She was doing very well on her own.

Chapter 5

The Spirit of Social Reform

Reading 18

The Hoosier School Master

Edward Eggleston

In the 1830s a wave of reforms swept the nation. With the extension of the franchise, society as a whole had a greater stake in the education of children. Educators like Horace Mann stressed the importance of free elementary instruction to teach future voters the heritage of the past and prepare them to be useful citizens. By 1850 the nation (outside of the South) had some 80,000 elementary schools and 3,500,000 students. Most frontier communities established schools as soon as possible. But Edward Eggleston, who taught in Indiana, suggests that not all schools were dedicated to book learning.

"Want to be a school-master, do you? You? Well, what would *you* do in Flat Crick deestrick, *I'd* like to know? Why, the boys have driv off the last two, and licked the one afore them like blazes. You might teach a summer school, when nothin' but children come. But I 'low it takes a right smart *man* to be school-master in Flat Crick in the winter. They'd pitch you out of doors, sonny, neck and heels, afore Christmas."

The young man, who had walked ten miles to get the school in this district, and who had been mentally reviewing his learning at every step he took, trembling lest the committee should find that he did not know enough, was not a little taken aback at this greeting from "old Jack Means," who was the first trustee that he lighted on. The impression made by these ominous remarks was emphasized by the glances which he received from Jack Means' two sons. The older one eyed him from the top of his brawny shoulders with that amiable look which a big dog turns on a little one before shaking him. Ralph Hartsook had never thought of being measured by the standard of muscle. This notion of beating education into young savages in spite of themselves, dashed his ardor.

He had walked right to where Jack Means was at work shaving shingles in his own front yard. While Mr. Means was making the speech which we have set down above, and punctuating it with expectorations, a large brindle bull-dog had been sniffing at Ralph's heels, and a girl in a new linsey-woolsey dress, standing by the door, had nearly giggled her head off at the delightful prospect of seeing a new school-teacher eaten up by the ferocious brute.

From *The Hoosier School Master* by Edward Eggleston. Published in 1871.

Between the disheartening words of the old man, the immense muscles of the young man who was to be his rebellious pupil, the jaws of the ugly bull-dog, and the heartless giggle of the girl, Ralph had a delightful sense of having precipitated himself into a den of wild beasts. Faint with weariness and discouragement, and shivering with fear, he sat down on a wheelbarrow.

"You, Bull!" said the old man to the dog, which was showing more and more a disposition to make a meal of the incipient pedagogue, "you, Bull! git aout, you pup!" The dog walked sullenly off, but not until he had given Ralph a look full of promise of what he meant to do when he got a good chance. Ralph wished himself back in the village of Lewisburg, whence he had come.

"You see," continued Mr. Means, spitting in a meditative sort of a way, "you see, we a'n't none of your saft sort in these diggins. It take a *man* to boss this deestrick. Howsumdever, ef you think you kin trust your hide in Flat Crick school-house I ha'n't got no 'bjection. But ef you git licked don't come on us. Flat Crick don't pay no 'nsurance, you bet! Any other trustees? Wal, yes. But as I pay the most taxes, t'others jist let me run the thing. You can begin right off a Monday. They a'n't been no other applications. You see it takes some grit to apply for this school. The last master had a black eye for a month. But, as I said, you can jist roll up and wade in. I 'low you've got pluck, may be, and that goes for a heap sight more'n sinnoo with boys. Walk in, and stay over Sunday with me. You'll hev to board roun', and I guess you better begin here."

Ralph did not go in, but sat out on the wheelbarrow, watching the old man shave shingles, while the boys split the blocks and chopped wood. Bull smelled of the newcomer again in an ugly way, and got a good kick from the older son for his pains. But out of one of his red eyes the dog warned the young school-master that *he* should yet suffer for all kicks received on his account.

"Ef Bull once takes a holt, heaven and yarth can't make him let go," said the older son to Ralph, by way of comfort.

It was well for Ralph that he began to "board round" by stopping at Mr. Means's. Ralph felt that Flat Creek was what he needed. He had lived a bookish life. But here was his lesson in the art of managing people. For who can manage the untamed and strapping youths of a winter school in Hoopole County has gone far toward learning one of the hardest of lessons. And twenty-five years ago, in Ralph's time, things were worse than they are now.

The older son of Mr. Means was called Bud Means. What his real name was Ralph could not find out, for in many of these families the nickname of "Bud" given to the oldest boy, and that of "Sis" which is the birthright of the oldest girl, completely bury the proper Christian name. Ralph was a general. He saw his first strategic point, which was to capture Bud Means.

After supper the boys began to get ready for something. Bull struck up his ears in a dignified way, and the three of four yellow curs who were Bull's satellites yelped delightedly and discordantly.

"Bill," said Bud Means to his brother, "ax the master ef he'd like to hunt coons. I'd like to take the starch out the stuck-up fellow."

"'Nough said," was Bill's reply.

"You durn't do it," said Bud.

"I don't take no sech a dare," returned Bill, and walked down to the gate, on which Ralph stood watching the stars come out, and wishing he had never seen Flat Creek.

"I say, mister," began Bill, "mister, they's a coon what's been a eatin' our chickens lately, and we're goin' to try ketch the varmint. You wouldn't like to take a coon hunt nor nothin', would you?"

"Why, yes," said Ralph, "there's nothing I should like better, if I could only be sure Bull wouldn't mistake me for the coon."

And so, as a matter of policy, Ralph dragged his tired legs eight or ten miles, on hill and in hollow, after Bud, and Bill, and Bull, and the coon. But the raccoon climbed a tree. The boys got into a quarrel about whose business it was to have brought the ax, and who was to blame that the tree could not be felled. Now, if there was anything Ralph's muscles were good for, it was to climb. So, asking Bud to give him a start, he soon reached the limb above the one on which the raccoon was. Ralph did not know how ugly a customer a raccoon can be, and so got credit for more courage than he had. With much peril to his legs from the raccoon's teeth, he succeeded in shaking the poor creature off among the yelping brutes and yelling boys. Ralph could not help sympathizing with the hunted animal, which sold its life as dearly as possible, giving the dogs many a scratch and bite. It seemed to him that he was like the raccoon, precipitated into the midst of a party of dogs who would rejoice in worrying *his* life out, as Bull and his crowd were destroying the poor raccoon. When Bull at last seized the raccoon and put an end to it, Ralph could not but admire the decided way in which he did it, calling to mind Bud's comment: "Ef Bull once takes a holt, heaven and yarth can't make him let go."

But as they walked home, Bud carrying the raccoon by the tail, Ralph felt that his hunt had not been in vain. He fancied that even red-eyed Bull, walking uncomfortably close to his heels, respected him more since he had climbed that tree.

"Purty peart kind of a master," remarked the old man to Bud after Ralph had gone to bed. "Guess you better be a little easy on *him*. Hey?"

But Bud designed no reply. Perhaps because he knew that Ralph heard the conversation through the thin partition.

Ralph woke delighted to find it raining. He did not want to hunt or fish on Sunday, and this steady rain would enable him to make friends with Bud.

I do not know how he got started, but after breakfast he began to tell stories. Out of all the books he had ever read he told story after story. And "old man Means," and "old *Miss* Means," and Bud Means, and Bill Means, and Sis Means, listened with great eyes while he told of Sinbad's adventures, of the Old Man of the Sea, of Robinson Crusoe, of Captain Gulliver's experiences in Liliput, and of Baron Munchausen's exploits.

Ralph had caught his fish. The hungry minds of these backwoods people, sick and dying of their own commonplace, were refreshed with the new life that came to their imaginations in these stories. For there was but one book in the Means library, and that, a well-thumbed copy of Captain Riley's Narrative, had long since lost all freshness.

"I'll be dog-on'd," said Bill emphatically, "ef I hadn't ruther hear the master tell them whoppin' yarns, than to go to a circus the best day I ever seed!" Bill could pay no higher compliment.

What Ralph wanted was to make a friend of Bud. It's a nice thing to have the seventy-four-gun ship on your own side, and the more Hartsook admired the knotted muscles of Bud Means, the more he desired to attach him to himself. So, whenever he struck out a peculiarly brilliant passage, he anxiously watched Bud's eye. But the young Philistine kept his own counsel. He listened but said nothing, and the eyes under his shaggy brow gave no sign. Ralph could not tell whether those eyes were deep and inscrutable, or only stolid. Perhaps a little of both. When Monday morning came Ralph was nervous. He walked to school with Bud.

"I guess you're a little skeered by what the old man said, a'n't you?"

Ralph was about to deny it, but on reflection concluded that it was always best to speak the truth. He said that Mr. Means's description of the school had made him feel a little downhearted.

"What will you do with the tough boys? You a'n't no match for 'em." And Ralph felt Bud's eyes not only measuring his muscles, but scrutinizing his countenance. He only answered:

"I don't know."

"What would you do with me, for instance?" and Bud stretched himself up as if to shake out the reserve power coiled up in his great muscles.

"I shan't have any trouble with you."

"Why, I'm the worst chap of all. I thrashed the last master myself."

And again the eyes of Bud Means looked out sharply from his shadowing brows to see the effect of this speech on the slender young man.

"You won't thrash me, though," said Ralph.

"Pshaw! I 'low I could whip you in an inch of your life with my left hand and never half try," said young Means with a threatening sneer.

"I know that as well as you do."

"Well, a'n't you afraid of me then?" and again he looked sidewise at Ralph.

"Not a bit," said Ralph, wondering at his own courage.

They walked on in silence a minute. Bud was turning the matter over.

"Why a'n't you afraid of me?" he said presently.

"Because you and I are going to be friends."

"And what about t'others?"

"I am not afraid of all the other boys put together."

"You a'n't! The mischief! How's that?"

"Well, I'm not afraid of them because you and I are going to be friends, and you can whip all of them together. You'll do the fighting and I'll do the teaching."

The diplomatic Bud only chuckled a little at this; whether he assented to the alliance or not Ralph could not tell.

When Ralph looked round on the faces of the scholars—the little faces full of mischief and curiosity, the big faces full of an expression which was not further removed than second-cousin from contempt—when young Hartsook looked into these faces, his heart palpitated with stage-fright. There is no audience so hard to face as one of school children, as many a man has found to his cost. Perhaps it is that no conventional restraint can keep down their laughter when you do or say anything ridiculous.

Hartsook's first day was hurried and unsatisfactory. He was not master of himself, and consequently not master of anybody else. When evening came there were symptoms of insubordination through the whole school. Poor Ralph was sick at heart. He felt that if there had ever been the shadow of an alliance between himself and Bud, it was all "off" now. It seemed to Hartsook that even Bull had lost his respect for the teacher. Half that night the young man lay awake. At last comfort came to him. A reminiscence of the death of the raccoon flashed on him like a vision. He remembered that quiet and annihilating bite which Bull gave. He remembered Bud's certificate, that "Ef Bull once takes a holt, heaven and yarth can't make him let go." He thought that what Flat Creek needed was a bull-dog. He would be a bull-dog, quiet but invincible. He would take hold in such a way that nothing should make him let go. And then he went to sleep.

In the morning Ralph got out of bed slowly. He put his clothes on slowly. He pulled on his boots in a bull-dog mood. He tried to move as he thought Bull would move if he were a man. He ate with deliberation, and looked everybody in the eyes with a manner that made Bud watch him curiously. He found himself continually comparing himself with Bull. He found Bull possessing a strange fascination for him. He walked to school alone, the rest having gone on before. He entered the schoolroom preserving a cool and dogged manner. He saw in the eyes of the boys that there was mischief brewing. He did not dare sit down in his chair for fear of a pin.

Everybody looked solemn. Ralph lifted the lid of his desk. "Bow-wow! wow-wow!" It was the voice of an imprisoned puppy, and the school giggled and then roared. Then everything was quiet.

The scholars expected an outburst of wrath from the teacher. For they had come to regard the whole world as divided into two classes, the teacher on the one side representing lawful authority, and the pupils on the other in a state of chronic rebellion. To play a trick on the master was an evidence of spirit; to "lick" the master was to be the crowned hero of Flat Creek district. Such a hero was Bud Means, and Bill, who had less muscle, saw a chance to distinguish himself on a teacher of slender frame. Hence the puppy in the desk.

Ralph Hartsook grew red in the face when he saw the puppy. But the cool, repressed, bull-dog mood in which he had kept himself saved him. He lifted the dog into his arms and stroked him until the laughter subsided. Then, in a solemn and set way, he began:

"I am sorry," and he looked round the room with a steady, hard eye—everybody felt that there was a conflict coming—"I am sorry that any scholar in this school could be so mean"—the word was uttered with a sharp emphasis, and all the big boys felt sure that there would be a fight with Bill Means, and perhaps with Bud—"could be so *mean*—as to—shut up his *brother* in such a place as that!"

There was a long, derisive laugh. The wit was indifferent, but by one stroke Ralph had carried the whole school to his side. By the significant glances of the boys, Hartsook detected the perpetrator of the joke, and with the hard and dogged look in his eyes, with just such a look as Bull would give a puppy, but with the utmost suavity in his voice, he said:

"William Means, will you be so good as to put this dog out of doors?"

Reading 19

Ten Nights in a Barroom

Thomas S. Arthur

Heavy drinking was common in colonial America. In 1763 Boston merchants estimated that every man, woman, and child consumed an average of four

From *Ten Nights in a Barroom* by Thomas S. Arthur. Published in 1854.

gallons of rum annually, and such heavy consumption continued throughout the nineteenth century. To combat this "evil," the first temperance society was organized in 1806 by a physician who was concerned about the harmful effects of alcohol. Many such societies flourished and countless temperance tracts were written, including the book, *Ten Nights in a Barroom,* the *Uncle Tom's Cabin* of the temperance movement. Satisfying the public's taste for the sensational, it was endorsed by many Sunday schools and was a long-time favorite theater presentation.

Following the direction from which the sound came, I entered one of the large drawing-rooms. The atmosphere was stifling, and all as dark as if it were midnight. Groping my way to a window, I drew back the bolt and threw open a shutter. Broadly the light fell across the dusty, uncarpeted floor, and on the dingy furniture of the room. As it did so, the moaning voice which had drawn me thither swelled on the air again; and now I saw, lying upon an old sofa, the form of a man. It needed no second glance to tell me that this was Judge Hammond. I put my hand upon him, and uttered his name: but he answered not. I spoke more firmly, and slightly shook him; but only a piteous moan was returned.

"Judge Hammond!" I now called aloud, and somewhat imperatively.

But it availed nothing. The poor old man aroused not from the stupor in which mind and body were enshrouded.

"He is dying!" thought I; and instantly left the house in search of some friends to take charge of him in his last, sad extremity. The first person to whom I made known the fact shrugged his shoulders, and said it was no affair of his, and that I must find somebody whose business it was to attend to him. My next application was met in the same spirit; and no better success attended my reference of the matter to a third party. No one to whom I spoke seemed to have any sympathy for the broken-down old man. Shocked by this indifference, I went to one of the county officers, who, on learning the condition of Judge Hammond, took immediate steps to have him removed to the Alms-house, some miles distant.

"But why to the Alms-house?" I inquired, on learning his purpose. "He has property."

"Everything has been seized for debt," was the reply.

"Will there be nothing left after his creditors are satisfied?"

"Very few, if any, will be satisfied," he answered. "There will not be enough to pay half the judgments against him."

"And is there no friend to take him in,—no one, of all who moved by his side in the days of prosperity, to give a few hours' shelter, and soothe the last moments of his unhappy life?"

"Why did you make application here?" was the officer's significant question.

I was silent.

"Your earnest appeals for the poor old man met with no words of sympathy?"

"None."

"He has, indeed, fallen low. In the days of his prosperity, he had many friends, so called. Adversity has shaken them all like dead leaves from sapless branches."

"But why? This is not always so."

"Judge Hammond was a selfish, worldly man. People never liked him much. His favouring, so strongly, the tavern of Slade, and his distillery operations, turned from him some of his best friends. The corruption and terrible fate of his son—and the insanity and death of his wife—all were charged upon him in people's minds; and every one seemed to turn from him instinctively after the fearful tragedy was completed. He never held up his head afterward. Neighbours shunned him as they would a criminal. And here has come the end at last. He will be taken to the Poor-house, to die there—a pauper!"

"And all," said I, partly speaking to myself, "because a man, too lazy to work at an honest calling, must needs go to rum-selling."

"The truth, the whole truth, and nothing but the truth," remarked the officer with emphasis, as he turned from me to see that his directions touching the removal of Mr. Hammond to the Poor-house were promptly executed.

In my wanderings about Cedarville during that day, I noticed a small, but very neat cottage, a little way from the centre of the village. There was not around it a great profusion of flowers and shrubbery; but the few vines, flowers, and bushes that grew green and flourishing about the door, and along the clean walks, added to the air of taste and comfort that so peculiarly marked the dwelling.

"Who lives in that pleasant little spot?" I asked of a man whom I had frequently seen in Slade's bar-room. He happened to be passing the house at the same time that I was.

"Joe Morgan," was answered.

"Indeed!" I spoke in some surprise. "And what of Morgan? How is he doing?"

"Very well."

"Doesn't he drink?"

"No. Since the death of his child, he has never taken a drop. That event sobered him, and he has remained sober ever since."

"What is he doing?"

"Working at his old trade."

"That of a miller?"

"Yes. After Judge Hammond broke down, the distillery apparatus and cotton spinning machinery were all sold and removed from Cedarville. The purchaser of what remained, having something of the fear of God, as well as regard for man, in his heart, set himself to the restoration of the old order of things, and in due time the revolving mill-wheel was at its old and better work of grinding corn and wheat for bread. The only two men in Cedarville competent to take charge of the mill were Simon Slade and Joe Morgan. The first could not be had, and the second came in as a matter of course.

"And he remains sober and industrious?"

"As any man in the village," was the answer.

I saw but little of Slade or his son during the day. But both were in the bar-room at night, and both in a condition sorrowful to look upon. Their presence, together, in the bar-room, half intoxicated as they were, seemed to revive the unhappy temper of the previous evening, as freshly as if the sun had not risen and set upon their anger.

During the early part of the evening, considerable company was present, though not a very select class. A large proportion were young men. To most of them the fact that Slade had fallen into the sheriff's hands was known; and I gathered from some aside conversation which reached my ears, that Frank's idle, spendthrift habits had hastened the present crisis in his father's affairs. He, too, was in debt to Judge Lyman—on what account, it was not hard to infer.

It was after nine o'clock and there was not half a dozen persons in the room, when I noticed Frank Slade go behind the bar for the third or fourth time. He was just lifting a decanter of brandy, when his father, who was considerably under the influence of drink, started forward, and laid his hand upon that of his son. Instantly a fierce light gleamed from the eyes of the young man.

"Let go of my hand," he exclaimed.

"No, I won't. Put up that brandy bottle,—you're drunk now."

"Don't meddle with me, old man!" angrily retorted Frank. "I'm not in the mood to bear any thing more from *you*."

"You're drunk as a fool now," returned Slade, who had seized the decanter. "Let go the bottle."

For only an instant did the young man hesitate. Then he drove his half-clenched hand against the breast of his father, who went staggering away several paces from the counter. Recovering himself, and now almost furious, the landlord rushed forward upon his son, his hand raised to strike him.

"Keep off!" cried Frank. "Keep off! If you touch me, I'll strike you down!" At the same time raising the half-filled bottle threateningly.

But his father was in too maddened a state to fear any consequences, and so pressed forward upon his son, striking him in the face the moment he came near enough to do so.

Instantly, the young man, infuriated by drink and evil passions, threw the bottle at his father's head. The dangerous missile fell, crashing upon one of his temples, shivering it into a hundred pieces. A heavy, jarring fall too surely marked the fearful consequences of the blow. When we gathered around the fallen man, and made an effort to lift him from the floor, a thrill of horror went through every heart. A mortal paleness was already on his marred face, and the death-gurgle in his throat! In three minutes from the time the blow was struck, his spirit had gone upward to give an account of the deeds done in the body.

"Frank Slade! you have murdered your father!"

Sternly were these terrible words uttered. It was some time before the young man seemed to comprehend their meaning. But the moment he realized the awful truth, he uttered an exclamation of horror. Almost at the same instant, a pistol-shot came sharply on the ear. But the meditated self-destruction was not accomplished. The aim was not surely taken; and the ball struck harmlessly against the ceiling.

Half an hour afterward, and Frank Slade was a lonely prisoner in the county jail!

Does the reader need a word of comment on this fearful consummation? No: and we will offer none.

Reading 20
The Circuit Rider

Edward Eggleston

The Methodist church was especially well suited to the frontier. The doctrine of the Methodists was very democratic and emphasized the gospel of grace and free will. The church espoused the belief that all men were equal before the Lord and that each individual must obtain his own salvation through conversion. Aiding the Methodists were circuit riders—individual itinerant preachers who held services and offered instruction in Methodist doctrine. These men traversed the backcountry on horseback, taking lodging and meals when and where they could get them. They were usually warmly welcomed by the isolated farmers, who were eager for any news or gossip

From *The Circuit Rider* by Edward Eggleston. Published in 1874.

they could offer. Edward Eggleston spent several years as a circuit rider in
Ohio and Minnesota.

More than two years have passed since Morton made his great sacrifice. You
may see him now riding up to the Hickory Ridge Church—a "hewed-log"
country meetinghouse. He is dressed in homespun clothes. At the risk of
compromising him forever, I must confess that his coat is straight-breasted—
shad-bellied as the profane call it—and his best hat a white one with a broad
brim. The face is still fresh, despite the conflicts and hardships of one year's
travel in the mountains of Eastern Kentucky, and the sickness and exposure
of another year in the malarious cane-brakes of Western Tennessee. Perils of
Indians, perils of floods, perils of alligators, perils of bad foods, perils of cold
beds, perils of robbers, perils of rowdies, perils of fevers, and the weariness of
five thousand miles of horseback riding in a year, with five or six hundred
preachings in the same time, and the care of numberless scattered churches in
the wilderness have conspired to give sedateness to his countenance. And yet
there is a youthfulness about the sun-browned cheeks, and a lingering expression of that sort of humor which Western people call "mischief" about the
eyes, that match but grotesquely with white hat and shad-bellied coat.

He has been a preacher almost ever since he became a Methodist. How
did he get his theological education? It used to be said that Methodist preachers were educated by the old ones telling the young ones all they knew; but
besides this oral instruction Morton carried in his saddle-bags John Wesley's
simple, solid sermons, Charles Wesley's hymns, and a Bible. Having little of
the theory and system of theology, he was free to take lessons in the larger
school of life and practical observation. For the rest, the free criticism to which
he was subject from other preachers, and the contact with a few families of
refinement, had obliterated his dialect. Naturally a gentleman at heart, he had,
from the few stately gentlemen that he met, quickly learned to be a gentleman
in manners. He is regarded as a young man of great promise by the older
brethren; his clear voice is very charming, his strong and manly speech and
his tender feeling are very inspiring, and on his two circuits he has reported
extraordinary revivals. Some of the old men sagely predict that "he's got
bishop-timber in him," but no such ambitious dreams disturb his sleep. He has
not "gone into a decline" on account of Patty. A healthy nature will bear heavy
blows. But there is a pain, somewhere—everywhere—in his being, when he
thinks of the girl who stood just above him in the spelling-class, and who
looked so divine when she was spinning her two dozen cuts a day. He does
not like this regretful feeling. He prays to be forgiven for it. He acknowledges
in classmeeting and in love-feast that he is too much like Lot's wife—he finds

his heart prone to look back toward the objects he once loved. Often in riding through the stillness of a deep forest—and the primeval forest is to him the peculiar abode of the Almighty—his noble voice rings out fervently and even pathetically with that stanza:

> "The dearest idol I have known,
>   Whate'er that idol be,
> Help me to tear it from thy throne
>   And worship only Thee!"

No man can enjoy a joke with more zest than he, and none can tell a story more effectively in a generation of preachers who are all good story-tellers. He loves his work; its dangers and difficulties satisfy the ambition of his boyhood; and he has had no misgivings, except when once or twice he has revisited his parents in the Hissawachee Bottom. Then the longing to see Patty has seized him and he has been fain to hurry away, praying to be delivered from every snare of the enemy.

He is not the only man in a straight-breasted coat who is approaching the county meeting-house. It is conference-time, and the greetings are hearty and familiar. Everybody is glad to see everybody, and, after a year of separation, nobody can afford to stand on ceremony with anybody else. Morton has hardly alighted before half a dozen preachers have rushed up to him and taken him by the hand. A tall brother, with a grotesque twitch in his face, cries out:

"How do you do, Brother Goodwin? Glad to see the alligators haven't finished you!"

To which Morton returns a laughing reply; but suddenly he sees, standing back of the rest and waiting his turn, a young man with a solemn, sallow face, pinched by sickness and exposure, and bordered by the straight black hair that falls on each side of it. He wears over his clothes a blanket with arm-holes cut through, and seems to be perpetually awaiting an ague-chill. Seeing him, Morton pushes the rest aside, and catches the wan hand in both of his own with a dry: "Kike, God bless you! How are you, dear old fellow? You look sick."

Kike smiled faintly, and Morton threw his arm over his shoulder and looked in his face. "I am sick, Mort. Cast down, but not destroyed, you know. I hope I am ready to be offered up."

"Not a bit of it. You've got to get better. Offered up? Why, you aren't fit to offer to an alligator. Where are you staying?"

"Out there." Kike pointed to the tents of a campmeeting barely visible through the trees. The people in the neighborhood of the Hickory Ridge Church, being unable to entertain the Conference in their homes, had resorted to the device of getting up a camp-meeting. It was easier to take care of the preachers out of doors than in. Morton shook his head as he walked with Kike to the thin canvas tent under which he had been assigned to sleep. The white spot on the end of Kike's nose and the blue lines under his finger-nails told plainly of the on-coming chill, and Morton hurried away to find some better shelter for him than under this thin sheet. But this was hard to do. The few brethren in the neighborhood had already filled their cabins full of guests, mostly in infirm health, and Kike, being one of the younger men, renowned only for his piety and his revivals, had not been thought of for a place elsewhere than on the camp-ground. Finding it impossible to get a more comfortable resting place for his friend, Morton turned to seek for a physician. The only doctor in the neighborhood was a Presbyterian minister, retired from the ministry on account of his impaired health. To him Morton went to ask for medicine for Kike.

"Dr. Morgan, there is a preacher sick down at the camp-ground," said Morton, "and—"

"And you want me to see him," said the doctor in an alert, anticipative fashion, seizing his "pill-bags" and donning his hat.

When the two rode up to the tent in which Kike was lodged they found a prayer-meeting of a very exciting kind going on in the tent adjoining. There were cries and groans and amens and hallelujahs commingled in a way quite intelligible to the experienced ear of Morton, but quite unendurable to the orderly doctor.

"A bad place for a sick man, sir," he said to Morton, with great positiveness.

"I know it is, doctor," said Morton; "and I've done my best to get him out of it, but I cannot. See how thin this tent-cover is."

"And the malaria of these woods is awful. Camp meetings, sir, are always bad. And this *fuss* is enough to drive a patient crazy."

Morton thought the doctor prejudiced, but he said nothing. They had now reached the corner of the tent where Kike lay on a straw pallet, holding his hands to his head. The noise from the prayer-meeting was more than his weary brain would bear.

"Can you sit on my horse?" said the doctor, promptly proceeding to lift Kike without even explaining to him who he was, or where he proposed to take him.

Morton helped to place Kike in the saddle, but the poor fellow was shaking so that he could not sit there. Morton then brought out Dolly—she was all his own now—and took the siight form of Kike in his arms, he riding on the croup, and the sick man in the saddle.

"Where shall I ride to, doctor?"

"To my house," said the doctor, mounting his own horse and spurring off to have a bed made ready for Kike.

As Morton rode up to the doctor's gate, the shaking Kike roused a little and said, "She's the same fine old Dolly, Mort."

"A little more sober. The long rides in the cane-brakes and the responsibility of the Methodist itinerancy, have given her the gravity that belongs to the ministry."

Such a bed as Kike found in Dr. Morgan's house! After the rude bearskins upon which he had languished in the backwoods cabins, after the musty feather-beds in freezing lofts, and the pallets of leaves upon which he had shivered and scorched and fought fleas and mosquitoes, this clean white bed was like a foretaste of heaven. But Kike was almost too sick to be grateful. The poor frame had been kept up by will so long, that now that he was in a good bed and had Morton he felt that he could afford to be sick. What had been ague settled into that wearisome disease called bilious fever. Morton staid by him nearly all of the time, looking into the conference now and then to see the venerable Asbury in the chair, listening to a grand speech from McKendree, attending on the third day of the session, when, with the others who had been preaching two years on probation, he was called forward to answer the "questions" always propounded to "Candidates for admission to the conference." Kike only was missing from the list of those who were to have heard the bishop's exhortations, full of martial fire, and to have answered his questions in regard to their spiritual state. For above all gifts of speech or depths of learning, or acuteness of reasoning, the early Methodists esteemed devout affections; and no man was of account for the ministry who was not "groaning to be made perfect in this life." The question stands in the discipline yet, but very many young men who assent to it groan after nothing so much as a city church with full galleries.

The strange mystery in which appointments were involved could not but pique curiosity. Morton having had one year of mountains, and one year of cane-brakes, had come to wish for one year of a little more comfort, and a little better support. There is a romance about going threadbare and tattered in a good cause, but even the romance gets threadbare and tattered if it lasts too long, and one wishes for a little sober reality of warm clothes to relieve a romance, charming enough in itself, but dull when it grows monotonous.

The awful hour of appointments came on at last. The brave-hearted men sat down before the bishop, and before God, not knowing what was to be their fate. Morton could not guess where he was going. A miasmatic cane-brake, or a deadly cypress swamp, might be his doom, or he might—but no, he would not hope that his lot might fall in Ohio. He was a young man, and a young man must take his chances. Morton found himself more anxious about Kike than about himself. Where would the bishop send the invalid? With Kike it might be a matter of life and death, and Kike would not hear to being left without work. He meant, he said, to cease at once to work and live.

The brethren, still in sublime ignorance of their destiny, sang fervently that fiery hymn of Charles Wesley's:

"Jesus, the name high over all,
    In hell or earth or sky.
Angels and men before him fall,
    And devils fear and fly.

"O that the world might taste and see,
    The riches of his grace,
The arms of love that compass me
    Would all mankind embrace."

And when they reached the last stanzas there was the ring of soldiers ready for battle in their martial voices. That some of them would die from exposure, malaria, or accident during the next year was probable. Tears came to their eyes, and they involuntarily began to grasp the hands of those who stood next them as they approached the climax of the hymn, which the bishop read impressively, two lines at a time, for them to sing:

"His only righteousness I show,
    His saving truth proclaim,
'Tis all my business here below
    To cry, 'Behold the Lamb.'

"Happy if with my latest breath
    I may but gasp his name,
Preach him to all and cry in death,
    'Behold, behold the Lamb!' "

Then, with suffused eyes, they resumed their seats, and the venerable Asbury, with calmness and with a voice faltering with age, made them a brief address; tender and sympathetic at first, earnest as he proceeded, and full of ardor and courage at the close.

"When the British Admiralty," he said, "wanted some man to take Quebec, they began with the oldest General first, asking him: 'General, will you go and take Quebec?' To which he made reply, 'It is a very difficult enterprise.' 'You may stand aside,' they said. One after another the Generals answered that they would, in some more or less indefinite manner, until the youngest man on the list was reached. 'General Wolfe,' they said, 'will you go and take

Quebec?' 'I'll do it or die,' he replied." Here the bishop paused, looked round about upon them, and added, with a voice full of emotion, "He went, and did both. We send you first to take the country allotted to you. We want only men who are determined to do it or die! Some of you, dear brethren, will do both. If you fall, let us hear that you fell like Methodist preachers at your post, face to the foe, and the shout of victory on your lips."

The effect of this speech was beyond description. There were sobs, and cries of "Amen," "God grant it," "Halleluiah!" from every part of the old log church. Every man was ready for the hardest place, if he must. Gravely, as one who trembles at his responsibility, the bishop brought out his list. No man looked any more upon his fellow. Every one kept his eyes fixed upon the paper from which the bishop read the appointments, until his own name was reached. Some showed pleasure when their names were called, some could not conceal a look of pain. When the reading had proceeded half way down the list, Morton heard, with a little start, the words slowly enounced as the bishop's eyes fell on him:

"Jenkinsville Circuit—Morton Goodwin."

Well, at least Jenkinsville was in Ohio. But it was in the wickedest part of Ohio. Morton half suspected that he was indebted to his muscle, his courage, and his quick wit for the appointment. The rowdies of Jenkinsville Circuit were worse than the alligators of Mississippi. But he was young, hopeful and brave, and rather relished a difficult field than otherwise. He listened now for Kike's name. It came at the bottom of the list:

"Pottawottomie Creek—W. T. Smith, Hezekiah Lumsden."

The bishop had not dared to entrust a circuit to a man so sick as Kike was. He had, therefore, sent him as a "second man" or "junior preacher" on a circuit in the wilderness of Michigan.

The last appointment having been announced, a simple benediction closed the services, and the brethren who had foregone houses and homes and fathers and mothers and wives and children for the kingdom of heaven's sake saddled their horses, called, one by one, at Dr. Morgan's to say a brotherly "God bless you!" to the sick Kike, and rode away, each in his own direction, and all with a self-immolation to the cause rarely seen since the Middle-Age.

They rode away, all but Kike, languishing yet with fever, and Morton watching by his side.

Reading 21

The Woman Question

Dorothea Malm

The era of reform before the Civil War witnessed the initial steps in the gradual emancipation of women. Until the nineteenth century it was accepted that a woman's place was in the home. Even a charming and talented woman like Abigail Adams was considered important only because she was the wife of John Adams. But as a result of changing attitudes, some progress for women was made. Female teachers began to be acceptable after 1800. Oberlin College opened its doors in 1833 as a coeducational institution. The first medical diploma earned by a woman was awarded in 1849. Yet the antagonism of men toward these limited advances was very great, as is reflected in the following selection.

"I only mean to admit that Phebe is not in advance of her times in the attainment of a purely rational approach to marriage."

"Thank God," he said. "But who is—or should be?"

"But she is all the same sensible enough to want to use the light of reason in judging her emotions—and yours—before letting herself go. And you should help her in that. You should not want her to come to you until she is sure of herself."

"I am sure enough for both of us."

"Oh, arrogant!" she said, shaking her head. "Oh, foolishly impetuous!"

"Never shake thy hoary locks at me in that tone of voice, I am not a foolish boy," he said imperturbably, "unless you are still a foolish girl, remember that."

"Oh, women are always older than men. As for your sister. As a matter of fact, I felt some slight guilt when you spoke of 'previous knowledge.' I met Miss Bonchurch in Boston . . ."

"Ah! You have met Julia." He took off his hat, pushed his hair back thoughtfully, and put his hat on again, pulling the brim to an angle even more reckless than before.

"She came to see our school, just before it closed for good, when she was in Boston visiting—I think—an aunt? Well, and she mentioned your interest in *my* sister," said Mary, pinching off a red blossom from the columbine that lay against her knee and nibbling one of its horns, whose tiny sweetness made her feel nine years old again. "She said nothing very much about it, but I did, I fear, gain the impression that you would inevitably be successful in carrying off any prize on which you had set your eye. Perhaps that has influenced my appraisal of your conduct. I guess I would have to agree with her," she added, looking up to study him with a sketcher's impersonal eye. He stood his ground, his shoulders to the oak, the thumb of one hand hooked into his trouser pocket, the other hand playing with a clump of dark glossy leaves that grew from the trunk of the tree just above his shoulder, but his face was for a moment as red as the columbine. "But that's no excuse, you know."

"And so I suppose I shall hear some more from Julia about woman's rights when I get home."

"I hope so."

"Bore from within is your motto, is it? Bore in every sense of the word!"

"If necessary," she said, smiling.

"You make me want to go to sea again!" he exclaimed, twitching up his white trousers and sitting down on a neighboring rock. "And it's all such nonsense! . . . The truth is, I can't see from one minute to the next what you are all making such a fuss about."

There sprang up in her an emotion that was in part pure zest for argument and partly real anger over that careless dismissal of a burden by one who had never borne it. "Can't you?" she said, her voice trembling slightly. "Well, consider this, sir. Consider this. Here we sit, side by side, two human beings. You are nine-and-twenty, I am nine-and-twenty; you earn your living, I earn my living; you are unmarried, I am unmarried. But you are considered to be a valuable member of the human community; and I am despised as an eccentric failure. Would that seem worth making a fuss about if you were me?"

He took off his hat and studied the inside of it, turning it about by the brim, his elbows on his knees. "Not if I had a noble alternative," he said at last.

"But all women do not marry," she reminded him.

"But for every woman there exists some man whose duty it is to provide her with her share of a home. A father . . . a brother . . . even," he added deliberately, giving her a sidelong glance that was as friendly as it was serious, "even a brother-in-law," but she missed the generous implication of that in her haste to proceed with her case.

"But suppose," she said eagerly, "suppose the woman is born for another destiny, a destiny outside the home! Suppose she has great talents as a doctor or a lawyer, or for business—why should she be required to smother them because of the accident of being born a woman rather than a man?"

"Should she not regard the accident of her sex as an act of Divine

Providence, equally with the accident of her talents? If God had meant her to use her talents outside the home, He would have made her a man."

"No, no, I cannot accept that. It is men who have made the conditions of society. It is men who have placed us in subjection with man-made laws."

"In subjection, or in shelter?"

"In subjection," she said roundly. "Even at best, we are not sheltered from everything—and at worst we are sheltered from nothing. On the contrary! But even if the shelter were complete and enduring, we should still want our freedom. We would rather sorrow in freedom than be happy as slaves. That is merely our right as women, it is our human right." She picked up a stone and threw it as hard as she could against a tree and then rubbed her fingers together to clean them of dirt and leaf mold.

"As slaves. . . . That's putting it a little high, isn't it?" he suggested, leaning languidly back on one elbow and looking around in enjoyment of the dark coolness and quiet and wild plant smells of the woods.

"I don't think so. Nor would you, if you were me." She looked at him, wide-shouldered, long-legged, sprawled at ease on his rock with no skirts to hinder him and no corsets to constrict him. "Let me put it to you this way—leaving out the question of dress for the moment," she interposed absently. "Let me—"

"Don't, oh, don't tell me that you hanker for a Bloomer?"

"Never mind that," she said, flushing. "Let me put it to you like this—now give your mind to the situation that I am going to picture. Suppose that from the moment *you* first opened your eyes to the world, you had found yourself confined in an artificial sphere of life that required you to be bashful, dependent, and uneducated, whatever your real capabilities might be. Suppose that as a boy you had learned that colleges existed—but that you were not allowed to enter them because you had had the bad luck to be born a boy instead of a girl. And suppose that in the whole world there were only four kinds of employment open to you as a man—that of a teacher, a tailor, a clerk in a store, or a menial servant. You could not be a merchant—nor could you go to sea. You could not become a doctor except by fighting your way through the united opposition of the whole scornful profession. You could not become a lawyer by any manner of means. You could not be a . . . a dentist. You could not enter politics. You could only be a teacher, a tailor, a clerk in a store, or a menial servant—and as such, wherever you were in competition with the triumphant law-making other sex, even through its weakest and stupidest representatives, you could expect to be paid—at best—only about one-third as much as they were being paid for the same work—not because your work was inferior, but only because you happened to be born a man. I am turning it about, you see."

"As for that," he said, interrupting, and changing his position on his rock to make himself even more indecorously comfortable, "there is the matter of social equity. Men must be paid more than women because they have families to support. The whole responsibility for supporting the home rests on the man."

"Not always, not always," she said as she waved an airy flight of midges away from her face—it was only her face that they could attack; the rest of her was well covered. "There are seamstresses who are supporting their families—or trying to do so—and they are not singled out for a larger wage on that account. But leaving that out, do you think then that wages should be distributed according to the needs of the workers, or according to their skill? That is, should a bachelor always receive less than a married man? And should a man with six children be inevitably paid more than the father of two, regardless of his competence?"

"It cannot be carried to that fine a point," he said judiciously. He looked up at the cool irregular pieces of blue sky showing in the depths of branches overhead. "There will always be cases of hardship. But as the world goes, most women are supported by men, whereas most men are not supported by women—most working women support only themselves—"

"*Can* support only themselves, with the wages that they are forced to accept. But let us not be distracted into side issues. Let us return to the case that I was presenting. Were the situation turned about, you, Mr. Bonchurch, would now be known as a male old maid, and you would be considered to have pitifully failed in your primary function—that of beguiling some lordly female into providing you with a home of your own—your only way of attaining one. They would be saying of you, 'Poor old William Bonchurch—still unmarried, poor soul,' though you were only twenty-nine! And it wouldn't mean, mind, that you hadn't found a woman who pleased you—it would mean that no woman had happened to condescend to select you as the object of her proposal of marriage."

"And so you want women to do the proposing? I see. I understand," he said with a grin.

"No! Please don't joke, it is a serious matter! I am asking you how you would like to be judged not on your character as a man and your accomplishments in your chosen work but solely on the basis of whether you had succeeded in getting yourself mated! Suppose your dignity and position in the world depended solely on that! Suppose it was felt that all your talents and energies could properly go only into the task of somehow or other getting yourself *married!*"

"Poor old Mary Whitby," he said, and he leaned over, found a biggish stone half buried in last year's moldering leaves, and gravely offered it to her.

"I confess I feel it," she said, smiling at the stone but allowing him to keep it. "But more than that I feel the indignity of *having* to feel it. Well, then. Consider also this. You succeed in your great project of life, you get yourself married—and all your earned and inherited property promptly becomes entirely the property of your wife. You can no longer lay a finger on it."

"That is no longer true in New York. The law of '48—"

"It is a beginning, but even New York has more to do in that line. And the other states, where there are no rich Dutch patroons to concern themselves over the dissipation of their great properties by dissolute sons-in-law, have everything to do," she said, disposing of that interruption with dispatch. "Well, to go on. Your wife starts spending most of her time in the saloons, and so, in order to avoid starvation for yourself and your children, you must find work—as a tailor or a—a washerman—for you would of course have the care of the children entirely on your hands, and so you could not go out as a store clerk or house servant—whereupon this drunken wife of yours has a legal right to take your tiny earnings from you by force and use them to buy more drink! Yes! It has happened!"

"I know it has," he agreed noncommittally.

"Furthermore, this drunken wife abuses you—beats you—knocks you about. At last you can endure it no longer, and so you obtain a divorce. And that divorce gives you only the right to withdraw your person from your home, the home that you have helped to make with the labor of your hands, leaving your children behind—"

"Which helps, I suppose, in some cases to prevent divorce."

"But that is not the point!" she said scorchingly, and then remembered her pedagogic patience. "The point is, sir, wherein does the protection of women lie in such a law, that deprives her of her children for no fault of her own? That obliges her to submit to brutal mistreatment for the sake of not leaving her children in the care of the brute who is mistreating her, that permits the husband to make a will leaving the guardianship of her children away from her, though she be of the highest character and of blameless reputation—I know of a particular case of that kind, a wicked tragedy—yes, and that gives him the right to pocket her earnings, that allows him to chastise her physically or lock her into a room to enforce obedience to his most trivial whims, that allows him to demand her services as a wife against her will, that allows him to bring her back by force like a runaway slave if she leaves him without legal cause—and in New York the legal cause is infidelity only! He may drink to excess, he may beat her, he may half starve her, he may work her beyond her strength, but she may not leave him unless she can prove a charge of infidelity! And who decides whether she has proved it? His fellow men!"

"No, but do go on turning it all about," he said in a lazy drawl. "I want to hear more of that poor washerman and his drunken brute of a wife!"

"I made a mistake in doing that. That makes a joke of it, and it is no joke, really, you know." She looked at him, and he impassively returned her look with an ambiguous sparkle in his dark eyes. "You know that, don't you?" He looked very solemn. "Where is the justice in such laws? And leaving justice out of it for the moment—but not forever—where is the protection in them?"

"Is there not protection in the law that says a wife may not be held responsible for a crime committed in her husband's presence?"

"*That!*" she cried. "Oh, that would be enough to keep me a spinster forever, if I had had a thousand chances to marry!" He laughed delightedly; she scowled. "That is the most insulting thing of all! It is no protection to be denied the possession of an independent will. That is merely degrading."

"And so," he said with a melancholy sigh, sitting up and brushing a bit of leaf litter from his sleeve, "you would have wives free to abandon their husbands and homes at will, free to hold their earnings and possessions separate from the common funds of the household, free to defy their husbands in public and private and live like tyrant queens, submissive to nothing but their own desires—"

"You talk as if women required a special protection against their evil instincts. Very well! But give men the same protection, then—I'm sure they need it quite as much! Oh, it is very odd. Women are the mothers of your children, the professed objects of your highest love, and yet you would treat them like weak-minded unruly children who cannot be trusted with money or with the power to make decisions for themselves or even with the custody of their own babies. . . . You don't even want them to be well educated! That is one side of it." She looked away through the slanted columns of gnarled trees into the deeper murmurous shadows of the woods. "The other side is even odder. Consider my father. He would never stoop to laying a finger on my mother in wrath, nor dream of claiming her earnings, and he would sooner die than undermine her authority over her children—yet he would not alter the laws that permit him to do such things. He thinks, I believe, of the chance that *might* have given him a wife who needed corporeal correction and who would misuse her savings and mislead her children—he never thinks of the chance that might have given my mother a husband who would wickedly and tyrannously use those powers on *her.* You talk of woman being the weaker sex! Yet it is man who demands the special protection of the law!"

"Oh, yes, you are very good at turning things about, Miss Mary!"

"No, I have turned nothing about there," she replied soberly. "It is perfectly true. Men claim to be superior in every way—in strength and in intellect—and yet they require the assistance of the law in maintaining their position of dominance—even in the privacy of their own homes, where they have personally selected the woman over whom they want to rule. . . . If I were a man, I should dispense with every inequity that favors me—every one—and then I should make my real superiority so plain that it could be denied by no one. Otherwise—otherwise it is nothing but a fraud, and the world would be the cleaner for having it exposed!"

Chapter 6

Manifest Destiny

Reading 22

The Shadow Catcher

James Horan

The Lewis and Clark expedition (1803–1806) called attention to the large numbers of furbearing animals in the Northwest, and Zebulon Pike's travels (1806–1807) did the same for the Southwest. In the years after 1815 fur trappers swarmed into the West to reap the rich harvest. These men, "a reckless breed of men," opened the vast area to permanent settlement; many of them guided the wagon trains of emigrants to their destination. The following is a résumé of the kind of fur trade that was common until the elimination of the beaver in the 1830s.

It is not easy at this point in our history, now that the fur trade has diminished so greatly, to appreciate how important it was in former times. When I found myself so unexpectedly a part of it, the fur trade was a leading branch of commerce in the western world and the only business transacted in the immense wilderness empire west of the Mississippi.

Though it had begun early in the eighteenth century, it did not assume large proportions until after the government published the reports of Lewis and Clark and Pike.

In the east we were well acquainted with the activities of John Jacob Astor, especially through Washington Irving's account of Astoria, his fort in Oregon Territory. After my uncle had pointed Astor out to me, on more than one occasion I saw him in Cherry's, dining by himself on a solitary chop and a glass of ale. For all the fortune he was reported to have made from the skins of the unfortunate beaver, he appeared to me a morose, lonely man who was constantly scheming to protect his fortune from brigands and interlopers.

When I arrived at the scene the Northwest fur trade was dominated by Hudson's Bay, which was contemptuously referred to by Montero and other free trappers as "the pious monster" or "the Trust."

With Manuel Lisa's Missouri Company dissolved, the major companies were General Ashley's and the French firms of Bernard Pratte and Auguste Chouteau. When Astor sold out Astoria to the Hudson's Bay people, he combined with the Columbia Fur Company to dominate the western scene. By 1830 he had elbowed out such giants as Smith, Jackson, and Sublette. The upper Missouri—Astor's domain—was still rich in beaver, but the prize was Oregon.

At the time of which I write, Hudson's Bay controlled the Northwest's fur trade. Their only rivals were the so-called free trappers, small bands of mountain men who were so jealous of their independence that to protect it they sometimes spent their whole winter fighting each other instead of trapping.

In the years I have been in the West I have known many of them, and have come to the conclusion that this strong desire for independence was only an excuse to engage in drinking bouts and savage brawls. At their rendezvous, a designated meeting place where they sold their furs and bought supplies, whiskey, and squaws, they practiced the worst kind of debauchery. I know many men who have lived among the tribes isolated from the outside world for long periods who did not revert to animals at the first opportunity. Those who did, I believe, had already been conquered by the wilderness. . . .

At the time of my arrival, the wealth of furs in beaver, otter, mink, and fox made the American West the richest empire the world has ever known. The three most accepted methods of obtaining furs were through traffic with the Indian Nations, by employing hunters and trappers as the larger companies did, or by buying directly from the free trappers.

But whatever source the trader favored, he generally paid in merchandise he carried with him—articles especially selected for the Indians, or for trappers and hunters, food and staples which could not be obtained out West, and tobacco and liquor.

Since American goods were so inferior that traders carrying them were refused admittance to Indian camps, all Indian trade goods were purchased from foreign companies, especially British. English houses maintained headquarters in New York and Boston to supply rifles, knives, and powder, while Oriental companies flooded New York with beads and imitation pearls. On all these goods American traders were taxed a high duty.

Why, then, did men risk fortunes and sacrifice their lives? Why were they consumed with such cupidity that they would sacrifice every man in their company? The answer lies in the now dusty ledgers of men like Asa Fleming.

Invoices show that merchandise in the Teton country, for example, was four hundred per cent of its original cost in the eastern market. The initial cost was swelled by interest, insurance, wagons, provisions for food until the buffalo country was reached, horses, mules, riding saddles, blankets, pack covers, halters, horseshoeing, and other expenses incidental to the transportation of the goods across the country.

Two thousand dollars could keep a well-equipped company of twenty hunters and ten engagés in the field for a year.

With average success, each hunter would take in one hundred and twenty beaver skins during this period, at a value in New York or Boston of one thousand dollars. Allowing the cost of the return journey the initial outlay of two thousand dollars would bring in a profit of sixteen thousand dollars. Of course, not every venture was a success; weather and the Nations wiped out more than one ambitious eastern merchant who had risked all on one company.

But fortunes could be made.

Only last winter, while the winds howled about our cabin, I checked through my records and was astonished to find that one expedition two years ago netted as high as seventy per cent profit on our investment. Last week a man in the Santa Fe trade told us he cleared forty per cent profit, while the average was between fifteen and twenty per cent.

Montero once estimated Asa Fleming's annual profit as in the neighborhood of one hundred thousand dollars. We had all jeered at this but now I believe his estimate was very conservative.

With such large profits to be gained, there is little wonder why men were willing to cheat, lie, and steal until that became their way of life.

Reading 23

Magnificent Destiny

Paul Wellman

As American pioneers moved westward, they entered the vast territory of Mexico in what is now the southwestern United States. This area was sparsely populated and the frontiersmen moved into it, claiming the best farmland. In Texas they had been granted the right to settle but were soon unhappy with Mexican rule and revolted. The Texas revolt was greatly aided by the assistance of Mexicans who were also unhappy with the administration in Mexico City. The decisive battle of the Texas Revolution was fought at San Jacinto (April 21, 1836), and what follows is a narrative recreation of it.

Up the slope toward the Mexican barricade toiled the thin single line of Texans, a strange, wild march of haggard men, knowing they were assailing an enemy of overwhelming numbers, knowing that only death awaited them if they did not win this day.

They did not keep formation, but each man sought, after a fashion, to remain in touch as close as possible with those on either side of him. At first they did not fire their rifles; and at the beginning the curve of the hilltop allowed them to advance some little distance before they were observed from the Mexican camp.

But then came a high warning cry from in front; bugles sounded and Mexican muskets began to thud. Even then the Texas rifles did not reply.

Back and forth before the scattered line galloped Houston on his white stallion, encouraging his men. Now they greeted him with hoarse wild shouts, for at last they knew their leader and for what he had planned and labored all along.

The big Mexican cannon roared. But its charge went too high, and the Texas line still surged forward.

On the right the Twin Sisters toiled up the slope, hauled by rawhide ropes at the hands of their thirty swearing attendants. Houston rode over toward them and Hockley saw his sword jerk in the direction of the enemy barricades.

He shouted orders: his men leaped to the guns, swung them about, and the Twin Sisters blasted their eruption of horseshoe fragments. Too close to miss. Part of the barricade ceased to exist, and with it the men behind it.

Down the Texas line Deaf Smith rode like the wind, his great howling voice crying, "Fight for your lives! Vince's bridge is down! Fight for your lives!"

The Texans needed no reminder that all retreat was cut off. They were as men already dead.

Off to the left came a shout: "Remember the Alamo!"

In an instant it was taken up, a terrible roar for vengeance, by every throat in the Texas line:

"*Remember the Alamo!*"

In that line also, Captain Seguin's company of Texas Mexicans, fighting loyally, rendered it in their own tongue:

"*Recuerden el Alamo!*"

Here and there men stumbled and fell as the muskets from the barricade increased their volume of sound and powder smoke blurred the whole enemy position.

The Texans were no longer walking. They began to run forward, each man at such speed as he could maintain, but each furious to get at the enemy.

Never in any battle was there such a charge as this. Dirty, savage fighters had forgotten life and looked only for death. No mere bravery here; it was exaltation, an irresistible dedication to conclusion, for a payment in blood long delayed.

Houston, riding in front of the line, felt carried out of himself, believed with all his soul that nothing could stand against this charge.

Saracen gave a shuddering leap, sank to the ground. Houston loosed his feet from the stirrups and sprang aside as the stallion collapsed dead, riddled by musket balls.

A soldier caught a horse for him; and the men cheered when they saw him mount again, unharmed.

Now for the first time the Texas rifles began to crackle. Behind the barricade gray-clad figures went down.

Twenty yards to the enemy line. Moseley Baker, a fighter for all his insubordination, was down. Junius Mottley, Rusk's aide, was down. Others were down. Reeling, with their blood spattering from them, the wounded tried to keep their feet, stumbling, no longer cheering, until they fell behind, too weak to go on.

In the drifting clouds of smoke the barricade appeared just ahead, and the din of the battle rose to a crescendo. Through the blinding fog the Texans rushed, fierce as wolves at the kill.

"Remember the Alamo!"

It had become a view halloo, a death yell.

Burleson's regiment simply rolled over the barricade. Off to the left Sherman carried the flank position with a storming rush and fell upon Cos's disorganized brigade just behind.

Houston felt a shock in his right foot. Nevertheless he lashed his horse with the reins to jump the parapet.

In mid-leap a bullet caught the animal in the head. It seemed to check in midair, then came to a crashing fall on the other side of the barricade.

Thrown heavily, Houston struggled up. He had a bullet in his ankle, low down. At the moment the wounded foot seemed numb rather than painful, but he could not rest his weight on it. Nevertheless when another horse—the third of the day—was brought to him, he managed to heave himself into the saddle.

Behind the Mexican barricades now raged vast confusion. The soldiers of Santa Anna had broken, and were fleeing; the Texans were "remembering the Alamo" with a ferocity appalling.

In spite of his wound Houston rode back and forth, trying to get his men into some semblance of order.

"Parade! Parade, men!" he kept shouting. But nobody appeared to hear him; or if they heard, they ignored him.

Blood-lust had reached a stage almost of insanity. In every direction Mexicans scattered, flying in panic, the chin straps of their caps askew, weapons thrown away. And the Texans bounded after them, slaughtering them.

Some of the fugitives fell on their knees, with a piteous cry:

"Me no Alamo, me no Alamo!"

It availed them nothing. Death was the penalty Santa Anna had exacted: death was the penalty his men suffered now.

In the wild riot of bloodshed there were some appalling sights. Houston saw a lieutenant go by him on the run, shouting, "Boys, *you* know how to take prisoners! Remember how they took them at the Alamo!"

Deaf Smith rode past in the melee, howling, "Knock their goddamn brains out!"

His horse stumbled or was shot, and he fell prostrate. A Mexican officer, still fighting, cut at him with a sword, but the scout, whose pistol was empty, threw the weapon in the man's face, dazing him, then killed him with his own saber.

A Texan slashed with his fifteen-inch bowie knife, catching a Mexican across the throat. The jugular was severed and a stream of blood jetted ten feet out as the man sank dying to the ground.

Here and there hand-to-hand combats took place, but the Texans, with their knives or clubbed rifles, were everywhere in the ascendancy. Brains were spattered out by great swinging blows of the guns. Wounded in many cases were stabbed to death where they fell.

Most of the Mexicans made no effort to resist, but simply fled for their lives, doubling, and dodging like rabbits in helpless terror.

Scores plunged into a morass, fifteen feet deep in soft mud, and there perished. Others attempted to swim a bayou, and were shot down by Texans standing on the bank, who made bets as to who would sink such and such a head.

Off toward the east Lamar's horsemen were ruthlessly cutting down fugitives.

One Mexican ran with a woman clinging to his arm. She was a camp follower, dressed in the loose trousers and jacket of a man, but her shape, and her way of running, and her long hair flying behind her, should have identified her as a woman to any but a blood-mad killer.

The Mexican was cut down by a Texan, and the woman halted beside his body, which was still kicking in the death throes. Apparently she was too bewildered to turn in any direction. Perhaps she thought that her sex might save her. But a crude-faced man in a leather hunting coat swung a great knife at her. Hilt-deep into the soft round of her belly the long blade plunged. She fell forward, with a little stricken whimper, and he finished her with a stab in the back.

But even the Texans were revolted by a crime so unnatural. To them the murder of a woman was a horror. The man who had done the deed disappeared and never was fully identified.

Uncle Jimmy Curtis knocked down a Mexican colonel with his clubbed gun.

"You killed Wash Cottle!" the oldster yelled. "Now I'm goin' to kill you an' make a razor strop out'n yore hide!"

Colonel Wharton intervened and helped the Mexican to his feet.

"Mount my horse behind me!" he said.

The officer understood the gesture better than the words. He obeyed, but an instant later Uncle Jimmy furiously shot him off the horse.

Everywhere men, begging for mercy, were unpityingly slain by the vengeful victors. Sickened by the blood and violence, Houston felt a new grave concern. If one of Santa Anna's other columns chanced to arrive while his army was in this state of desperate confusion, disaster could be the only result.

But the men were utterly out of hand. Long weeks of built-up hatred were having a merciless outlet.

To one blood-spattered crowd rushing by he called out half-humorously: "Gentlemen! I applaud your bravery, but damn your manners!"

A sensation of faintness came over him. He looked down at his wounded foot. Blood there. A ragged hole in the boot, and from it a scarlet stream was oozing.

For the first time he was conscious of intense pain.

One of the surgeons saw he was wounded and offered to dress his hurt.

Houston shook his head. "No. I'll have it attended to when I get back to our camp. I can last till then." And he inquired politely, "Did you suffer any damage in the assault, Doctor?"

The surgeon shook his head.

Beside his horse stood Major Hockley, looking up at him anxiously.

The last contingent of Mexican troops with any kind of cohesion was being surrendered by its commander, Colonel Almonte.

The sun was setting, red in the west.

The Battle of San Jacinto was over: won.

A sudden blackness seemed to close about Houston. When he recovered consciousness he was lying on the ground. He had fainted from loss of blood into George Hockley's arms.

Reading 24

The Time of the Gringo

Elliott Arnold

With the ever westward movement of the United States, it was inevitable that the American frontier would clash with the Mexican frontier. Because the very restrictive economic policies of the Spanish and (after 1821) Mexican governments made consumer goods scarce and exorbitantly priced, American traders saw an excellent opportunity to make large profits, sometimes as high as 300 percent, in bringing textiles and hardware items to areas such as Santa Fe. With the trade door opened, this clash was speeded up immensely. American merchants and trade meant more than just economic activity. As the Taos priest, Antonio Martinez, warns Mexican Governor Manuel Armijo, the "time of the gringo" was upon them.

Martínez swirled the brandy in the glass. "Do you believe you can rid New Mexico of the ascendancy of the Americans? Can one turn back the clock?"

"You imply that the infiltration of gringos is part of historical process, padre," the Governor said. "I do not agree with you. The gringos have infected our life, but it has been done because of our carelessness. That can be corrected."

"Can it, excelencia? I wonder." The priest looked at him intently. "It appears to me that this is the time of the gringo. They are strong and we are weak. They are young and we are old."

"I am stronger than they are," Don Manuel said.

"Your army is stronger than their army, Don Manuel. That is true. But I do not speak of armies and battles. I speak of the imprint one people makes on another. You may defeat the gringo army, but this other fight will be the more difficult one. Soldiers may be beaten, but ideas are elusive things. One cannot turn muskets and cannon on them. For almost twenty-five years the gringos have brought in their ideas along with their merchandise. Those ideas in big ways and in little ways have taken hold. The time of the gringo truly began when the first wagon rolled in from the prairie. The merchants have been more dangerous than the soldiers who come today. Today the soldiers come only to take formal possession of what the gringos have been nibbling on since the Spaniards were kicked out of Mexico."

"And I will remove their food and send them from the table!"

"I pray with all my soul that you do so, excelencia!"

Don Manuel looked at him curiously. "Why, padre? I have listened to you for many years. You have had liberal ideas, almost revolutionary ideas, too liberal for a country controlled by Mexicans. The thoughts you hold on edu a-tion, on freedom, on treatment of the wild Indians, your desire for newspapers and periodicals such as the one you yourself published, all these things are closer to the thinking of the gringos than to the thinking of your own people. In a sense you have been an alien among Mexicans, padre, a lonely and discontented alien. I should not have been surprised to hear that you would welcome the gringos."

The priest stared moodily at the floor. "In some ways I do, Don Manuel," he said in a low voice.

Don Manuel gave a short laugh. "You believe that *I* am torn by doubts and am undecided, padre, and yet compared with you I am a man of single purpose. You would hail the gringos because they would bring with them laws and practices of which you approve. But you also know your stature as a priest would be lessened in a land of heretics and that your political powers would be taken away forever. I grieve for you, padre. I would not exchange my problems for yours."

Reading 25

The Wine of San Lorenzo

Herbert Gorman

As the Mexican War (1846–1848) progressed, many Mexicans became disgusted with the poor leadership, the lack of proper supplies, and the general futility of their nation's war effort as exemplified in the Battle of Buena Vista (February 1847), the major battle of the war. There the Mexican forces were defeated not only because they had no food but also because the Mexican gunpower was so inferior that cannon balls often reached the Americans on the first bounce. Furthermore, Mexican officers thought of war in terms of cavalry charges with lances and flashing sabres and did not realize that the superiority of American firepower made such tactics obsolete. This selection depicts a scene between two Mexican nationals who are concerned because General Winfield Scott's army was marching overland from Vera Cruz to Mexico City.

The bishop was receiving visitors in his library and more waited impatiently in the gloom of the stone-tiled hall where the masklike faces of long-dead clerics peered through smoke-darkened varnish. Don Isidro, therefore, after leaving his name with the harassed young priest by the door passed on through the house and into the small garden where he seated himself on a pink-stone bench inset with blue and white tiles. Against the farther wall the espadañas were in bloom and a plump padre marched up and down the gravel walk peering with weak eyes at an open book that he held in his hand and mumbling softly to himself. The padre had a long nose that trembled sensitively with the moving of his lips. It was quiet, almost too quiet, in the garden. The customary subdued lisp of the fountain was silent and the usual birds that chattered about the espaliered fruit trees had sought other hunting grounds. Don Isidro crossed his hands on his stomach, sighed and closed his eyes. The thought flitted through his head that he was growing old but it vanished almost as rapidly as it came. It was like the flash of a fish glimpsed in translucent water. The sun, mounting to the midday, pressed balmily against his legs and he wondered somewhat testily why he could not relax as he always had relaxed on a cool sunny day. A scraping sound on the path reached his ears and he supposed it was the plump padre until he sensed someone sitting down beside him and opened his eyes to see the bishop.

Don Isidro struggled to his feet and sat down again.

"I slipped out through the garden door," explained the bishop, smiling slightly. "Let them stew in there for a bit. One of Isunza's aides is waiting. I'll keep him long enough to make sure that he misses his dinner."

He studied Don Isidro's face with his sharp little eyes.

"What is it?" he asked. "Did you walk out here? If the information you seek is what I think, it is quite true. It must be all over the city by this time."

Don Isidro cleared his throat.

"I bring you greetings and affection from my family," he said formally and then his lower lip thrust out. "We have been defeated?"

"Decidedly," answered the bishop tranquilly. "At the pass of the Cerro Gordo."

His observant eyes fastened on the meandering padre who had accelerated his mumbling and was crossing himself constantly.

"Brother Eugenio is fencing with the devil again," he remarked dryly. "He must have had bad dreams last night. Do you know, he comes to me and confesses his dreams?"

Don Isidro was not interested in Brother Eugenio.

"Well, what happened?" he demanded with supposed impatience. "What are the particulars of the action? You have had reports?"

"I can give you a minute or two only," said the bishop, pursing his bloodless lips and tugging at his ear with a bony forefinger and thumb. "There are half a dozen people waiting in there to report or beg favors. Yes, I have had reports. They are not complete, Don Isidro, but here is the story as I have patched it together."

He yielded to his old habit of closing his eyes as though he could marshal his facts better by shutting out the visible world.

"The Americans began their advance from Vera Cruz on April eighth," he said. "On the eleventh they reached the National Bridge. During this thirty-seven-mile march through torrid country nothing was done to harass or stop them because nothing could be done. We had neither the men and equipment nor the time to raise fortifications or barricades close to the coast. Besides, La Viga, who commanded this district, is a zote, a numskull, and his superior, Canalizo, is a windbag. Santa Anna, coming down from Jalapa, hit upon the pass at the Cerro Gordo, which as you probably don't know, is on his own land, as the appropriate place to make a stand. He may be a windbag, too, but he is not a numskull. Strongly fortifying the heights overlooking the road by the Cerro Gordo he rested his right on a ravine with almost perpendicular sides several hundred feet high and his left on the Cerro Gordo which rises more than nine hundred feet above the river. His entire line faced hills along which extended for miles the Vera Cruz-Jalapa road, the only road possible for artillery. Vázquez of the Ingenieros informs me that it was a good position and should have held."

He opened his eyes and glanced inquiringly at his nephew.

"I know the Cerro Gordo," declared Don Isidro for want of something better to say. "It's about sixty miles from the coast and would seem to have been an excellent place to make a stand. What happened? Didn't the general have sufficient forces?"

"He must have had at least twelve thousand men," said the bishop.

"Then, in the name of Heaven——" began Don Isidro with some excitement.

"Wait," interrupted the bishop. "There are more elements necessary for success in warfare than men. I am an apostle of peace but I have wit enough to know that. For instance, generals. For instance, a plan. For instance, morale. That last, the most important of all, Santa Anna did not have. True, he had men. True, he had a sort of plan . . . although, according to Vázquez, it was based too much on assumption and vitiated by a disregard of particulars. For instance, there was a forward hill called La Atalaya which the engineers argued should be fortified and strongly held. Santa Anna sent twenty-five men to it. Robles, believing the Americans could turn the main position, wanted fortifications on the extreme left. Santa Anna said, 'No.' Santa Anna said that a rabbit couldn't get through. Santa Anna, as usual, was too cocksure."

"The morale of the troops must have been bad," remarked Don Isidro gloomily. "But why? What—"

"Why?" repeated the bishop quickly. "Ah, I have been hearing about that all morning. Their morale was bad from a complexity of causes. The narrow camp was too crowded with cottages, tents, huts and market booths and the results was a confusion that made everybody irritable. Swarms of insects kept the men awake all night. The water supply was insufficient and the pulque was so green that it gave those who drank it diarrhea. A sort of cholera swept the camp and the exposure brought on lung troubles. There wasn't enough to eat. But worst of all was the hopeless feeling about the Americans. The men from the north recalled how they had been forced to turn their backs on the Americans at Palo Alto, the Resaca, Monterrey and La Angostura and the men from the south had seen Vera Cruz and San Juan de Ulúa capitulate. In short, they regarded the Americans as invincible. And it didn't help any when Santa Anna began shooting captured deserters. According to Vázquez, even the officers talked privately about disaster. All the tinder of a panic was there. Only the spark was needed."

Don Isidro groaned.

"Go on," he said. "I suppose I might as well hear about the spark."

The bishop made a slight gesture of impatience.

"We are not an objective people," he declared. "We do not scrutinize; we feel. Our impulses are always our undoing. Discipline, Don Isidro, we lack discipline. The story of the Cerro Gordo appears to be a story of the lack of discipline, of leadership, of will. Certainly, we had the troops . . ."

His voice trailed off into silence and he observed the marching figure of the padre with some distaste.

"The story?" he said after a moment. "It is like most of our stories. The Americans attacked and we resisted but not enough. They took two tactically important hills and a height. They did what our generals had declared impossible, turned our left. We trusted to the fact that there was no road there. They hacked a road through the chaparral. They outshot us, outmaneuvered us, outfought us. We broke and ran. They killed a thousand of us, captured three thousand prisoners including several generals, more than four thousand stand of arms, about forty cannon, a large amount of ammunition, most of the army funds and . . . Santa Anna's wooden leg."

He erupted into a short laugh.

"Isn't that good?" he demanded. "Santa Anna's wooden leg!"

Don Isidro refused the levity.

"It is terrible," he said somberly. "Some sort of infernal luck seems to go with the Americans. What are we going to do now? Do you think . . . ?"

The bishop became grave.

"Perhaps the Americans are too unimaginative to accept defeat," he answered. "Perhaps we are too volatile to achieve victory. What are we going to do? Well, what would you do?"

"At Jalapa . . . " began Don Isidro.

"The Americans are in Jalapa," interrupted his uncle.

"We must fight again," said Don Isidro heavily. "Surely, Santa Anna will make a stand at La Hoya. The pass is more than a mile long and the road runs between steep mountains. Santa Anna can . . ."

"You don't understand," explainted the bishop patiently. "The Americans are beyond La Hoya. Santa Anna ran away. His troops are streaming along the National Highway and all the side tracks and mountain paths. The vanguard of the fugitives is passing through Puebla now. It is a rout."

Don Isidro fingered his heavy underlip.

"Then . . . " he stuttered. "Oh . . . but . . . the Americans will enter the city."

"Of course they will," said the bishop. "They will enter the city. They will pass through the city. They will go through San Martin. They will pass Ixtaccíhuatl and Popocatépetl and cross the Río Frío. They will reach the Valley of Mexico. Why? Because there is nothing to stop them. Nothing at all. Except a moral reason. And Texas and California are worth more to them than moral reasons. They are practical men."

Don Isidro half-heard him. He clenched his big fists.

"We must make a stand," he asserted. "Where is Santa Anna? What is Isunza doing? We can fight a battle at Ojo de Agua or Nopalucan. The city is full of men and if, as you say, troops are passing through . . ."

"Vázquez tells me Santa Anna is at Orizaba," said the bishop sharply. "I have no doubt but that he will arrive here in due time. He always does. He will ask for money and for men. He will not get either."

"If he organizes quickly . . . " began Isidro and then the meaning of the bishop's last words struck him like a bolt of lightning.

"What's that?" he cried in a loud voice. "What did you say?"

"We've had enough of General Santa Anna," said the bishop. "That is what I say."

Don Isidro glanced with angry perplexity at his uncle.

"Who is there to take his place?" he inquired in a shaking voice.

The bishop turned his irritated fox-face to the sunny sky.

"He would bleed us white if he could," he said. "I beg you to recall what happened in Mexico City. Forced loans from the Church, eh? Well, they found little enough in my strongboxes. I was forewarned and when the troops came the funds of the bishopric of Puebla were safely hidden elsewhere. Oh, I saw to it that a few pesos were left. Just enough to drive the officials wild. The sacrilege . . ."

"That was the work of Gómez Farías!" exclaimed Don Isidro. "That was the work of a government that has ceased to exist. Have you forgotten that when Santa Anna returned from the . . . er . . . action at La Angostura he found the capital in a state of insurrection and put down that insurrection and took over the presidency and saw that the obnoxious laws were repealed? After all . . ."

"The Church paid him two million five hundred thousand pesos for that," broke in the bishop.

"The Church raised that much money in the name of patriotism to carry on the war," declared Don Isidro. "Why, there wasn't a priest in Mexico who didn't bless the name of Santa Anna in March."

"Well, it is April now," said the bishop baldly. "Besides, you do not understand. Santa Anna bled us when he passed through Puebla and he will try to bleed us again when he returns. He will not succeed. This is a city of peace. The Poblanos do not want to fight. We shall make such arrangements with the Americans as we please and Santa Anna can retreat to the capital and make his stand there . . . if he can raise enough troops."

Don Isidro stood up in amazement and then immediately sat down again.

"Are you informing me that Puebla will put up no defense against these gringo invaders?" he asked in a precise voice.

"That is exactly what I am informing you," replied the bishop. "This is a City of God."

"And Mexico?" demanded Don Isidro in the same precise voice.

The bishop shrugged his shoulders.

"Mexico is in the hands of God," he answered.

The two men sat and stared at each other for a half minute.

"No one loves Mexico, the Mexican people, more than I do, more than the Church does," declared the bishop calmly, "but wisdom always should be a part of love. We should not lose sight of the larger good when we are faced by the smaller vexation. My people are simple people and they are weary of violent struggle. The políticos in Mexico City made this war and they can finish this war. It was not made in Puebla. I do not say that we are waging an unjust war, for we are fighting invaders and that is always just. We are fighting imperialistic buccaneers. But I do say that it is not the duty of Puebla to offer resistance. Do you imagine we want our holy monuments bombarded, our people slain, our communal life smashed? No, my dear nephew, Puebla will not fight. I shall see to that."

"It is the duty of every Mexican patriot to fight to the last man," exploded Don Isidro. "We should raise barricades in the streets, fortify the houses, hold the Americans until a new army, an overwhelming army, is raised in the valley."

"It sounds very noble," remarked the bishop, "but it won't work out. The army would split and the parts would fight against each other; the generals would conspire and the políticos would defraud."

"It seems that we were more united under the viceroys than we are now," said Don Isidro bitterly.

"It is quite possible," agreed the bishop tranquilly. "A strong hand has its virtues."

"Submitting without a struggle is no evidence of strength," declared Don Isidro roughly. "I shall go to Isunza and ask him to resist."

The bishop smiled slightly.

"You may do what you please, Don Isidro," he said in a friendly voice. "You will merely waste your time. As I am wasting my time now."

He stood up.

"Don't let the American advance worry you too much," he continued. "They are not quite savages."

"I shall go to Isunza," repeated Don Isidro stubbornly as he rose heavily from the bench.

"Is there any more information I can give you?" asked the bishop politely. "I'm afraid you will have to wait for particulars of the fighting at the Cerro Gordo. Well . . ."

He took a step toward his side door.

"How is María Catalina?" he asked perfunctorily.

"Isunza will *have* to do something," declared Don Isidro. "It is impossible that he should . . ."

Anger bereft him of speech. The bishop moved down the path toward his villa.

"Visit me any time," he said cordially. "Come tomorrow. Or this evening. God bless you, my son."

His purple robe disappeared through the narrow portal.

Don Isidro stalked toward the house door and bumped violently into the strolling padre, knocking the book out of his hand.

"Por Dios . . . !" he began and then skirted the stooping figure in grim silence. He was repressing an almost uncontrollable desire to kick the padre right in the middle of his broad backside.

He was so angry as he walked along the road to the city that he hardly observed the gathering traffic flowing toward the plaza. The jingle of chains, bridle bits, spurs and sabers sounded musically in the clear air and the soft pounding of horses' hoofs in the gray dirt made a muffled drumlike undertone. He heard it as at a distance. Without being conscious of looking he was aware that these mounted men were cavalrymen, fragments from the Húzares, the Fifth of Morelia and the Ninth of Coraceros. There were men on foot, too, but they were like trees or bushes to him. He pushed brusquely by them as he had always pushed by pedestrians all his life . . . without care or excuse. He was angry and he was sufficiently detached to be aware of his anger and to wonder at it. He could not attribute all this inner rage to the fact that the serenity of his existence had been destroyed. No, it was more than that now . . . though that had been enough to begin with. It was Mexico. It was the pusillanimity of men. It was the dubious prospect. It was the damned criminality of it all. It was . . .

He bumped heavily against a burro and cursed inwardly.

Could it be patriotism, an awakened sense of the wrongs perpetrated against his land, say, that was boiling up within him and rousing his fury? He had never considered patriotism as a passion in itself but rather as a lip service for foreigners, a necessary intimation of one's honored place in time. One did not emphasize it for that would have been vulgar. It was indicated, insinuated, suggested as something that should be taken for granted. That, perhaps, was because it had never presented itself to him as a burning issue at Las Golondrinas and in Mexico City it had seemed to be no more than the angry shouts or crafty gestures of conflicting politicians and ambitious generals. It had slightly sickened him, then. He had been safe and removed at Las Golondrinas and patriotism there, now that he thought of it, was merely fidelity to himself. It had been fidelity to himself as far back as he could remember. Yes, even in those distant days when he had desired to raise a company of peons and ride off into the hills after the rebel Francisco de Paula. He had reacted then as youths of his caste reacted. It was not so much patriotism, not so much a profound affection for Ferdinand VII and the regime of the viceroys, as it was a desire to maintain his own culture and way of life, his privileged place in time, that roused him to such a pitch that his alarmed father had sent him to Spain. No, that was not patriotism. And after the battle of La Angostura (which he was convinced was a defeat) his irritation had not been patriotism. He had been merely inconvenienced by his wife's fear and hysteria and the moil and trouble of transferring a household through the difficult terrain to Puebla. It was the indignities that he had endured. It was a feeling, he imagined, that the padre back there in the garden would have experienced if he had actually kicked him in his backside.

But, then. Yes . . . no. At La Angostura, or Buena Vista, or whatever the history books would call it, the Mexican soldiers had fought and according to all secondhand tales they had fought well. At least, they had stopped the Americans dead in their tracks. Or had the Americans stopped *them* dead in their tracks? It was all mixed up. It didn't matter, though. What did matter was that the Mexicans had fought . . . and fought well. Now, the bishop and his cuadrilla of bootlickers proposed to hand Puebla over to the Americans without firing a gun. That was it! That was what put him in a rage. It was the shoddy acquiescence in defeat, the calculated surrender, the shameful understood *bargain* and not defeat in itself that put him in a rage. If that was patriotism, why, it was patriotism. It was pride, too. It was the pride of keeping a vow, or doing what one said one would do, of facing the worst without flinching, of being consistent. The Republic had accepted this war; the soldiers had marched forth singing "Adiós"; the populace had cheered and breathed defiance against the gringos; the Church had put its hand down into its pocket and produced funds to carry on the campaign. Let them all stand up to it, then. Let them stand up to it. Let them stop thinking about their precious skins and their concealed money boxes and their personal jealousies and . . . stand . . . up . . . to . . . it!

If he was to be made uncomfortable there might as well be a worthy reason for it. And if there was a worthy reason the rest of them (and that included the Church, by God!) should accept their responsibilities and face the music whether it was a triumphal march or a funeral dirge. One did not mix politics and war. Or religion, either. War was like a sponge. It sucked up everything into itself and that was all that there was to it. One did not postpone a war in order to fight an election. The enemy would not co-operate. Por Diós! There *was* an election coming along in May. A presidential election. Don Isidro groaned. Was that the reason that the bishop . . . ? These old manipulators . . . ! But, no. What good would it do Santa Anna's candidacy to hand Puebla over to the Americans? What benefit would the Church acquire by defeating Santa Anna? He was the only general in Mexico who even attempted to fight a battle. It would be instructive to know more about the man. Curious personality. Oh, undoubtedly an opportunist. But . . . "City of God," indeed! "Not the duty of Puebla to offer . . ." His rage flared up again as he swung sturdily into the sunlit streets.

I'll go straight to Isunza, he thought. I'll tell the bag of fat that he has sworn a certain oath to the Republic and that it is his duty to fortify the city, barricade the roads and put men with muskets behind the barricades. He can do it. Look, troops are pouring into the plaza now. There must be hundreds of them. Isunza must do that. We'll fight. I'll fight with the rest of them. Then it won't matter whether the Americans take Puebla or not. At least, we shall have fought. We shall have kept our vow and God will take care of the consequences. Then . . . Suddenly a new Mexico danced in his mind, a Mexico of united citizenry, of one oath, of combined will and purpose, of . . . As though directed by an invisible guide he turned his large head and saw a row of Indians sitting with their backs against a rose-pink wall, their sombreros tipped over their eyes, their blankets raised across their mouths. Not even the excitement of scores of fugitive soldiers hurrying along the streets could rouse them from their detached and somnolent observation. They were like the hills beyond the city, like the mountains, like Malinche, Orizaba, Ixtaccíhuatl and Popocaté-petl, immovable and stubborn and distantly contemptuous. What did it matter to them if the Americans entered the city? Nothing had mattered to them since Cortés with his frightening horses had passed this way and gone on to Cholula where the temple to Quetzalcóatl was raised. Nevertheless . . . He would go to Isunza anyway and tell him that Puebla must fight. It was something he could not say with any degree of firmness to his uncle, the bishop, but he could say it to Isunza. That bag of fat!

Reading 26

Gold in California

Todhunter Ballard

The discovery of gold in California in 1848 climaxed the spirit of Manifest Destiny. The lure of gold and the hope of immediate riches triggered one of the great mass internal migrations in the history of America. More than 250,000 people made their way to the gold fields in a few years. This selection tells what happened when a Wilmington, Ohio, newpaper owner contracted gold fever. The creation of companies to help finance the trip was typical of the times. The reading also depicts the resistance that many women had toward the mad adventures of their husbands.

Until the discovery of gold ours had been an ordered household and the town in which we lived a quiet, regulated, unhurried community. I don't recall that there had even been many political differences, since almost everyone was anti-slavery and most favored the Mexican War.

But it seemed that an unseen force erupted from the center of the earth, changing men and women overnight from their contented daily norm to a fevered restlessness.

Several of the young unmarried men took off for the East seeking ships to take them to the gold fields, but for the most part the town's imagination was caught up in George Muller's gold company.

Our shop printed up the stock certificates. I came in to find Old Ike running them off carefully from the plates he had laboriously carved. They weren't fancy, just sheets of stiff, coated paper printed with black ink. They showed a miner with a pick on his shoulder, and the fine print stated that in return for ten dollars the holder was granted a one thousandth interest in the gold discovered by the Clinton Mining Company.

The company had been organized the week before, with my uncle as president and George Muller manager. Their purpose was to raise ten thousand dollars, the sum to be used to outfit a party of ten volunteers who would be sent westward to the gold country.

These ten were to keep one half of the gold they found. The other half was to be shipped east and divided among the investors. It was also understood that any investor who chose, after the company was established, would be free to go west himself and take his place in the diggings.

To cinch his argument George Muller had built a mining machine. He had gotten the idea from his uncle who had done some mining in Georgia. It was an ingenious affair with a screen to take out the larger rocks, and a tray beneath it, mounted on leather straps, which was moved back and forth in a small tank of water by means of an eccentric and a hand crank.

Ike shut off the press and slowly filled his pipe.

"What do you think of them, Austin?" He indicated the pile of still damp stock certificates with a wave of the pipe stem.

"They're right pretty," I said.

"Um."

"Don't you think so? You made the plates."

"Best I could do with what I had. Still, I don't cotton much to the idea."

"What's wrong with it?"

He took time to light the pipe. "Well, several things. First off, who are the ten men they're going to send?"

I hadn't heard. After that first meeting at our house the group had gathered at George Muller's, and neither Dave nor Tommy had been able to listen in.

"Second, how they going to make certain them fellows will send back that half of the gold?"

I didn't know that either.

"Third, how they going to get there?"

I had the answer to that one. I mentioned the eight routes across the country, naming the mountain passes.

Ike grunted. "I went out to Santa Fe in thirty-one and it was a rough trip, and the men I was with knew what they was doing. There ain't no one in this town who does. And the trail north of that, the one the folks for Oregon have been using, is a lot worse from all I hear."

"Then you aren't going?"

He grunted again. "Oh, I'll probably go, when I have a mind. But then I never did have much sense nohow."

I heard my aunt saying almost the same thing that night at dinner. Relations between her and my uncle had become more strained each day as the agitation for the trek increased.

"I simply cannot understand you," she said as she placed the boiled dinner on the table. "Here you have about the best house in town. And the county newspaper. You are looked up to and respected, and why you should lend your name to anything as wild as this scheme of George Muller's is beyond me."

Uncle Ben was spreading freshly churned butter on a thick slice of new bread. He laid the knife and the bread down on the red-checked tablecloth.

"Please, let's not discuss it in front of the children."

"They're going to know soon enough. I was talking to Rebel and Ephraim this afternoon. They are very concerned."

My uncle said dryly, "Your brothers live in a state of constant concern. They are a little conservative, don't you think?"

"If you call showing good sound sense being conservative, they certainly are. As they point out it was rather absurd for us to take California in the first place, and perfectly idiotic to think that people will want to stay in that Godforsaken land once they have dug up all the gold."

My uncle picked up his bread slowly. He spoke mildly but I was not deceived, he always spoke mildly when he was making a telling point.

"I seem to remember that your grandfather came out to Virginia with the shirt on his back and no baggage."

Aunt Emeline flushed. "What's that to do with it?"

"And your father came over the mountains, settled first in Kentucky and then moved on up here."

"So?"

"If your grandfather had stayed in England where would you be? If your father had stuck there in Virginia where he owned not one acre of ground what would you and your brothers have now?"

"But they didn't."

"So"—Uncle Ben leaned forward—"let's not let the spirit of adventure die in two generations. There's a lot of interesting land between here and California, but before Austin dies most of it will be filled up."

"Now I know you are insane. And about this gold company: Who are the ten men you intend to send?"

"We haven't chosen them yet."

"And what makes you think that if they find any gold at all they will ship it three thousand miles back here?"

He looked up at her then and I saw a look on his face that I had never seen there before, a tight strain.

"We've taken care of that. It was decided this afternoon. George and I are going with them."

Goose pimples raised the hair on my arms, but before I could let out a whoop the sudden chill silence of the room stabbed me. Then came Aunt Emeline's long, ragged gasp.

"Ben Garner. You don't mean it."

My uncle bowed his head. "I certainly do."

She sat in a state of shock, unable to find the words she needed, the words which were trying to thrust out of her.

"You would go away and leave me?"

He looked at her, harried. "I am not leaving you. I'll send for you and the children as soon as we get established, as soon as I find a proper place for you to live."

She rose and left the table and the room. Later I heard her crying in the darkness of her bedroom. Caroline heard it too. Caroline came and crawled into bed with me. Her nightgown crept up to her skinny knees and her feet were like lumps of ice as she pressed them against mine.

"Austin, I'm scared."

I was scared too, but I couldn't admit it to a seven-year-old girl.

"What are you scared of, sissy?"

I knew, although I did not know the proper words at the time. She was scared for her security, of the crumbling of the family structure which had made us immune to the doubts and fears that harassed some of the kids we knew.

My uncle had gone downtown, and when he came back I heard his feet on the uncarpeted stairs. Caroline had gone to sleep in my arms. I could feel the bones of her thin body through the flannel gown. I knew that she was not supposed to be in bed with me. My aunt had not let us sleep in the same bed for the last three years, but I didn't want to make any noise.

My uncle's steps were uncertain and he bumped into the doorjamb as he turned into the main bedroom. I heard the scratch of the match and saw the quick light reflected in the hall, and heard my aunt's horrified voice.

"You've been drinking."

I couldn't make out the mumbled answer at first, then he said,

"It's enough to make a man want to drink, Emeline, when his wife sets herself against him."

"Ben."

"It's something I've got to do, Emmy." His voice broke and I knew that he was crying, and that was as great a shock to me as anything else. "You've got to understand, Emmy. I wasn't meant to just sit here all my life and write how many hogs Silas Appleby raised, or how Mrs. Sommers won the prize at the church supper."

"Ben Garner."

"Please understand. I'm thirty-one, Emmy, and I've never been anywhere or seen anything."

"Let's talk about it in the morning."

"No. I've got to talk about it now."

"I've never seen you drunk before. What will I tell the ladies at the . . ."

"To hell with the temperance women."

Silence.

"I sold the paper. Sold it to Malcolm Reed."

"You didn't."

"I did. We went to Fellow's saloon and sealed the bargain. He's going to take over the first of February."

She began to cry again. I heard him trying to sooth her. Then he blew out the light and I heard him try to comfort her, but the sobs continued until I went to sleep.

In the morning Aunt Emeline was unusually silent, but by then I hardly noticed. I couldn't wait to get to school and spread the news. My uncle Ben was going to California and so was I, as soon as he found us a home there.

By the time the bell rang I had the whole place in an uproar. Dave and Tommy Muller resented the attention I was getting, claiming rightly that their father had originated the idea of sending a company of men West, but nobody really listened to them.

After school I raced to the print shop, expecting to find Old Ike as excited as I was. Instead he looked as if the press had just fallen apart.

"What's the matter with you?"

He rubbed the side of his head with an ink-stained hand, leaving black streaks across his ear.

"Your uncle shouldn't have done it."

"Say he was going to California?"

"No. Sold his paper. Some of the men who pledged money to the gold company are already backing out."

I stared at him, stunned. "But why?"

"Your aunt's brothers. They've been busying around town all day, talking to one man after another. They're calling it a golden bubble, hollering that it's going to bust."

"But what for?"

Ike looked both ways to make sure he wasn't overheard.

"Your aunt," he said, "she doesn't want your uncle to go."

"I know that, but . . ."

"So she's got her brothers doing everything they can to stop him."

"Nobody listened to them before."

"They wasn't really fighting it then, just being cautious. But they're the bankers. They got a mortgage on about half the houses in this town, and most of the businessmen owe them money. And when you owe a man money you'd maybe better heed him."

This was a new idea to me, the power of money.

I said, "That's a mean trick."

"Don't you ever tell your uncle," he warned.

"Why not, if it's a mean trick?"

"You ain't old enough to understand," he said. "Women got their own method of doing things, their own way of figuring what's right and wrong. Ain't one woman in a thousand thinks her husband has got real good sense. They connive to catch a man and once they got him they ain't satisfied with the way he is. They can't leave him the way the good Lord made him, they got to plump for an alteration job."

"Is that the reason you didn't get married?"

He hesitated for a long moment. "I was married." he said.

He'd never mentioned it before. I said, "What happened to her?"

"I don't rightly know."

I didn't understand. "How come?"

He scratched his nose thoughtfully as if he couldn't make up his mind if he was wise in telling me.

"She was a French gal, down in New Orleans when I was down there with Andy Jackson. I wasn't much more than a button and she wasn't as old as me. Anyhow, we up and got married and after the fighting stopped I wanted to bring her North, only she wouldn't come."

"So you came without her?"

"Well, not right away. She was as cute as a bug's ear and it was kind of fun having her around. I stayed maybe six months. Her pa was dead and she and her maw had an old house with balconies and such, right at the edge of the Quarter. They tried to dress me up and make me a gentlemen, only I couldn't take it. I lit out one night and never went back."

I didn't say anything. I knew by the look on his face that he wasn't thinking of me, that he was thinking back nearly forty years.

I didn't tell my uncle what the Wards were doing, but it wasn't surprising that he found out. Very little goes on in a town the size of ours that most people don't know about shortly.

It happened three nights later. I'd been out milking the cow and feeding old Jimmy, our carriage horse. It had been a warm day and the snow had nearly vanished. I went through the back porch and into the summer kitchen. In winter my aunt used this for a cold room, since there was no heat, and the milk crocks were lined up before the tin bathtub which we used only during the summer months.

I had begun to fill the crocks from the bucket of warm milk that steamed lightly in the chill air. I heard them come into the kitchen from the dining room. Caroline was spending the night with one of her friends and I suppose they thought I was still in the barn.

"Why did you do it to me?" It was the first thing I heard my uncle say. "How could you do such a thing behind my back?"

My aunt's tone was too low to hear but I realized that something terrible was the matter. Uncle Ben sounded like a small child, not angry but hurt, puzzled, completely unbelieving and bewildered.

"Everyone in town is laughing at me."

"Ben"—I now had no difficulty in hearing her—"you are acting like a fool."

"Sure," he said bitterly. "Your two brothers have gone from one end of the county to the other telling everyone that I am a fool. So why shouldn't I act like one? Tell me why?"

"You'll thank them and me once you've had time to think it over."

"I'm not going to have time."

"What do you mean by that?"

"I'm going to California. I said I would and I am going."

"You can't go. Why, everyone has deserted that crazy company, everyone but George Muller."

"That makes no difference. I am going." I heard him cross the kitchen and pull open the back door.

"Ben, if you leave this house . . ."

She did not say what would happen. She didn't have the chance for he slammed the door and I heard his boots as he stamped away.

He didn't come home until late. My Aunt Emeline fed me in stony silence. I don't know whether or not she knew that I had overheard them. I ate rapidly and then ducked up the back stairs to my room. For a long time I heard her moving around in the kitchen below me, and then the house grew still.

Reading 27

The Way West

A. B. Guthrie

Not all Americans prompted to move west by the spirit of Manifest Destiny
went to California. Thousands made their way over the Oregon Trail to take
advantage of the rich soil in the Oregon Territory. They suffered hardships
common to many overland travelers: scurvy, cholera, lack of water, and
Indian attack. Thousands never reached the promised land but found instead an early grave along the trail. Those who survived endured many trials
and tribulations, as the following selection suggests.

Drive, plod, push, tug, turn the wheels. Eat dust, damn you! Eat mud. Swim
in sweat and freeze at night. Work the sun up. Work it down. Keep rolling.

Watch the stock. Fix the wagons. Unload, load, unload. Sleep dead like
a brute while the wheels keep turning in your head, and then get up and go.
Drive, plod, push, tug. Damn the dor bugs. Damn distance. Damn gullies,
streams, trees. Keep going. Three cheers for Oregon.

Fall into bed at night and feel your wife's warmth and know her back is
turned. Know it and not care, except deep in you where you keep your hates.
Let the knotted muscles melt. Let your mind drift. Let women come into it,
like the girl, Mercy McBee. As a man thinketh in his hearth, so is he. All right,
so is he. Let sleep flow over you, if you can.

Drive, plod, push, tug, turn the wheels. Eat dust, damn you! Eat mud.
Swim in sweat and freeze at night. Work the sun up. Work it down. Wear the
body limp. Keep moving.

Chapter 7

Slavery

Reading 28

Marching On

James Boyd

As the tide of public opinion changed regarding slavery, Southerners bitterly resented the attacks upon it by Northerners who knew little or nothing about the institution. To counter these attacks, Southerners especially enjoyed making a comparison between the status of well-cared-for blacks and the abject poverty of white factory workers in the North. The rather naïve attitudes of Northerners toward blacks and slavery is reflected in the following selection in the comment of a Boston college student visiting the South. The reply by the black on the question of freedom was predictable under the circumstances, since uneducated slaves did not always understand the concept of freedom.

"My brother just came home from college. He broke down from over-work, he told Papa, and Mr. Higgins has come with him. . . ."

"To try," Mr. Higgins interposed, "to help him make up some of the ground he lost while he was overworking."

James eyed him with less respect. The fellow was only some kind of schoolmaster after all. He needn't to carry such a high head. Perhaps they made more of schoolmasters in Boston. The man's suit of clothes must have cost thirty dollars.

Mr. Higgins now addressed himself seriously to James. He knocked the ash off his cigar in preparation. James stepped on it to put out any chance spark among the pine-needles.

"It is very interesting," said Mr. Higgins, "to see the South after having read so much of it."

"Yes, seh," said James. "What all have you read?" he inquired politely.

"There is a great deal being written in the North," Mr. Higgins answered, "about the South. No doubt you have heard of the interest there in slavery?"

"Not much," James said. "Oh," he added casually, "I've heard that the abolitionists are stealing niggers." Again she laughed. Mr. Higgins stroked his whiskers.

"But surely," he said, "as a practical man you must have some opinion on the question of slavery."

James would have liked to make some profound observation, but he could merely say, "Well, the niggers are here and that's about all there is to it."

"But you do not esteem them highly," said Mr. Higgins with an air of discovery.

"Esteem?" James nearly grinned right in the stranger's face. But he only said, "Well, niggers is just niggers."

"But surely," Mr. Higgins was persistent, "they would develop into something better in a state of freedom."

That was too much. The man, beside being curious out of all reason, was a born fool.

"I'd like to see every free nigger shot," he answered briefly.

"Ah, indeed," Mr. Higgins' ruddy, complacent face first looked shocked, then glowed with conscious morality. "I suppose you slave owners all feel that way."

"We don't own any niggers," James answered shortly.

"But surely—" Mr. Higgins began.

"But we want to keep them in their place," James cut in with an air of finality and turned away to her. What ailed this Yankee, anyway, standing here asking nit-wit questions and leaving the lady out altogether?

"I hope your brother's health is better," he said.

"I'm sure it will be soon," she answered. "it was just a case of too many cigars and sherry cobblers, I'm afraid, and perhaps some faro mixed in."

It was delightful to hear her run on like this as if he were a real friend instead of—instead of what? Not a stranger, that could not be possible. Yet what? While these thoughts passed through his head, Mr. Higgins' wandering eye had fallen on Logan and Ray who, having paused in their rail-piling to drink in the splendors of the party in the phaeton, now fell most assiduously to work again.

"By Jupiter!" he said, "there are two black boys now. I'd like to talk to them. Do you suppose they'd mind?" She gave him an amused and hopeless look.

"I reckon they can stand it." She started to call them over but Mr. Higgins was already on his way to the pile of rails.

"Well, what do you think of our Northern friend?" she asked.

"I expect he's a mighty clever gentleman," James answered evasively.

"Charles says that there are lots of them like that in Boston," she announced.

"Is that so?" He gave difficult but sincere credence to this information. He was about to add that Boston must be a mighty curious place, when she broke in.

"Let's listen to what he says." James nodded. There was intimacy in this.

"Well, my friends, you seem sufficiently contented," Mr. Higgins remarked; his voice was loud and jovial without sounding at ease. The negroes stopped work and stood, their eyes downcast, their hands hanging, half smiling in a depreciating manner. In his embarrassment Logan gripped the sand with his black toes, while the yellow negro, Rav, raised his eyes to the level of Mr. Higgins' waistcoat and licked his lips with his tongue.

"I said you seem sufficiently contented," said Mr. Higgins. The two stood as before, except that the smiles vanished and left them abject,—not that they did not aim to please this white man, but the crisply spoken syllables and the flatness of his intonation left them at sea as to whether the stranger intended greeting, question, or reproof. Mr. Higgins attributed their silence to profound and secret grief.

"I suppose your life, however, is hardly as easy as it seems." Rav, the thin yellow negro, did not reply. He knitted his brows in thought. He was beginning to have an inkling of the stranger's meaning. But Logan, the Guinea negro, though completely stunned by Mr. Higgins' speech and manner, spoke up promptly. It was necessary, he felt, that something should be done to placate this curious apparition. He therefore grinned widely with simulated merriment and thinly veiled anxiety, and muttered, "Yasso. Truth, too. Yasso. Ha!"

Mr. Higgins was somewhat disconcerted by the apparently insupportable delight with which Logan acknowledged a truth which one would think must be for him profoundly mournful. But he persisted.

"I suppose you would rather be free, eh?" He looked at each of them in turn. This time Rav understood but still he did not answer. He stole a glance at young Charles Prevost on the seat of the phaeton and at Charles' sister standing beside James Fraser. When he did speak it was with pleased self-importance but guardedly.

"Dat depen', suh, on de circumstance. Yes, suh, it depen' mightily. A heap of free niggers mighty bad off." Observing that Logan was straining to catch the meaning, Rav condescended to interpret for him. "White gent'man say, you want to be free?"

Logan's fixed grin vanished. He popped his eyes out in astonishment.

"Who? Me? Free? No." A look of triumphant cunning crossed his face as though he had detected a trap which had been skilfully set to catch him. "Whar rations come fum den?"

"Ah, I see," said Mr. Higgins slowly in a tone painfully at variance with his words. He moved back to the phaeton.

"Extraordinary chaps, these black fellows, Charles."

Charles Prevost, who had been leaning down and talking to the young lady in the back of the phaeton, glanced up. His face, showing softly white beneath the shadow of his broad hat, had a look at once gallant and astute, but underlying these superficial aspects it held a boyishness, a sweetness, a fundamental and indestructible innocence which, without effort, without knowledge of its power, or even of its own existence, would be able, James Fraser reluctantly admitted, to draw to itself the hearts of many men and women.

"I reckon they seem like that to you," he said to Mr. Higgins. "But then you seem so to them, too, I expect." He smiled with a simple amusement which robbed his words of irony.

Reading 29

The Red Cock Crows

Frances Gaither

Despite efforts to justify slavery on moral grounds and despite the claim that most blacks were happy in bondage, the South lived in constant terror of a slave insurrection. All Southern states had laws against slaves handling guns under any circumstances, and many mistresses kept huge dogs in their bedrooms while the master was away. The Denmark Vesey insurrection in 1822 cost 37 Negro lives and that of Nat Turner In 1831 some 120 Negro lives. This selection describes the terror in a Southern town when rumors of a slave uprising are heard.

Adam Fiske, skirting far around the lights and the milling crowds, entered the jail yard by the back gate without meeting anyone, but he found the back door locked. He knocked, softly at first, and called the jailer in a guarded voice. "Mr. Patton! Mr. Patton!" And then he tried calling Jody. But it was no use. The Negroes upstairs, crazed with fright, were raising bedlam, and the streets in every direction resounded with shouts and running feet and even hammering and sawing. Growing bolder, Adam pounded loudly on the jail door and even tried kicking it. But it held as solid as rock. While he stood, irresolute, trying to make up his mind what to do next, a man came around the corner of the building with a torch in his hand. The streak of flame, with its tail of black, oily smoke curling after it was for an instant blinding. Adam stared at it and blinked.

"What you think you're doin'?" the man with the torch demanded.

His face, though grotesque, distorted by the leaping flame held above his head, was yet familiar, a face seen often about Scott's Bluff whenever idlers congregated—down by the river when a boat was landing or leaving, at Dutch Pete's if the weather was cold or rainy, and, on summer days, in whichever store porch the shade at that hour blessed. Adam recognized the fellow as one of the town loafers the moment his eyes got used to the torchlight. But he had entirely forgotten the youth's name, if indeed, he had ever known it.

"Good-evening, Mr.——"

"I say: what you doin'? Tryin' to bust in the door?"

"I wanted to see Mr. Patton," said Adam.

"Oh. You wanted to see Mr. Patton." It was mimicry of the crudest, most insulting sort. And the accompanying grin seemed to writhe with purposed insolence across the flame-lit face before the young man turned and, waving his torch back and forth in signal, shouted: "Hit's just the Shandy school-teacher payin' a little back-door call on Sheriff Ed."

From beyond the corner rushed pell-mell his customary cronies, the whole galaxy of the town's choicest ruffians: a famous drunkard, red-faced above his beard, a bully much dreaded for his skill at gouging, and a half dozen more, all yelping away like hounds on a scent.

"Sheriff Ed's right busy, sir. He got a hangin' to see to. Was you wantin' something special?"

"How come you sneak round the back way, Professor?"

"Mebbe it's them niggers upstairs you come to call on?"

"Nigger-lover."

The specific jibes Adam hardly heard; but he did not miss the threat in the tones of voice and in the hostile faces pressing closer and closer at the foot of the steps. As he braced himself for attack a shadowy figure clambered over the board fence, crossed the yard, vaulted into the little porch and came trotting to Adam's side.

"You all right, Mister?" sounded a gentle, slurred whisper.

"For God's sake," said Adam. "I thought I told you to keep back."

At sight of a new victim the fun started all over.

"Well, do tell. Ef'n here ain't our *little* Yankee!"

"You a nigger-lover, too, Yank?"

"Sure he is. Didn't you hear him down to Dutch Pete's? Didn't you hear him say, far as he see, niggers got as good a right to be free as white men?"

"You say that, Kentucky?"

Suddenly Adam strode down the steps into their midst. Surprised, perhaps, they fell back before him, and one of them said, some of the mockery gone out of his voice:

"If you mean it—about seeing Sheriff Ed—ain't no reason why you can't. He's right around the corner, yonder."

Then the youth with the torch obligingly took the lead. Adam followed, with his unwanted young friend trotting at heel, breathing hard; and the rest pressed in behind, jostling one another and still jeering but with, it really seemed, a diminishing ferocity.

Beyond the corner of the jail the ruddy, wavering light of massed torches made every person and even every tree and house wall seem fantastic and instable—as a stick seen under water looks more like a snake than a stick. Near by some men with hatchets and axes were knocking the boards off the high jail fence. People crammed the street, the vacant lot over the way and the tavern porches, upstairs and down. There were even men on the rooftops, strung along the ridgepoles. And, at the moment Adam came around the corner and chanced to look up, three little boys skittered crazily down a shingled slope and fetched up, laughing, against a tall chimney. Every fence in the neighborhood had its row of figures roosting on it like buzzards on deadened tree limbs. And all the torchlit faces, rank on rank, from the edge of the road to the highest roof ridge, were turned watchful and intent upon the jail yard, where those men were demolishing the fence and several others with short lengths of board and hammers were securing a barrel to the bed of a wagon.

"Gentleman to sce you, Sheriff Ed."

Sheriff Ed and Deputy Jody with their hands bound and their holsters empty, stood near one of the rear wagon wheels, under guard of Messrs. Purdy, the steam-doctor, and Clint Stokes of the Pole Cat Creek neighborhood. Sheriff Ed smiled sheepishly as Adam, shoved violently from behind, strove not to collide with him.

"Howdy, Mr. Fiske. Well, it sure ain't our fault, Mr. Fiske. You and me sure done what we could to pertect them pore wretches up yonder."

Adam following Sheriff Ed's upward glance had a glimpse of dark hands crisped about iron bars, of dark foreheads and white rolling eyes at every window. The sight brought back to his ears, too, the pandemonium of terror still raging up there. It had never stopped of course—he had only ceased for a little while to hear it. Now it broke again in anguish on his ears. I looked over Jordan and what did I see. Sweet Jesus, tell Ol' Satan lemme go. Look down, oh Lord, look down. What was singing, what, prayer, and what, spontaneous lamentation, he could not make out.

"Mr. Fist! Mr. Fist!"

The hissing appeal came from directly above where he stood. He saw a dark arm in a pale, soft sleeve thrust out between the bars, Sack's arm. It reached downward, the palm and groping fingers outspread in pleading.

"Mr. Fist, please, sir, Mid ready now tell all he know. Mid, he say git Mas Troop here and he swear he tell the nekkid truth."

Jeers answered her.

"The truth! Mid? That Mid been lyin' so long he wouldn't reckernize the truth did he meet it in the big-road."

"You tell Mid git ready to travel."

Laughter mingled with catcalls and piercing whistles drowned out Sack's voice, but her arm remained dangling outside the window and now and then it jerked convulsively like a chicken's body just after the head has been tweaked off. Adam edged closer to the sheriff.

"Mr. Patton," he urged, "isn't there something to be done even yet? Someone we can send for who can make this crowd listen to reason?"

"This crowd! Reason!" Sheriff Ed shook his head and his eyes dilated. "If you know what's good for you, Mr. Fiske, you'll lay low. This ain't no picnic. This here's a mob. Hit's out for blood. An' it just as soon have yours and mine as any."

"All right, Sheriff Ed," a mighty voice interrupted. "Here's that rope. Will you take a look at the noose?"

Whitehead, the auctioneer, pushed in through the crowd around the wagon, a coil of new hemp rope wound loosely around his bent arm, and held a looped end out toward the sheriff, at the same time testing with his own hands the ease with which the noose slipped. He had somehow ripped the buttons off his gingham shirt and it hung open to the waist, showing the dark pelt on his chest, rank as young cane in a brake.

"All right, Sheriff?"

The sheriff shrugged his shoulders and moved his head impatiently.

"Hit ain't just the noose I'm worried about, Whitehead. You know as good as I do, the best noose in the world ain't gonna give you a proper hanging without you got good and sufficient drop. And how you gonna git good and sufficient drop without you got a gallows is past me. Moreover, I'm a Christian and I believe ever' man, black or white, ought to have the chance to cleanse his soul before he go to meet his Maker."

Surprisingly, to Adam Fiske at least, the nearest spectators loudly cheered this simple credo. And the cry, "Git a preacher," rising close at hand, spread through the crowd, echoing and re-echoing with increasing urgency.

"Don't send him off 'thout a preacher to pray with him, Whitehead. It ain't human."

"A nigger got a soul same as you and me."

The pressure became, minute by minute, so insistent that Whitehead set a ladder against the barrel in the wagon, clambered aloft and sent forth his clarion voice.

"We done sent for the preacher—sent for him same time we sent for this here rope. He ought to be coming along any minute. Have a little patience, can't you?"

After Whitehead had climbed down to the ground again, he came and took the keys from Sheriff Ed's belt and went off with them around the corner of the jail in the direction of the back door. A few minutes later he reappeared above, at Sack's window, with a lamp in his hand. There he thrust her aside, and, having set the lamp down, lowered the noose end of the rope to dangle outside against the brick wall. At the same time he shouted:

"How's that, Sheriff Ed? Is that good and sufficient drop?"

The sheriff stared up in a worried way, walked off a few steps, looked up again and came back.

"Hey, you fellows," he said to the men in the wagon, "get out a minute, will you? And, some of you, run this wagon close in under that there rope."

The wagon was pushed and backed and hacked about until the center of the barrel upright in the box came beneath the rope. Then the sheriff asked Mr. Purdy if he would please climb the ladder and stand on the barrel head. Mr. Purdy obliged. The sheriff, viewing him speculatively in relation to the rope, called up to the window.

"Pull in a little, Whitehead. Hit hangs a mite too long, to my way of thinking."

Jody put in.

"Mid ain't anywhere near as little as Purdy, Sheriff Ed. Mid's more my height."

There followed some argument in the crowd, which ended in Jody's hands being untied and his taking Purdy's place on the barrel head. Then the noose was lowered and raised and lowered again, with many people advising and criticizing. Throughout these proceedings Sheriff Ed worked irritably at his rope-cuffed hands and fussed under his breath.

"Hit ain't no gallows, however you fix it," he fumed.

He was a man of mercy, he said, and if a life was to be taken he believed in taking it easy-like. Even a catfish, now. A catfish the meanest fish on earth to handle. You'd near 'bout as well git mixed up with a rattlesnake as have a catfish fin you. You got to kill him. But you take and slam a cat against the side of the boat or bang its head out with an oar like some men do, hit ain't kind, any way you look at it. All you got to do is put your foot on its back and give it one quick jab with a sharp knife through the skull and. . .

"Look at it now, Sheriff," boomed Whitehead from above. "That any better?"

"I reckon," said Sheriff Ed without enthusiasm. "Only now you got it *too* short, look like. What you aimin' to do—jerk his head right off like they done to that highwayman down to Allenport in spring term of court?"

Whitehead played out a little more rope. Then he asked Jody, who still stood on the barrel, if he would please take hold just above the noose and bear his full weight down on the rope to make sure it was fast at the upper end. And, by the time that test was satisfactorily concluded, the preacher arrived, Bible in hand; and the crowd, parting to let him through, grew suddenly quiet. Even the Negroes wailing at the barred windows overhead hushed when they looked down and saw the black-clad figure crossing the street. In the swift silence the preacher's elderly, genteel voice sounded with startling clearness.

"I wonder, Sheriff, if someone could get me a lamp?"

"There's a lamp up there, sir," said Sheriff Ed. "And you'll find the back door open. Just go ahead on up. Mr. Whitehead, he's got the keys and he'll show you which cell you want."

While the preacher was up there, reading the Bible and praying with Mid, Whitehead came down, stood again near the sheriff and discussed with him in whispers the problem of whether to hitch the mules to the wagon before or after placing the noose. The grim argument hissed and spluttered along in the strange hush and at the end Sheriff Ed's voice once more complained, high and fretful:

"Still and all, hit ain't no gallows."

At last the preacher came out again. He was a wisp of an old gentleman, with pink, crinkled skin and a clean white beard. He was wiping his forehead with a big, snowy handkerchief and his frail old hand was trembling. Whitehead greeted him in a loud, blusterous manner.

"Well, is he ready, Reverend? Is he ready for his journey?"

The shouted question beat up against the barred windows and loosed there a new torrent of grief and terror. As the Negroes' raving rolled forth again there surged through the waiting crowd an answering clamor. Git it over, Whitehead. We can't wait all night. Git goin'.

"Mr. Patton, sir," besought the preacher, patting away the beads of sweat that kept forming on his pink, crinkled forehead, "this must be stopped. In the name of our Saviour, sir. We cannot allow them to execute a poor demented creature."

Adam Fiske started.

"Demented?" he echoed. "Did you say demented, sir?"

"Oh—it's Mr. Fiske. How do you do, sir? Yes, that poor boy's crazy. I'm sure he is—oh, he must be—only a madman could have such ideas in his head. He's absolutely convinced someone has conjured him. Believe me, gentlemen, a Christian community cannot contenance the hanging of an insane person. . . ."

"Hush, sir," said Sheriff Ed sadly. "You just as well's to save your breath. They're bringing him now."

Mid, with his hands tied behind him, was led out by two of the gang who a little earlier had heckled Adam Fiske at the back door, the notorious drunkard and the chief of all gougers. Mid was beyond speech, almost beyond walking. His head rolled about on his shoulders. His knees wobbled and bent. He lurched now to this side, now to that, and was yanked up by each guard in turn. They got him to the wagon and the foot of the ladder leaning between the wheels and there were about to hoist him up when Sheriff Ed rebuked them sharply.

"Hold on. Ain't you got a scrap of decency? The mules ain't even here yet. Ain't no use puttin' him up there just to be stared at."

Several youths with much shouting and clanking of chains fetched the mules at the double-quick, backed them up to the axle-tree and fastened the traces. Clint Stokes sprang to the wagon seat and seized the whip. The two guards forced Mid up the ladder. Whitehead mounting behind kept him from falling.

Adam made an attempt to get away but he was wedged fast in the forward shoving crowd. Mid, atop the barrel at last, swayed dizzily, supported by Whitehead, who stood on the top rung of the ladder. Then Whitehead adjusted the noose, released his hold on Mid, climbed down, and lifted the ladder away. Stokes cracked his whip and the mules lunged forward. As the wagon moved under him, Mid fell to his knees, beating the air with his bound wrists. The barrel rocked and, insecurely fastened after all, tore loose with a sound of ripping planks and toppled. Mid's feet kicking out wildly for it and even his arms, fettered and helpless, clutching at it as he fell, the rope, somehow, not taut yet.

Adam shut his eyes. Sheriff Ed cursed.

"I knowed hit'd be a mess," he said. "I said hit wa'n't no proper way to hang a man."

A weight lurched against Adam. He put out his arms and kept the young Kentuckian from falling to the ground. Somebody laughed.

"Well, I be a son of a gun, ef'n Kentucky ain't fainted. Hey, Kentucky, this the first hanging you was ever at? You can come to now, sister. Hit's safe to look now. Mid done quit twitching, nearly 'bout it. . . ."

Adam helped the boy over to the jail wall and waited while he braced himself against the bricks and vomited. Then Adam took out his watch and looked at it in a passing flutter of torch flame. Two fifteen. He held it to his ear. It was ticking away as strongly as ever. It was just twenty minutes since he had left his room at the tavern.

Reading 30

"Follow the Drinkin' Gourd"

The song "Follow the Drinkin' Gourd" was widely used as a guide for runaway slaves seeking freedom in the North or Canada. Symbolically, the "drinkin' gourd" was the Big Dipper pointing the way northward, and the "great big river" designated the river route northward. "Peg Leg Joe" was a legendary white leader of the Underground Railroad, and the phrase "left foot, peg foot, traveling on" referred to Peg Leg's wooden leg that was used to mark the road to freedom. Use of the song was common until its meaning was betrayed to the white masters.

When the sun comes back and the first quail calls,
Follow the drinkin' gourd.
For the old man is a-waitin' for to carry you to freedom,
If you follow the drinkin' gourd.

Chorus:
Follow the drinkin' gourd.
Follow the drinkin' gourd.
For the old man is a-waitin' for to carry you to freedom,
If you follow the drinkin' gourd.

The river bank will make a very good road,
The dead trees show you the way.
Left foot, peg foot, traveling on,
Follow the drinkin' gourd.

Where the great big river meets the little river,
Follow the drinkin' gourd.
For the old man is a-waitin' for to carry you to freedom,
If you follow the drinkin' gourd.

Reading 31

Follow the Drinking Gourd

Frances Gaither

As Northern abolitionists increased their efforts to free the slaves, Southern-ers retaliated with slave patrols on roads and railroads to intercept all blacks without a pass. Still, the slaves were able to pass the word among them-selves how one could flee all the way from Alabama to the North. The following is an example of how one black utilized the song "Follow the Drinkin' Gourd" in his quest for freedom.

Once he got up to mend the fire, found there was no more wood and started to the woodpile. Outside, he forgot what his errand was and stood, uncertainly peering out upon the tree-shadowed street. Many of the cabins had already quieted down for the night. The firelight oozing out between their logs and under their doors had dimmed to a thin, steady phosphorescence. But from others livelier fires sent forth a rippling brightness, and voices still sounded in talk or song. Next door Pleasant's harp was playing brightly.

Pleasant probably did not know the words or meaning of the song he played. The five to whom that secret belonged were far away from Hurricane tonight. Poldo was perhaps the only man left on Hurricane who knew the secret of the song. Standing still in the pale starlight which poured down on the open dooryard, he tried to fit the proper words to the notes that came twinkling from Pleasant's harp. To his surprise he could not do it. It made him uncomfortable not to be able to call back the song when he wanted to. . . .

Pleasant's mouth organ shifted to a dance tune, one of Antoine's. And patting feet and clapping palms struck up a muffled accompaniment. Some-how, Poldo remembered his errand and turned to the woodpile. Back indoors, seated on his stool, he lapsed once more into blankness. Several times sounds from outside pierced in to him: two young women rallying each other from opposite doorways; a boy sent to the spring for water, whistling his dog up for company; some men loitering past, joking and laughing. Then at last the hush of sleep settled down on the Quarter. Poldo's fire was dying again and he got up, absently, to replenish it. In the very act of reaching for a light-wood knot, he paused and straightened up, listening.

Standing so, ears cocked to the profound stillness, he began to murmur under his breath in foolish and querulous pleading, like a child resisting authority: Hurricane my home. Hurricane where I's born at. What'd I leave Hurricane for? I wouldn't know what way to go. I ain't half listen that night Mr. Joe talk all that runaway stuff. I forgit what all he say—like I forgit that ol' bad-luck song o' his. . . .

Grumbling and muttering, he began to move about the room. He spread a big handkerchief on the table, shook upon it what was left of the meal he had earlier ground, added a gourdful of shelled corn, a potato the children had overlooked in the ashes, the scraps of food left over from his own supper, the slab of bacon from its hook, and carefully tied all together inside the handkerchief. Then he felt in his pockets, fingering one by one his small store of coins, his knife, tobacco, pipe. When he touched paper, he drew forth his soiled, crumpled pass, stared at it a moment and then went over and dropped it into the fire. Standing to watch the bit of paper flare and then blacken and crumble away, he continued his grumbling argument: Man be a fool run off from Hurricane this night. Sheriff and his dogs liable be here soon in the mornin'. Man sho be out o' his mind make them ol' hounds a fresh warm trail to follow.

Yet he went on with his preparations: put his extra shoes on the table by the handkerchief-wrapped parcel of food; took a blanket from one of the beds, found a bit of plow line and made a knapsack of a sort. At the last he raked the fire back carefully, opened the door and fastened it again behind him. He had ceased his grumbling now, but his step, as he moved off down the sleeping street was slow and plodding, the step of a man driven forth.

His feet bore him along an old, little-traveled footpath leading down through Old Spring Hollow and up toward the back-land and Shields' Deadening. On the ridge at the edge of the piney woods, he stopped and looked back across his homeland. Under the starry sky, the woods and fields of Hurricane were a shapeless mass of shadow, with little streaks of milky mist washing over the lowest places: Old Spring and New Spring and the farther fields at the edge of the bottom. A sob broke from him. And then he turned and plodded on under the high pines.

A little before day he passed a cabin in a clearing. Through the open door he could see a woman getting breakfast by lamplight. The trail he had been following ended here. But just beyond, he knew a little branch that led down into Buzzard Creek Bottom. He found the stream as daylight was breaking and set off along it. Dawn made him think of Three S. Just about now Three S. would be mounting the stump before the door of his old house to give out his orders. He would call Poldo's name and get no answer. He would think that Poldo had overslept and send somebody to wake him. When Three S. knew for sure that Poldo was gone, he would know that what Miss Maggie had said about him was true.

When Poldo came to the creek, he turned right, working his way up stream. It was slow going through the swampy, thickly grown bottom, without a path to follow. Now and then a rotten log broke under him and sent him knee-deep in mire, Still he floundered on. Sunlight began at last to strike thin blades down through the sticky green gloom. He was sweating hard. But he did not stop until he came to an old dead tree thrusting up fingerlike from a sandy point. Beyond the tree was a clump of laurel and titi. He had never seen the place before, but recognition flashed somewhere inside of him.

He dropped his blanket knapsack off his back, got down on his knees and crawled under the bushes. There, clearly, was the place where an overturned skiff had lately lain. The ground was still dark with damp and the vegetation was killed in unmistakable outline. Crawling out again, he saw where the skiff had been launched. The leaves and brush were trampled for some distance about and there was the slash the keel had cut across the yard-long shingle. Near the foot of the dead tree were the ashes of a campfire.

Coffee and Lem and the others had made the fire, of course, cooked their bacon and corn pone at it only yesterday. But Poldo hardly knew how he came to be standing here now in his turn. What evil force had drawn him here against his will? It was all very well for the five traveling together, singing their secret song in lonely swamps, rehearsing the directions they had received for the journey, sharing the squirrels and rabbits they would trap, sharing every danger, one man posted as sentinel while the others slept. It would be a different thing to attempt that journey alone, hungry and afraid, day after weary day, unsure of every mile, maybe getting lost or shot at or hunted down with dogs. . . .

Suddenly Poldo turned his back on the creek and began to run, without his bundle, hardly looking where he set his feet, stumbling, falling, scrambling up and running on, sobbing aloud: Please s'r, Mr. Littleberry. I wants to be where you at. I take my whippin' for runnin' off. I knows I done wrong. You the onliest friend I got. I tell you all I know 'bout that peg-leg fellow make our hands run off. Hurricane my home. Hurricane where I's born. . . .

Just outside the bottom a white man was plowing in a little deadening and a woman in the doorway of a log cabin was scattering corn to a flock of "Dominecker" chickens. Seeing the two white people brought Poldo to an abrupt halt. Checked just inside the sheltering woods, he peered out for some minutes before he realized that this was the same cabin he had passed before sunup, the same woman he had seen getting breakfast. His panting sobs quieted after a bit and he heard water gurgling along through the woods a little way off. He stumbled toward the sound. When he had drunk deeply and doused cool water over his head, he plodded back down the branch to the creek and then fought his sweating way up the creek again to the sandy point, the bare, skeleton tree and his bundle lying untouched on the ground where he had dropped it.

Standing once more on the small hidden beach appointed as the first day's hiding-place, he looked carefully at the dead tree, as at first he had failed to do. And now he found there, painted plainly on the naked trunk at a level with his eyes, the outline of a human foot and a small rude circle. As he stared at the painted sign, he began to hear, word by word, names of rivers, names of places, names of stars—all as clear and natural as if spoken now close at his ear in a mild friendly voice. The Tombigbee is a plain road all the way to north Alabama. From there it's only a stone's throw to the Tennessee. And the Tennessee's another clear road to follow. At the mouth of it, a red-haired man with a squint kept a woodyard. He would gladly hire any wayfarer, white or black, to cut his wood. And the first time a black man was alone with him, it was necessary only to say, "I'm a friend of Peg-leg Joe's," to be put across the Ohio that very night and landed at the first station on the Underground. . . .

Poldo could even see the homely gesture Mr. Joe had made as he pointed his pipestem at the heavens. Do you know the name of that star, Poldo? The country between the Alabama and the Tombigbee is a ticklish stretch, I own, but even there a man need not get lost if he keeps an eye on that star. . . .

The trembling went out of his legs. He slipped down on the sand, pillowed his head on the blanket roll and went at once to sleep. It was mid-afternoon when he waked, sweating with fright. He started up in panic again, straining his ears for the barking of dogs, the sound of men's voices. Sheriff's coming, he reckoned darkly, sheriff and his dogs, close on Poldo's tracks now. But it must have been only a bad dream that had wakened him, after all; for, when he raised himself on his elbow, tensely listening, all he could hear was a gentle sighing through the high tops of the cypresses. He sank back on his pillow and, turning to let his eyes rest on the painted sign, he lay quite still to wait for evening.

At sundown, he opened his bundle and ate the potato and corn bread. When he had eaten, he stood up, heaved his bundle to his back and moved off through the oozy, tangled creek bottom. In the river at the creek mouth he found a raft. That was lucky of course. Yet it hardly surprised him. Now, he could half believe that Mr. Joe, knowing Poldo would not leave with the others, had provided the raft on purpose for him.

It was fully night on shore, but out in the middle of the river daylight lingered. There the water, mud-colored by day, shone now like polished silver. It still reflected some last color from the opposite sky. It would be another hour before a raft, venturing out from the shadows alongshore, could cross the open river unseen. Poldo sat down to wait. He watched the color fade out of the western heavens and the river beneath. After the color was gone, the sheen on the water dimmed and vanished, too. On his left, dark and shapeless beyond the pallid shield, lifted Hurricane Bluff. On his right, by leaning forward, he could see another bluff, lower than Hurricane, with fewer trees on top and a cluster of shed roofs cutting the sky. That was Waycross Landing. Above the horizon, just between the Waycross Landing sheds and the opposite shore, the Drinking Gourd brightened steadily. It was standing on its handle as when Mr. Joe had showed it to him, its uppermost side pointing to the North Star.

A word shaped itself in Poldo's mind and found its way to his tongue. "Free." He spoke it aloud, but questioningly, unsure of its flavor. Then he put another, homelier word beside it. "Free nigger. Uh, uh, uh."

The groans gave place to a low, shy laugh. And he went on repeating the two words, trying them out, now with one shading, now with another, like an actor conning a new part. Now he tried them windily, swaggeringly, like Antoine; now, with complaisance faintly edged with derision, like Mr. Littleberry, perhaps, or Captain Clisbee; and then he spoke them with the surprise and awe which he, Poldo, in his own person, honestly felt. . . .

At last he reckoned it was dark enough. He scrambled down the bank, untied the raft, sprang aboard and pushed off, poling hard until he felt the current take him. Then he dropped to his knees and laid the pole down beside him. It was a good place to cross. The mirrored image of the Buzzard Creek woods sheltered him all the way down into the shadow of Hurricane Bluff, a vast pool of darkness. Both banks were inky black as far as he could see. There wasn't so much as a woodyard on the river between Hurricane and Waycross. And the opposite shore for several miles in both directions was unpeopled swamp. Yet his heart quickened painfully as he passed from the protecting gulf of Hurricane's shadow on to the unsheltered expanse at the middle of the river.

There it was much brighter than he had bargained for. The vault of sky and the depths of water glittered dizzyingly. In fear of the revealing stars, he stretched out flat and shut his eyes. Lying so, he heard the swamp frogs' chorus swell slowly louder, felt at last a shadow like airy fingers laid over his eyelids, and then the raft crashed noisily into reeds. He seized the pole. One thrust brought him bump against cypress knees. He caught hold, swung his blanket-wrapped bundle onto the dark shore and leaped after it. He stopped long enough to drag the raft well inside the margin of canes, hiding it as well as he could and tying it firmly. And then, hoisting his bundle to his back, he set off up river.

Reading 32

Fire Bell in the Night

Constance Robertson

The Underground Railroad aided runaway slaves in their flight through the free states into Canada. From 1840 to 1861 this secret and shifting network was operated by dedicated abolitionists, even though the Fugitive Slave Act, passed in 1850, made such assistance a federal crime. Perhaps only 1,000 slaves a year benefited from its work, but it offered hope to the slaves and was an abomination to Southerners. The following selection tells of its operation in upstate New York and suggests the diversity of the people involved in this humanitarian enterprise.

On that night—and on every night, rain or shine, hot or cold, winter or summer or spring or autumn—a strange thing was happening. Along the shores of Lake Erie men were pushing out in boats, carrying dark passengers; beside the sand beaches of Lake Ontario men hid in clumps of bushes, awaiting the sound of oars and a soft whistle from across the water; on the Suspension Bridge—The Bridge, it was called, simply, as far south as the rice fields of Georgia and South Carolina—two men, perhaps, or a woman with three children, or an old woman alone, were hurrying to reach the northern shore of the river.

At the windows of darkened, remote farmhouses, hands were raised to knock softly. The windows would slide up, open a crack.

"Who's there?"

"A friend with friends."

Then, after a moment, footsteps would sound, the shed door would open, and a half dozen men would enter, treading softly.

In a hundred kitchens, lamps were lit at midnight, women would pull the shades and hurry from buttery to stove, warming up food. They would load the table and draw up the chairs, and a company of dark-skinned men would sit down—hesitating at first to sit with white folks—until hunger made them snatch at the good food, gulp down the fresh milk, tear at the leg of a chicken.

Along dark roads, late at night, horses were trotting, pulling covered wagons, three-seated Liberator wagons crowded with passengers, closed carriages, peddlers' carts, open lumber wagons filled with loads of straw that in turn covered other loads. Men with their hats pulled down over their eyes, and their coat collars turned up to hide their faces, drove rigs along at a fast clip. They must get to wherever they were going before daylight.

Next morning, in a barn thirty miles away, a quiet man in a wide-brimmed Quaker hat would harness his sleek team to the family carryall and drive it up to the front door. Out would come a party of ladies, all neatly dressed in gray with Quaker bonnets and veils over their faces. Demurely they would mount the horse block and step into the carriage. The driver would cluck to his team, the carriage would roll out of the drive and away through the streets of the village, as innocently as you please. The driver would nod and raise his whip to salute a friend, the ladies would bow, the strangers hanging around the post office or the village store would glance at them and then away.

Or, south of the Line, men might be cutting their way through swamps. They would come to a stream and creep along its banks until they found a skiff tied to a stump. Then they would turn, perhaps, and an owl would be heard to cry in the night, hooting softly under the leaves of the forest, until one by one, three men, two women, gaunt, frightened, stopping to listen when a twig snapped, when a dog howled, would glide through the shadows until they came to the boat. They would get into the boat and oars would move, carefully, silently, until the boat reached the northern bank of the river.

On railroad trains there were passengers huddled in seats they had not paid for. When they raised dark hands to pull their collars closer around their ears, the hands trembled. Conductors on the cars where they sat never looked at them; never asked for their tickets. If a noisy group of men—their hats cocked rakishly, perhaps; with handsome black mustaches, and wearing holsters at their belts—came into the cars, then the conductor would mutter a word to the passengers in the rear seat. "Slave catchers. Get to the last car." Or, perhaps, he would hurry them off at the next station.

On boats, paddling up the coast from Baltimore, from Philadelphia, from Charleston, black men were hiding, crouched in empty barrels, or down behind a pile of boxes, trying not to cough in the acrid stink of smoke, trying not to breathe when the inspectors came around, trying to look like a bale of cotton, down amongst the cargo.

Or perhaps, on this very night, a black man was lying in a box, pressing his mouth against the tiny, bored holes in the side of the box to get air—more air—for his bursting lungs. If he could hold out, if he could bear the darkness and the bruising of his body and the choking in his lungs, he would be carried, tossed by porters into a wagon, jolted over the cobblestones in the street, carried along to a house. Then he would feel the box tilting again—now he was fairly standing on his head—as the box jolted up steps and he would hear a door close. At the last he would hear pounding; the wood beside his cheek would shiver, nails would screech as they came out, and finally the cover of the box would be opened. For a moment he would only want to breathe. Nothing else mattered; not the voices of his friends, not food, not water, not even the freedom he had been thinking about so hard in the darkness of the box. Only air. Then hands would touch him, faces bend over him, he would feel himself being lifted, carried—tenderly, this time—and the journey would be over.

In New York, in Vermont, in Ohio and Michigan and Illinois and Indiana, strange men came into the towns and villages. Tall, lean men wearing fine linen and nankeen pantaloons, and speaking in soft slurring accents; short heavy men, in rough clothes, with mud spattered on their riding boots; marshals with badges on their coats and new derringers in their belts. They would come in a posse, half a dozen of them, riding hard into the village just at dusk, reining short before the village lockup, leaping from their horses and running up the steps to see the head man.

Sometimes they did not stop in the village, but rode, hell for leather, out the sand road, galloping up Johnny-Cake Hill in a cloud of white dust, to stop at a farmhouse where their boots clattered across the kitchen porch. They would track mud and dirt over the scrubbed floors inside pulling beds apart, pawing through closets, ransacking the attic, tumbling the woodpile in the cellar, mad as hornets if they did not find a black girl with a baby.

"She came this way," they would say, pounding on the kitchen table. "We have reliable information that she came to this farm tonight. If you're concealing her, it'll be the worse for you."

But the farmer and his wife knew nothing about any slave girl and her baby.

"Keep your damned cattle at home if you want them," the farmer would say, grinning.

And his wife would reprove him. "Now, Asahel," while the angry men stamped out of her disordered kitchen.

Chapter 8

The Civil War

Reading 33

War Is Kind

Stephen Crane

Before the guns of the Civil War cooled at Appomattox Court House, 618,-000 men gave "their last full measure of devotion." In this most costly of all America's wars, 360,000 men from the North and 258,000 from the South lost their lives. Stephen Crane, the author of one of the most realistic novels of the Civil War, *The Red Badge of Courage,* asks in the following poem if such great losses were justified. The author uses irony to question the chivalric values of the Middle Ages which are used to justify war.

Do not weep, maiden, for war is kind.
Because your lover threw wild hands toward the sky
And the affrighted steed ran on alone,
Do not weep.
War is kind.

Hoarse, booming drums of the regiment,
Little souls who thirst for fight,
These men were born to drill and die.
The unexplained glory flies above them,
Great is the battle-god, great, and his kingdom—
A field where a thousand corpses lie.

Do not weep, babe, for war is kind.
Because your father tumbled in the yellow trenches,
Raged at his breast, gulped and died,
Do not weep.
War is kind.

Swift blazing flag of the regiment,
Eagle with crest of red and gold,
These men were born to drill and die.
Point for them the virtue of slaughter,
Make plain to them the excellence of killing
And a field where a thousand corpses lie.

Mother whose heart hung humble as a button

From *War Is Kind* by Stephen Crane. Published in 1899.

On the bright splendid shroud of your son,
Do not weep.
War is kind.

Reading 34

Marching on

James Boyd

The following selection is a view of events in North Carolina after Lincoln's election to the Presidency. Lincoln, who was not even on the ballot in ten Southern states, had received only 40 percent of the popular vote. Although most Southern states took a "wait-and-see" attitude toward Lincoln, South Carolina threatened to leave the Union and finally did secede in December 1860. It was the opinion of many Southerners that they could depart in peace —that the North would not fight the secession—because they believed that Southern society was basically superior to that of the North. They attributed this superiority to Southern chivalry and had nothing but contempt for the Yankee traders.

The papers next day told how the Yankees had elected the Black Republican as President. Men spoke about it grimly. Let Lincoln himself say what he pleased about wishing the South well, it was an Abolition trick. No more than a threat as yet, but North Carolina was on guard. At the first sign of interference the Abolitionists would learn a thing or two.

It soon appeared, however, that the people in South Carolina were not disposed to wait until they were trampled on. Before Christmas they had withdrawn from the Union and set up for themselves. That was going a little strong maybe, some of the older men said, but after all they had a right to if they wanted to. It was their own affair.

Christmas itself was a dreary and uneasy day. James had wanted to go home and stay over New Year's but the shops just now were working overtime. The order had come that everything on wheels was to be put in shape, so he had only the day—a day of cold, clammy rain and streaks of sea-driven mist.

The air seemed heavy with foreboding. Only the children shot off their fire-crackers with accustomed gusto and the negroes by immemorial privilege paraded the streets that night in fantastic dress and costume, singing, dancing and shouting "Christmas gif'!"

In the swift weeks that followed five more States left the Union, and meeting together at Montgomery formed a confederacy. As far as Wilmington and the Cape Fear were concerned that settled it. A thrill ran through the people. Here was a government of the South—a Southern Nation—springing into being, an Empire of their own, free from fetters, threats, and impositions of sanctimonious, greedy aliens, free to develop, to achieve dignity, prosperity, and glory according to the Southern genius. And it was all so simple: they had but to withdraw from the Union as was their privilege, to leave the government where they were now a meanly used, misunderstood minority, and join their strength to the new nation whose sympathy by birth, by breeding, by tradition, would be forever theirs. It was all so simple. How could any man hold back? They had the right and, anyhow, the Yankees wouldn't fight; a race of shop-keepers and bluenosed elders, they valued their skins as highly as their pocket-books. Their government right now was paralyzed, distracted; their politicians, even their President, Old Buchanan, sought frantically to patch up some shabby compromise, to keep by trickery and trading what they could not keep by force. They would negotiate, palaver as long as there was hope, but they would not fight. A gentleman from Charleston, sent to encourage North Carolina, had stood up before five thousand people on the Court House steps. Hawk-eyed, pale and passionate, he had pulled a handkerchief from his tight broadcloth sleeve, a handkerchief far smaller and finer than Major Pettibone's. He had held it aloft, a fluttering wisp of cambric.

"My friends!" he had cried, "They won't fight! Bullies have ever been cowards since the world began. They won't fight. With this handkerchief I'll guarantee to wipe up every drop of blood that's spilled."

"You need not be alarmed," he had added loftily. "You need not hesitate. There can be no doubt nor danger in an issue between southern chivalry and northern traders." He clenched his hand aloft, then pointed to the north, "Have not our representatives at Washington for years challenged Yankee politicians to make good their low slanders, to defend their vulgar and cow-ardly abuse on the field of honor? How often has such a challenge been accepted? And when our representative, Mr. Brooks, had chastised a Yankee senator who had insulted his family with all the vulgar ingenuity of an edu-cated gutter-snipe but who dared not risk his skin to back his charges, what happened? Was there a Yankee in the North who dared to raise a hand in the whipped dog's defence? And then you remember Preston Brooks' triumphal progress through the South. Why did we all accord him honor? Because he represented, typified the thousands of good men in the South who stand ready to back their names with their lives." His voice turned coldly derisive. "And against these thousands not one man of that calibre could be found in the whole pitiful Yankee nation." Pitch by pitch he raised them to frenzy; the crowd became a roaring, boiling sea of straining eyes and mouths, of waving hats and sticks and banners, so that when old Judge Seagrove, climbing painfully up the steps, had waited, wonderfully gray and grim and old, until the shouting ceased, and had then begun in his dry, cracked voice, "North Carolina has never in the past found it necessary to be shown her duty by emissaries from elsewhere. With all personal respect to our distinguished visitor, I therefore say that we should ask ourselves why is it necessary now?" he was checked by an angry murmur. He kept on manfully; through the growing tumult fragments of sentences still reached them. "No government has ever been designed with an implied provision for its own destruction. . . . What you propose is revolution and that, of course, is an inherent right. . . . But on what pretext will we go before the world?" Then some one shouted, "Hurrah for Southern rights!" A band struck up. They formed broad, lurching columns that stretched from curb to curb and marched away down Market Street. James Fraser, his arms linked with Bill and the switch-engine boy, looked backward as he tramped away. Judge Seagrove in his rusty black coat still stood on the Court House steps alone. His eyes strained after the retreating crowd as though he were never to see one of them again. Below him the gentleman from South Carolina, encircled by ribbons and leghorn hats, was being smothered under flowers.

The abolitionist Lincoln was inaugurated without incident though there had been sufficient talk of Southern plots to scare him into stealing into Washington City by night and secretly. Meanwhile the South Carolinians had mobilized and with their forces had ringed in Fort Sumter at the harbor's mouth at Charleston, had cut it off until it should capitulate, the flag come down and the last Yankee be driven from their soil.

Reading 35

Gone with the Wind

Margaret Mitchell

In the minds of many Southerners the idea of a war with the North could only be characterized as romantic. Most importantly, they did not and could not understand the features of modern warfare which called for a reliance upon industrial might. Southerners viewed war in terms of dashing cavalry charges and flashing sabres and did not foresee the impact of changing technology on warfare. Nor did they have any comprehension of the virtually limitless supply of men in the North. In *Gone with the Wind* Rhett Butler points out these factors and calls the Southern gentlemen's attention to the fact that the North held 81 percent of the nation's factories, incuding those producing war matériel.

Under the arbor, the deaf old gentleman from Fayetteville punched India.

"What's it all about? What are they saying?"

"War!" shouted India, cupping her hand to his ear. "They want to fight the Yankees!"

"War, is it?" he cried, fumbling about him for his cane and heaving himself out of his chair with more energy than he had shown in years. "I'll tell 'um about war. I've been there." It was not often that Mr. McRae had the opportunity to talk about war, the way his women folks shushed him.

He stumped rapidly to the group, waving his cane and shouting and, because he could not hear the voices about him, he soon had undisputed possession of the field.

"You fire-eating young bucks, listen to me. You don't want to fight. I fought and I know. Went out in the Seminole War and was a big enough fool to go the Mexican War, too. You all don't know what war is. You think it's riding a pretty horse and having the girls throw flowers at you and coming home a hero. Well, it ain't. No, sir! It's going hungry, and getting the measles and pneumonia from sleeping in the wet. And if it ain't measles and pneumonia, it's your bowels. Yes sir, what war does to a man's bowels—dysentery and things like that—"

The ladies were pink with blushes. Mr. McRae was a reminder of a cruder era, like Grandma Fontaine and her embarrassingly loud belches, an era everyone would like to forget.

"Run get your grandpa," hissed one of the old gentleman's daughters to a young girl standing near by. "I declare," she whispered to the fluttering matrons about her, "he gets worse every day. Would you believe it, this very morning he said to Mary—and she's only sixteen: 'Now, Missy . . .' " And the voice went off into a whisper as the granddaughter slipped out to try to induce Mr. McRae to return to his seat in the shade.

Of all the group that milled about under the trees, girls smiling excitedly, men talking impassionedly, there was only one who seemed calm. Scarlett's eyes turned to Rhett Butler, who leaned against a tree, his hands shoved deep in his trouser pockets. He stood alone, since Mr. Wilkes had left his side, and had uttered no word as the conversation grew hotter. The red lips under the close-clipped black mustache curled down and there was a glint of amused contempt in his black eyes—contempt, as if he listened to the braggings of children. A very disagreeable smile, Scarlett thought. He listened quietly until Stuart Tarleton, his red hair tousled and his eyes gleaming, repeated: "Why, we could lick them in a month! Gentlemen always fight better than rabble. A month—why, one battle—"

"Gentlemen," said Rhett Butler, in a flat drawl that bespoke his Charleston birth, not moving from his position against the tree or taking his hands from his pockets, "may I say a word?"

There was contempt in his manner as in his eyes, contempt overlaid with an air of courtesy that somehow burlesqued their own manners.

The group turned toward him and accorded him the politeness always due an outsider.

"Has any one of you gentlemen ever thought that there's not a cannon factory south of the Mason-Dixon Line? Or how few iron foundries there are in the South? Or woolen mills or cotton factories or tanneries? Have you thought that we would not have a single warship and that the Yankee fleet could bottle up our harbors in a week, so that we could not sell our cotton abroad? But—of course—you gentlemen have thought of these things."

"Why, he means the boys are a passel of fools!" thought Scarlett indignantly, the hot blood coming to her cheeks.

Evidently, she was not the only one to whom this idea occurred, for several of the boys were beginning to stick out their chins. John Wilkes casually but swiftly came back to his place beside the speaker, as if to impress on all present that this man was his guest and that, moreover, there were ladies present.

"The trouble with most of us Southerners," continued Rhett Butler, "is that we either don't travel enough or we don't profit enough by our travels. Now, of course, all you gentlemen are well traveled. But what have you seen? Europe and New York and Philadelphia and, of course, the ladies have been to Saratoga" (he bowed slightly to the group under the arbor)."You've seen the hotels and the museums and the balls and the gambling houses. And you've come home believing that there's no place like the South. As for me, I was Charleston born, but I have spent the last few years in the North." His white teeth showed in a grin, as though he realized that everyone present knew just why he no longer lived in Charleston, and cared not at all if they did know. "I have seen many things that you all have not seen. The thousands of immigrants who'd be glad to fight for the Yankees for food and a few dollars, the factories, the foundries, the shipyards, the iron and coal mines—all the things we haven't got. Why, all we have is cotton and slaves and arrogance. They'd lick us in a month."

For a tense moment, there was silence. Rhett Butler removed a fine linen handkerchief from his coat pocket and idly flicked dust from his sleeve. Then an ominous murmuring arose in the crowd and from under the arbor came a humming as unmistakable as that of a hive of newly disturbed bees. Even while she felt the hot blood of wrath still in her cheeks, something in Scarlett's practical mind prompted the thought that what this man said was right, and it sounded like common sense. Why, she'd never even seen a factory, or known anyone who had seen a factory. But, even if it were true, he was no gentleman to make such a statement—and at a party, too, where everyone was having a good time.

Stuart Tarleton, brows lowering, came forward with Brent close at his heels. Of course, the Tarleton twins had nice manners and they wouldn't make a scene at a barbecue, even though tremendously provoked. Just the same, all the ladies felt pleasantly excited, for it was so seldom that they actually saw a scene or a quarrel. Usually they had to hear of it thirdhand.

"Sir," said Stuart heavily, "what do you mean?"

Rhett looked at him with polite but mocking eyes.

"I mean," he answered, "what Napoleon—perhaps you've heard of him? —remarked once, 'God is on the side of the strongest battalion!' "

Reading 36

Casey

Ramona Stewart

The federal draft act of March 3, 1863 offered exemption from service upon
the payment of three hundred dollars. Such distinction between rich men's
money and poor men's blood angered those who could not afford to buy
their way out of service. On July 13 a mob attacked a draft headquarters in
New York City, and soon a full-scale riot was on that raged for four days. In
many respects it was a race riot, as Irish laborers attacked Negroes. Police,
firemen, and militia failed to calm the mob, and it was not until regular troops
were brought in that the riot was suppressed. The following describes the
dimensions of the riot.

But they never got to the saloon. Once on the street, they saw crowds and a
great milling of men and horses on Third Avenue.

"What's that now?" Casey said.

Scanlon squinted. "An accident with cars?"

It was the street railway cars surely. There was a line of them piling up
along the street. "Come, let's see," Casey said and they trotted to the Avenue.
But as they drew closer, they saw it wasn't any kind of accident at all. One
of the drivers was just then throwing down the reins and jumping to join the
crowd.

"By Jaysus, it's Frank," Casey said. "Now we'll find out what's up." He
and Scanlon pushed through and Casey grabbed his brother's arm.

"What's going on?" Casey yelled.

"I don't know," Frank shouted back. "Unless they're sore about the draft.
They was standing on the tracks so as not to let us pass."

"But you jumped down by yourself," Casey said. "I saw you do it."

"An' how much further would I get if I had a call to join the martyrs?"
Frank said.

He had a point. Before him three cars were stopped southward bound and
two more going north. They were empty of passengers, the horses cropping
grass along the tracks.

"Take a look around you, man," Frank said and Casey turned and took
a look.

At first they seemed the same crowd as at fires—factory men and butchers, cart drivers, day laborers, a few women now too, rough drabs who'd been leaning out the windows and had come down to join the fun. Poking up at a distance, he saw a crudely lettered placard reading NO DRAFT, so Frank was right. That was what it was about. But they didn't seem dangerous, except perhaps the sheer weight of them. There were several hundred now where earlier there'd been a dozen. And they'd been gathering a few weapons—paving bricks, but here and there a man had a bowie knife in his belt. He saw one rusty musket. The rest had sticks and stones. And all were drinking. He wondered where they'd got the money, till across the street he saw they'd pushed into a saloon and got a keg. The keeper wasn't chancing a refusal and the wrecking of his place.

But saloonkeepers didn't stand for that. He'd be sending a boy running out the back to get the cops. Then Casey realized that was strange, too—with a mob stopping cars and pushing into the saloons, he'd have expected cops already. He turned back to Scanlon and then he stopped.

A couple of the men were laying axes to a telegraph pole. Hypnotized, the crowd watched till the pole plunged into a tangle of wires and a great cheer went soaring to the dull, hot sky. He knew then what was different. The crowds at fires were half good-humored and half angry, and so was this one; but at the fires the fun and fury was scattered. This one was stopping cars and cutting wires; it had an enemy and purpose.

"The draft," he said, and Scanlon clapped his shoulder.

"The goddamn draft," Scanlon said as if he was talking to himself, working out the possibilities.

Casey felt a thrill go through him. It felt like whiskey did, the people rising. Five hundred years of oppression was in his blood as in the others, and now it struck back at a cruel law.

"On to Headquarters!" a man was bawling.

Draft headquarters, of course, Casey thought, it was all leading up to strike at headquarters. But there were two drawings today, one on Broadway, one on Third. The crowd hesitated and argued.

"What's it matter?" Scanlon yelled.

And that was true. The essential was momentum, so the crowd didn't die but kept in motion, engulfing new recruits till it grew into a mob. In another moment, the crowd felt the need to move itself. Without decision being made, it began to surge ahead. Dragging telegraph wires and rolling the beer keg, the men headed north toward the drawing at the provost marshal's office.

They went slowly, stopping to raid grogshops and shinny up poles to hack down more wires. There were no cars running now. And over on Second Casey saw they were stopped, too. Looking through a cross street, he saw one of the cars with two drunks jigging on its roof.

And then at Forty-fourth, the forerunners stopped, backing up the men behind as a kind of sigh ran through them. Casey felt gooseflesh creep up his arms when he saw what it was—a mob, not in hundreds but in thousands, was waiting there already.

"Holy God," Scanlon breathed and Casey felt Frank lose his balance and brush against him. Next they moved like a brook rushing down to join the sea.

The police were at last in evidence, some sixty of them. But with that kind of mob they could only bar the doors. They'd tried to stop the sacking of the saloon beside the draft office. The windows were out and the shuttered door ripped down. Beer kegs were set on the street. Men knelt beside them, wetting themselves in the beer.

What was odd was the sense of waiting. The blinds of the draft office were still drawn.

"What time is it?" Scanlon asked and Casey tried to guess. What with the telegraph wire cutting and the detour they'd made to a piano factory to demand the men be let out to join them or they'd burn it down, they must have taken two hours to move twenty-five blocks.

"After ten," he said.

"The drawing was to start at nine," Scanlon said. "They must have called it off."

It was likely, Casey thought. He wondered should he head back to the Comet to find Maguire. The great insurrection was turning into a drunken holiday. Already a man beside them had shaped some telegraph wire into a cane and was doing a minstrel dance around it.

Then the window blinds shot up inside, and the mob came quivering to life. It roared defiance and a stone went sailing through the draft window. Sweeping the police aside, a dozen men brought a pole and battered down the front door. In the back of the crowd Casey looked for Scanlon and saw him wriggling his way toward the front. In a second he was gone through the door and up the stairs. A big woman in a shawl came elbowing her way in on Casey and while he shoved her from his way, Frank disappeared on him too. The crowd was surging forward and it took all his strength to keep on his feet. He lost track of what was happening then, only struggled and pushed back and felt himself dragged forward by the rip. A woman screamed and he knew she'd gone down but there was no hope for her at all.

Suddenly he was at the entrance, and in the instant caution touched him for all his gooseflesh and the pull within him. Catching hold of the wall, he held to it and let those after him go by. He began pushing sideways, keeping close to the wall, until the mob's tug lessened and, finding himself in an eddy, he dragged clear and came out before the ruined saloon.

For a moment, he looked up at the sky and sucked in air. Across the way he saw the women hanging out the tenement windows above a carriage factory and stables. From overhead came a shower of glass. He ducked inside the saloon as the sound of wrecking started—a chair was pitched from the draft office, and the leg of a desk as the axes went to work. In a few moments more came a great yell of triumph—the draft wheel, he supposed, or maybe not, for the yell had changed to screaming. Wondering had the cops put up a fight, he ducked outside to see, but they were most of them still there, looking nervous, their locust clubs at the ready.

The mob rushed out faster than it had gone dashing in. Looking up, Casey saw the windows were all knocked out but he had to make a run across the street before he saw the first spurt of flame licking up a wall and leaping toward the air. My God, he thought, the wires are down. From old training, he nearly ran to let his engine company know. But there was another pull inside him that resisted the draft as much as Scanlon; let the office burn, they'd only got what they'd deserved.

The cops felt different. At the first sight of fire, they started striking back with their locust sticks, battering at the heads and shoulders as they struggled through the door. The women inside went on screaming. Outside a man went down. Soon Casey heard a shot and then another. He took cover again, this time inside the stables where the horses were rearing in their stalls.

There were some good horses there. One gray mare in particular, lunging and neighing. He liked a horse like that. Cuban maybe by the looks of her. She looked like Restell's Cuban thoroughbreds. So he slammed the front doors shut and bolted them, then coaxed the horses from their stalls and out the back alley and two blocks over to another stable.

When he came back, the street was changed. The carriage factory and the tenement apartment above it had gone up. The women who'd been hanging out the windows were pushing through the mob holding their children.

By then the fire companies had sighted the smoke and were dragging their hose carts and engines through. Hearing a roar go up, he found an empty keg and climbed atop it to see if Pacific Engine was arriving but it was only men struggling. They'd got somebody down, he figured. When the underman wriggled free, Casey saw a well-dressed man about sixty. They caught him again and bore him down. Then the crowd moved in.

"Jaysus," he said, crawling down from the keg. It was the police superintendent. He must have been touring the draft offices and blundered in without a guard.

By two o'clock Casey was covered with ash and hauling the Pacific engine rope through the crowd that stretched down Third Avenue. He was so tired he kept slipping on the cobbles and he felt like half the things he'd seen were from his dreams. There had been Decker, the chief fire engineer, who'd arrived with the Pacific. He'd mounted a broken table and gave a speech to great cheering. The mob had turned friendly for Decker. It was sweet to watch, the way he softened that great beast so they let the handpumps move in.

They let Casey and the other firemen fall to work. It didn't take long because there was so little left to save, but the search for victims in the char took longer. They found a dozen, dead and injured, and the crowd carried off the living.

When Scanlon showed up, he was drunk and God only knew where he'd been since he'd rushed in the draft office, but his pockets were stuffed with enrollment slips. So he wouldn't be picked up and shot, Casey grabbed them and scattered them on the bloody street. He seized Scanlon by the arm and led him back to the Pacific where he set him to winding hose. At the familiar feel of the leather, Scanlon went on with it by himself. They packed up the Pacific and started hauling her home.

But they'd not gone a block before they heard shots to the south and next moment, to the west, a plume of smoke was rising.

"It's not far, let's take her boys," his foremen shouted. "Step out lively!"

With a groan, Casey put a hand back to the tongue and guided her around the corner.

It was the old Bull's Head Market Hotel. When they arrived the door was off its hinges, its windows out, and it was blazing like a pine torch while the cattle from its stockade stampeded across the market barriers. Frightened steers were rushing off while the mob trailed away with the bar stock and every portable—chairs and vases, the guests' clothing . One old crone went by him with a cage of canaries. He supposed they were from the lobby.

He saw Horse and Paddy Sullivan staggering off with an iron safe. The aproned bartender came running after them but Horse only turned and struck him once and he went down.

"Holy Christ, it's Horse and Paddy," Casey said, turning to Scanlon. But Scanlon had already dropped the rope and was staggering off to lend a hand with the safe.

Mose Barry came jumping from the blazing stoop and dashed off with a gold-framed picture. Casey looked around. The whole Arsenal Gang was there looting, and perhaps it had done the firing too. Staggering through the smoke was the Pig Girl carrying an armload of hoop-skirt dresses. As he watched, disbelieving the visions, she jumped down the stoop, fending off a steer that turned the corner sharp. She took out down the street and caught up with

Horse and Scanlon. Heaving the dresses about her neck like a boa, she reached down to help with the safe and they turned a corner out of sight.

They gave up trying to make the firehouse. The crowd south was too thick and besides smoke was rising every way they looked. Turning north, they bucked a mob that was chasing a pickpocket. They were after him by hundreds. A dozen were knocked down and trampled. Casey hauled a woman to her feet. Her arm was hanging limp and blood was streaming down her cheek but she was laughing.

”Yer the boy, my chicken!” she kept screaming in his face till he let her go and she dropped.

The fire bells had been ringing in his ears so long he was floating on the sound and gone lunatic like the rest. He dragged the rope, unwound the hose, manned the brakes, and dragged out bodies. Part time he had the sense he was jumping surf at Coney Island but he was just rising and falling with the fire bell.

Passing the Colored Orphan Asylum, he came abruptly to his senses and saw it sharp and clear; the big white frame house with green shutters, surrounded by lawn and shade trees, the graveled carriage path invaded by the mob that had swarmed over the picket fence. They'd trampled the vegetable garden and ruined the flowers as they howled for the nigger brats and rows of dark, childish faces peered down at them from the windows.

Already two files of children were marching out and the faces at the windows were vanishing. But before the last child was gone, the men were at the door. Beds, chairs and tables began flying out the windows to the mob waiting below. Then a pack of screaming drunks took out across the grass to get the children.

"Take them!" Casey's foreman shouted and the company grabbed up spanners and hose nozzles just as Chief Decker's special company came trotting into sight hauling hose carts and pumpers. Together they waded in, and when the drunks were driven back, Decker threw his company round the children, standing guard with poles and axes. When the parlor curtains began blazing, they couldn't move without deserting the children, so they watched as the house went up, sending sparks flying into the trees.

The mob was brawling over children's toys when Maguire drove by in his buggy. He jumped to the gravel and looked sickly at the fighting that was going on over the lawn. A young whore lay bleeding with the knife wound in her breast and Maguire stooped to look but she was dead. He rose and came to the firemen's circle about the small, dark children.

"All safe?" Maguire asked.

"So far," Decker said.

"Better get them to the station house," and Decker nodded. "I'll take the buggy on around and meet you there."

As the companies began to move with Decker in the lead and the children filing hand in hand, the firemen in the rear dragging their hose carts and pumpers, Casey fell out of line and walked Maguire to his buggy. He was still dressed in his Saratoga outfit, the cream sporting top hat and light trousers giving off the expensive air of fast horses, French cuisine and mint juleps beneath the trees. But his face was gray like a man who's been hit in the stomach.

"My God," he said.

Casey nodded. He was still seeing frightened rows of eyes along the windows. He said: "They'll be bringing in the troops?"

"They're going to have to. Pull them out of Gettysburg," Maguire said. He turned again to the young whore. They were tying a rope to her foot and two men were dragging her off. One of her belled red boots was left behind on the grass.

"They've got the armory at Twenty-first," Maguire said. "I don't know they'll keep it long, but long enough to get rifles and cartridges. The Harlem tracks are torn up. There's hell to pay in Greenwich Village."

That brought Casey up. "What's going on in the Village?"

Maguire nodded at the smoldering Asylum. "What do you think? The niggers."

Casey nodded. There was a big Negro section near Claire. And he'd seen Scanlon himself blaming Petey for the draft.

"They've started hanging," Maguire said. "Dragging them out of the houses, man or woman don't make no difference. Might hang you too, if you've got one hid."

Casey ran an arm across his sweaty forehead. He hadn't worried about Claire. She'd know enough to lie low. But he'd forgotten that she had Ruby.

"Jump in the buggy. I'll drive you over," Maguire said, meaning the station house.

"I can't now," Casey said. He turned and started off.

"Casey!" Maguire yelled. He must have thought the day had turned his head.

There was no use telling Maguire; it would offend his sense of morals. He started running down the gravel path with Maguire's shouts echoing in his ears.

Reading 37

A Horseman in the Sky

Ambrose Bierce

The American Civil War not only divided the nation—it often divided families as well. Several of Mrs. Lincoln's relatives fought for the South, and it was not too unusual for brother to meet brother on the battlefield or for first cousins to arrest each other. These occurrences were most common in the border states of Missouri, Kentucky, and Maryland. In those areas, as in the locale of this story, western Virginia, there was a bitter division over which side was right, and, as the following selection brings out, several members of a family may have been in the Blue and Gray.

I

One sunny afternoon in the autumn of the year 1861 a soldier lay in a clump of laurel by the side of a road in western Virginia. He lay at full length upon his stomach, his feet resting upon his toes, his head upon the left forearm. His extended right hand loosely grasped his rifle. But for the somewhat methodical disposition of his limbs and a slight rhythmic movement of the cartridge-box at the back of his belt he might have been thought to be dead. He was asleep at his post of duty. But if detected he would be dead shortly afterward, death being the just and legal penalty of his crime.

The clump of laurel in which the criminal lay was in the angle of a road which after ascending southward a steep acclivity to that point turned sharply to the west, running along the summit for perhaps one hundred yards. There it turned southward again and went zigzagging downward through the forest. At the salient of that second angle was a large flat rock, jutting out northward, overlooking the deep valley from which the road ascended. The rock capped a high cliff; a stone dropped from its outer edge would have fallen sheer downward one thousand feet to the tops of the pines. The angle where the soldier lay was on another spur of the same cliff. Had he been awake he would have commanded a view, not only of the short arm of the road and the jutting rock, but of the entire profile of the cliff below it. It might well have made him giddy to look.

The country was wooded everywhere except at the bottom of the valley to the northward, where there was a small natural meadow, through which

From *Tales of Soldiery and Civil War* by Ambrose Bierce. Published in 1891.

flowed a stream scarcely visible from the valley's rim. This open ground looked hardly larger than an ordinary door-yard, but was really several acres in extent. Its green was more vivid than that of the inclosing forest. Away beyond it rose a line of giant cliffs similar to those upon which we are supposed to stand in our survey of the savage scene, and through which the road had somehow made its climb to the summit. The configuration of the valley, indeed, was such that from this point of observation it seemed entirely shut in, and one could but have wondered how the road which found a way out of it had found a way into it, and whence came and whither went the waters of the stream that parted the meadow more than a thousand feet below.

No country is so wild and difficult but men will make it a theatre of war; concealed in the forest at the bottom of that military rat-trap, in which half a hundred men in possession of the exits might have starved an army to submission, lay five regiments of Federal infantry. They had marched all the previous day and night and were resting. At nightfall they would take to the road again, climb to the place where their unfaithful sentinel now slept, and descending the other slope of the ridge fall upon a camp of the enemy at about midnight. Their hope was to surprise it, for the road led to the rear of it. In case of failure, their position would be perilous in the extreme; and fail they surely would should accident or vigilance apprise the enemy of the movement.

II

The sleeping sentinel in the clump of laurel was a young Virginian named Carter Druse. He was the son of wealthy parents, an only child, and had known such ease and cultivation and high living as wealth and taste were able to command in the mountain country of western Virginia. His home was but a few miles from where he now lay. One morning he had risen from the breakfast-table and said, quietly but gravely: "Father, a Union regiment has arrived at Grafton. I am going to join it."

The father lifted his leonine head, looked at the son a moment in silence, and replied: "Well, go sir, and whatever may occur do what you conceive to be your duty. Virginia, to which you are a traitor, must get on without you. Should we both live to the end of the war, we will speak further of the matter. Your mother, as the physician has informed you, is in a most critical condition; at the best she cannot be with us longer than a few weeks, but that time is precious. It would be better not to disturb her."

So Carter Druse, bowing reverently to his father, who returned the salute with a stately courtesy that masked a breaking heart, left the home of his childhood to go soldiering. By conscience and courage, by deeds of devotion and daring, he soon commended himself to his fellows and his officers; and it was to these qualities and to some knowledge of the country that he owed his selection for his present perilous duty at the extreme outpost. Nevertheless, fatigue had been stronger than resolution and he had fallen asleep. What good or bad angel came in a dream to rouse him from his state of crime, who shall say? Without a movement, without a sound, in the profound silence and the langour of the late afternoon, some invisible messenger of fate touched with unsealing finger the eyes of his consciousness—whispered into the ear of his spirit the mysterious awakening word which no human lips ever have spoken, no human memory ever has recalled. He quietly raised his forehead from his arm and looked between the masking stems of the laurels, instinctively closing his right hand about the stock of his rifle.

His first feeling was a keen artistic delight. On a colossal pedestal, the cliff, —motionless at the extreme edge of the capping rock and sharply outlined against the sky,—was an equestrian statute of impressive dignity. The figure of the man sat the figure of the horse, straight and soldierly, but with the repose of a Grecian god carved in the marble which limits the suggestion of activity. The gray costume harmonized with its aerial background; the metal of ac-coutrement and caparison was softened and subdued by the shadow; the animal's skin had no points of high light. A carbine strikingly foreshortened lay across the pommel of the saddle, kept in place by the right hand grasping it at the "grip"; the left hand, holding the bridle rein, was invisible. In sil-houette against the sky the profile of the horse was cut with the sharpness of a cameo; it looked across the heights of air to the confronting cliffs beyond. The face of the rider, turned slightly away, showed only an outline of temple and beard; he was looking downward to the bottom of the valley. Magnified by its lift against the sky and by the soldier's testifying sense of the formidable-ness of a near enemy the group appeared of heroic, almost colossal, size.

For an instant Druse had a strange, half-defined feeling that he had slept to the end of the war and was looking upon a noble work of art reared upon that eminence to commemorate the deeds of an heroic past of which he had been an inglorious part. The feeling was dispelled by a slight movement of the group: the horse, wihout moving its feet, had drawn its body slightly backward from the verge; the man remained immobile as before. Broad awake and keenly alive to the significance of the situation, Druse now brought the butt of his rifle against his cheek by cautiously pushing the barrel forward through the bushes, cocked the piece, and glancing through the sights covered a vital spot of the horseman's breast. A touch upon the trigger and all would have been well with Carter Druse. At that instant the horseman turned his head and looked in the direction of his concealed foeman—seemed to look into his very face, into his eyes, into his brave, compassionate heart.

Is it then so terrible to kill an enemy in war—an enemy who has surprised a secret vital to the safety of one's self and comrades—an enemy more formidable for his knowledge than all his army for its numbers? Carter Druse grew pale; he shook in every limb, turned faint, and saw the statuesque group before him as black figures, rising, falling, moving unsteadily in arcs of circles in a fiery sky. His hand fell away from his weapon, his head slowly dropped until his face rested on the leaves in which he lay. This courageous gentleman and hardy soldier was near swooning from intensity of emotion.

It was not for long; in another moment his face was raised from earth, his hands resumed their places on the rifle, his forefinger sought the trigger; mind, heart, and eyes were clear, conscience and reason sound. He could not hope to capture that enemy; to alarm him would but send him dashing to his camp with his fatal news. The duty of the soldier was plain: the man must be shot dead from ambush—without warning, without a moment's spiritual preparation, with never so much as an unspoken prayer, he must be sent to his account. But no—there is a hope; he may have discovered nothing—perhaps he is but admiring the sublimity of the landscape. If permitted, he may turn and ride carelessly away in the direction whence he came. Surely it will be possible to judge at the instant of his withdrawing whether he knows. It may well be that his fixity of attention—Druse turned his head and looked through the deeps of air downward, as from the surface to the bottom of a translucent sea. He saw creeping across the green meadow a sinuous line of figures of men and horses—some foolish commander was permitting the soldiers of his escort to water their beasts in the open, in plain view from a dozen summits!

Druse withdrew his eyes from the valley and fixed them again upon the group of man and horse in the sky, and again it was through the sights of his rifle. But this time his aim was at the horse. In his memory, as if they were a divine mandate, rang the words of his father at their parting: "Whatever may occur, do what you conceive to be your duty." He was calm now. His teeth were firmly but not rigidly closed; his nerves were as tranquil as a sleeping babe's—not a tremor affected any muscle of his body; his breathing, until suspended in the act of taking aim, was regular and slow. Duty had conquered; the spirit had said to the body: "Peace, be still." He fired.

III

An officer of the Federal force, who in a spirit of adventure or in quest of knowledge had left the hidden *bivouac* in the valley, and with aimless feet had made his way to the lower edge of a small space near the foot of the cliff, was considering what he had to gain by pushing his exploration further. At a distance of a quarter-mile before him, but apparently at a stone's throw, rose from its fringe of pines, the gigantic face of rock, towering to so great a height above him that it made him giddy to look up to where its edge cut a sharp, rugged line against the sky. It presented a clean, vertical profile against a background of blue sky to a point half the way down, and of distant hills, hardly less blue, thence to the tops of the trees at its base. Lifting his eyes to the dizzy altitude of its summit the officer saw an astonishing sight—a man on horseback riding down into the valley through the air!

Straight upright sat the rider, in military fashion, with a firm seat in the saddle, a strong clutch upon the rein to hold his charger from too impetuous a plunge. From his bare head his long hair streamed upward, waving like a plume. His hands were concealed in the cloud of the horse's lifted mane. The animal's body was as level as if every hoofstroke encountered the resistant earth. Its motions were those of a wild gallop, but even as the officer looked they ceased, with all the legs thrown forward as in the act of alighting from a leap. But this was a flight!

Filled with amazement and terror by this apparition of a horseman in the sky—half believing himself the chosen scribe of some new Apocalypse, the officer was overcome by the intensity of his emotions; his legs failed him and he fell. Almost at the same instant he heard a crashing sound in the trees— a sound that died without an echo—and all was still.

The officer rose to his feet, trembling. The familiar sensation of an abraded shin recalled his dazed faculties. Pulling himself together he ran rapidly obliquely away from the cliff to a point distant from its foot; thereabout he expected to find his man; and thereabout he naturally failed. In the fleeting instant of his vision his imagination had been so wrought upon by the apparent grace and ease and intention of the marvelous performance that it did not occur to him that the line of march of aërial cavalry is directly downward, and that he could find the objects of his search at the very foot of the cliff. A half-hour later he returned to camp.

This officer was a wise man; he knew better than to tell an incredible truth. He said nothing of what he had seen. But when the commander asked him if in his scout he had learned anything of advantage to the expedition he answered:

"Yes, sir; there is no road leading down into this valley from the southward."

The commander, knowing better, smiled.

IV

After firing his shot, Private Carter Druse reloaded his rifle and resumed his watch. Ten minutes had hardly passed when a Federal sergeant crept cautiously to him on hands and knees. Druse neither turned his head nor looked at him, but lay without motion or sign of recognition.

"Did you fire?" the sergeant whispered.

"Yes."

"At what?"

"A horse. It was standing on yonder rock—pretty far out. You see it is no longer there. It went over the cliff."

The man's face was white, but he showed no other sign of emotion. Having answered, he turned away his eyes and said no more. The sergeant did not understand.

"See here Druse," he said, after a moment's silence, "it's no use making a mystery. I order you to report. Was there anybody on the horse?"

"Yes."

"Well?"

"My father."

The sergeant rose to his feet and walked away. "Good God!" he said.

Chapter 9

Reunion

Reading 38

Good Old Rebel

Innes Randolph

The bitterness that had developed between the North and South in the
decade before the Civil War fanned to a white heat during the conflict, and
this hatred could not be turned off simply because the fighting stopped. Both
sides continued to express their attitudes in many ways. Northern hatred was
an integral part of the harsh radical reconstruction plan. Southern hatred was
nurtured inwardly for many generations and was expressed through many
outlets, including this song.

Oh, I'm a good old Rebel,
Now that's just what I am;
For this fair land of Freedom
I do not care a dam.
I'm glad I fit against it—
I only wish we'd won,
And I don't want no pardon
For anything I've done.

I hates the Constitution
This great Republic, too;
I hates the Freedmen's Buro,
In uniforms of blue.
I hates the nasty eagle,
With all his brag and fuss;
The lyin', thievin' Yankees,
I hates 'em wuss and wuss.

I hates the Yankee Nation
And everything they do;
I hates the Declaration
Of Independence, too.
I hates the glorious Union,
'Tis dripping with our blood;
I hates the striped banner—
I fit it all I could.

I followed old Marse Robert
For four years, near about,

Got wounded in three places,
And starved at Pint Lookout.
I cotch the roomatism
A-campin' in the snow,
But I killed a chance of Yankees—
I'd like to kill some mo'.

Three hundred thousand Yankees
Is stiff in Southern dust;
We got three hundred thousand
Before they conquered us.
They died of Southern fever
And Southern steel and shot;
I wish it was three millions
Instead of what we got.

I can't take up my musket
And fight 'em now no more,
But I ain't goin' to love 'em,
Now that is sartin sure.
And I don't want no pardon
For what I was and am;
I won't be reconstructed,
And I don't care a dam.

Reading 39

Main Travelled Roads

Hamlin Garland

The following selection tells something of the struggle of the farm wives left behind in the North. As usual, it was the woman who had to do the day-by-day chores, care for the children, and, most difficult of all, wait for her husband to come home. The return of the private in the North was a sober affair as the weary and often battle-scarred veteran made his way home. The government did not provide transportation home for the soldier; in fact, he was lucky even to get his fare home. Furthermore, the soldier could not look forward to the generous GI benefits that the government now extends to its

From *Main Travelled Roads* by Hamlin Garland. Published in 1890.

veterans.

The nearer the train drew toward La Crosse, the soberer the little group of "vets" became. On the long way from New Orleans they had beguiled tedium with jokes and friendly chaff; or with planning with elaborate detail what they were going to do now, after the war. A long journey, slowly, irregularly, yet persistently pushing northward. When they entered on Wisconsin territory they gave a cheer, and another when they reached Madison, but after that they sank into a dumb expectancy. Comrades dropped off at one point or two points beyond, until they were only four or five left who were bound for La Crosse County.

Three of them were gaunt and brown, the fourth was gaunt and pale, with signs of fever and ague upon him. One had a great scar down his temple, one limped, and they all had unnaturally large, bright eyes, showing emaciation. There were no hands greeting them at the station, no banks of gayly dressed ladies waving handkerchiefs and shouting "Bravo!" as they came in on the caboose of a freight train into the towns that had cheered and blared at them on their way to war. As they stood at the station, the loafers looked at them indifferently. Their blue coats, dusty and grimy, were too familiar now to excite notice, much less a friendly word. They were the last of the army to return, and the loafers were surfeited with such sights.

The train jogged forward so slowly that it seemed likely to be midnight before they should reach La Crosse. The little squad grumbled and swore, but it was no use; the train would not hurry, and, as a matter of fact, it was nearly two o'clock when the engine whistled "down brakes."

All of the group were farmers, living in districts several miles out of the town, and all were poor.

"Now, boys," said Private Smith, he of the fever and ague, "we are landed in La Crosse in the night. We've got to stay somewhere till mornin'. Now I ain't got no two dollars to waste on a hotel. I've got a wife and children, so I'm goin' to roost on a bench and take the cost of a bed out of my hide."

"Same here," put in one of the other men. "Hide'll grow on again, dollars'll come hard. It's going to be mighty hot skirmishin' to find a dollar these days."

"Don't think they'll be a deptuation of citizens waitin' to 'scort us to a hotel, eh?" said another. His sarcasm was too obvious to require an answer.

Smith went on, "Then at daybreak we'll start for home—at least, I will."

"Well, I'll be dummed if I'll take two dollars out o' *my* hide," one of the younger men said. "I'm goin' to a hotel, ef I don't never lay up a cent."

"That'll do f'r you," said Smith; "but if you had a wife an' three young uns dependin' on yeh—"

"Which I ain't, thank the Lord! and don't intend havin' while the court knows itself."

The station was deserted, chill, and dark, as they came into it at exactly a quarter to two in the morning. Lit by the oil lamps that flared a dull red light over the dingy benches, the waiting room was not an inviting place. The younger man went off to look up a hotel, while the rest remained and prepared to camp down on the floor and benches. Smith was attended to tenderly by the other men, who spread their blankets on the bench for him, and, by robbing themselves, made quite a comfortable bed, though the narrowness of the bench made his sleeping precarious.

It was chill, though August, and the two men, sitting with bowed heads, grew stiff with cold and weariness, and were forced to rise now and again and walk about to warm their stiffened limbs. It did not occur to them, probably, to contrast their coming home with their going forth, or with the coming home of the generals, colonels, or even captains—but to Private Smith, at any rate, there came a sickness at heart almost deadly as he lay there on his hard bed and went over his situation.

In the deep of the night, lying on a board in the town where he had enlisted three years ago, all elation and enthusiasm gone out of him, he faced the fact that with joy of home-coming was already mingled the bitter juice of care. He saw himself sick, worn out, taking up the work on his half-cleared farm, the inevitable mortgage standing ready with open jaw to swallow half his earnings. He had given three years of his life for a mere pittance of pay, and now!—

Morning dawned at last, slowly, with a pale yellow dome of light rising silently above the bluffs, which stand like some huge storm-devastated castle, just east of the city. Out to the left the great river swept on its massive yet silent way to the south. Bluejays called across the water from hillside to hillside through the clear, beautiful air, and hawks began to skim the tops of the hills. The older men were astir early, but Private Smith had fallen at last into a sleep, and they went out without waking him. He lay on his knapsack, his gaunt face turned toward the ceiling, his hands clasped on his breast, with a curious pathetic effect of weakness and appeal.

An engine switching near woke him at last, and he slowly sat up and stared about. He looked out of the window and saw that the sun was lightening the hills across the river. He rose and brushed his hair as well as he could, folded his blankets up, and went out to find his companions. They stood gazing silently at the river and at the hills.

"Looks natcher'l, don't it?" they said, as he came out.

"That's what it does," he replied. "An' it looks good. D' yeh see that peak?" He pointed at a beautiful symmetrical peak, rising like a slightly truncated cone, so high that it seemed the very highest of them all. It was touched by the morning sun and it glowed like a beacon, and a light scarf of gray morning fog was rolling up its shadowed side.

"My farm's just beyond that. Now, if I can only ketch a ride, we'll be home by dinner-time."

"I'm talkin' about breakfast," said one of the others.

"I guess it's one more meal o' hardtack f'r me," said Smith.

They foraged around, and finally found a restaurant with a sleepy old German behind the counter, and procured some coffee, which they drank to wash down their hardtack.

"Time'll come," said Smith, holding up a piece by the corner, "when this'll be a curiosity."

"I hope to God it will! I bet I've chawed hardtack enough to shingle every house in the coolly. I've chawed it when my lampers was down, and when they wasn't. I've took it dry, soaked, and mashed. I've had it wormy, musty, sour, and blue-mouldy. I've had it in little bits and big bits; 'fore coffee an' after coffee. I'm ready f'r a change. I'd like t' git holt jest about now o' some of the hot biscuits my wife c'n make when she lays herself out f'r company."

Well, if you set there gabblin', you'll never *see* yer wife."

"Come on," said Private Smith. "Wait a moment boys; less take suthin'. It's on me." He led them to the rusty tin dipper which hung on a nail beside the wooden water-pail, and they grinned and drank. Then shouldering their blankets and muskets, which they were "takin' home to the boys," they struck out on their last march.

"They called that coffee Jayvy," grumbled one of them, "but it never went by the road where government Jayvy resides. I reckon I know coffee from peas."

They kept together on the road along the turnpike, and up the winding road by the river, which they followed for some miles. The river was very lonely, curving down along its sandy beds, pausing now and then under broad basswood trees, or running in dark, swift, silent currents under tangles of wild grapevines, and drooping alders, and haw trees. At one of these lovely spots the three vets sat down on the thick green sward to rest, "on Smith's account." The leaves of the trees were as fresh and green as in June, the jays called cheery greetings to them, and kingfishers darted to and fro with swooping, noiseless flight.

"I tell yeh, boys, this knocks the swamps of Loueesiana into kingdom come."

"You bet. All they c'n raise down there is snakes, niggers, and p'rticler hell."

"An' fighting men," put in the older man.

"An' fightin' men. If I had a good hook an' line I'd sneak a pick'rel out o' that pond. Say, remember that time I shot that alligator——"

"I guess we'd better be crawlin' along," interrupted Smith, rising and shouldering his knapsack, with considerable effort, which he tried to hide.

"Say, Smith, lemme give you a lift on that."

"I guess I c'n manage," said Smith, grimly.

"Course. But, yo' see, I may not have a chance right off to pay yeh back for the times you've carried my gun and hull caboodle. Say, now, gimme that gun, anyway."

"All right, if yeh feel like it, Jim," Smith replied, and they trudged along doggedly in the sun, which was getting higher and hotter each half-mile.

"Ain't it queer ain't no teams comin' along," said Smith, after a long silence.

"Well, no, seein's it's Sunday."

"By jinks, that's a fact. It *is* Sunday. I'll git home in time f'r dinner, sure!" he exulted. "She don't hev dinner usually till about *one* on Sundays." And he fell into a muse, in which he smiled.

"Well, I'll git home jest about six o'clock, jest about when the boys are milkin' the cows," said old Jim Cranby. "I'll step into the barn, an' then I'll say: '*Heah*! why ain't this milkin' done before this time o' day?' An' then won't they yell!" he added, slapping his thigh in great glee.

Smith went on. "I'll jest go up the path. Old Rover'll come down the road to meet me. He won't bark; he'll know me, an' he'll come down waggin' his tail an' showin' his teeth. That's his way of laughin'. An' so I'll walk up to the kitchen door, an' I'll say, '*Dinner* f'r a hungry man!' An' then she'll jump up, an'——"

He couldn't go on. His voice choked at the thought of it. Saunders, the third man, hardly uttered a word, but walked silently behind the others. He had lost his wife the first year he was in the army. She died of pneumonia, caught in the autumn rains while working in the fields in his place.

They plodded along till at last they came to a parting of the ways. To the right the road continued up the main valley; to the left it went over the big ridge.

"Well, boys," began Smith, as they grounded their muskets and looked away up the valley, "here's where we shake hands. We've marched together a good many miles, an' now I s'pose we're done."

"Yes, I don't think we'll do any more of it f'r a while. I don't want to, I know."

"I hope I'll see yeh once in a while, boys, to talk over old times."

"Of course," said Saunders, whose voice trembled a little, too. "It ain't *exactly* like dyin'." They all found it hard to look at each other.

"But we'd ought'r go home with you," said Cranby. "You'll never climb that ridge with all them things on yer back."

"Oh, I'm all right! Don't worry about me. Every step takes me nearer home, yeh see. Well, good-by, boys."

They shook hands. "Good-by. Good luck!"

"Same to you. Lemme know how you find things at home."

"Good-by."

"Good-by."

He turned once before they passed out of sight, and waved his cap, and they did the same, and all yelled. Then all marched away with their long, steady, loping, veteran step. The solitary climber in blue walked on for a time, with his mind filled with the kindness of his comrades, and musing upon the many wonderful days they had had together in camp and field.

He thought of his chum, Billy Tripp. Poor Billy! A "minie" ball fell into his breast one day, fell wailing like a cat, and tore a great ragged hole in his heart. He looked forward to a sad scene with Billy's mother and sweetheart. They would want to know all about it. He tried to recall all that Billy had said, and the particulars of it, but there was little to remember, just that wild wailing sound high in the air, a dull slap, a short, quick, expulsive groan, and the boy lay with his face in the dirt in the ploughed field they were marching across.

That was all. But all the scenes he had since been through had not dimmed the horror, the terror of that moment, when his boy comrade fell, with only a breath between a laugh and a death-groan. Poor handsome Billy! Worth millions of dollars was his young life.

These sombre recollections gave way at length to more cheerful feelings as he began to approach his home coolly. The fields and houses grew familiar, and in one or two he was greeted by people seated in the doorways. But he was in no mood to talk, and pushed on steadily, though he stopped and accepted a drink of milk once at the well-side of a neighbor.

The sun was burning hot on that slope, and his step grew slower, in spite of his iron resolution. He sat down several times to rest. Slowly he crawled up the rough, reddish-brown road, which wound along the hillside, under great trees, through dense groves of jack oaks, with tree-tops far below him on his left hand, and the hills far above him on his right. He crawled along like some minute, wingless variety of fly.

He ate some hardtack, sauced with wild berries, when he reached the summit of the ridge, and sat there for some time, looking down into his home coolly.

Sombre, pathetic figure! His wide, round, gray eyes gazing down into the beautiful valley, seeing and not seeing, the splendid cloud-shadows sweeping over the western hills and across the green and yellow wheat far below. His head dropped forward on his palm, his shoulders took on a tired stoop, his cheek-bones showed painfully. An observer might have said, "He is looking down upon his own grave."

. . .

A man in a blue coat, with a musket on his back, was toiling slowly up the hill on the sun-bright, dusty road, toiling slowly, with bent head half hidden by a heavy knapsack. So tired it seemed that walking was indeed a process of falling. So eager to get home he would not stop, would not look aside, but plodded on, amid the cries of the locusts, the welcome of the crickets, and the rustle of the yellow wheat. Getting back to God's country, and his wife and babies!

Laughing, crying, trying to call him and the children at the same time, the little wife, almost hysterical, snatched her hat and ran out into the yard. But the soldier had disappeared over the hill into the hollow beyond, and, by the time she had found the children, he was too far away for her voice to reach him. And, besides, she was not sure it was her husband, for he had not turned his head at their shouts. This seemed so strange. Why didn't he stop to rest at his old neighbor's house? Tortured by hope and doubt, she hurried up the coolly as fast as she could push the baby wagon, the blue-coated figure just ahead pushing steadily, silently forward up the coolly.

When the excited, panting little group came in sight of the gate they saw the blue-coated figure standing, leaning upon the rough rail fence, his chin on his palms, gazing at the empty house. His knapsack, canteen, blankets, and musket lay upon the dusty grass at his feet.

He was like a man lost in a dream. His wide, hungry eyes devoured the scene. The rough lawn, the little unpainted house, the field of clear yellow wheat behind it, down across which streamed the sun, now almost ready to touch the high hill to the west, the crickets crying merrily, a cat on the fence near by, dreaming, unmindful of the stranger in blue——

How peaceful it all was. O God! How far removed from all camps, hospitals, battles lines. A little cabin in a Wisconsin coolly, but it was majestic in its peace. How did he ever leave it for those years of tramping, thirsting, killing?

Trembling, weak with emotion, her eyes on the silent figure, Mrs. Smith hurried up to the fence. Her feet made no noise in the dust and grass, and they were close upon him before he knew of them. The oldest boy ran a little ahead. He will never forget that figure, that face. It will always remain as something epic, that return of the private. He fixed his eyes on the pale face covered with ragged beard.

"Who *are* you, sir?" asked the wife, or, rather, started to ask, for he turned, stood a moment, and then cried:

"Emma!"

"Edward!"

The children stood in a curious row to see their mother kiss this bearded, strange man, the elder girl sobbing sympathetically with her mother. Illness had left the soldier partly deaf, and this added to the strangeness of his manner.

But the youngest child stood away, even after the girl had recognized her father and kissed him. The man turned then to the baby, and said in a curiously unparternal tone:

"Come here, my little man; don't you know me?" But the baby backed away under the fence and stood peering at him critically.

"My little man!" What meaning in those words! This baby seemed like some other woman's child, and not the infant he had left in his wife's arms. The war had come between him and his baby—he was only a strange man to him, with big eyes; a soldier, with mother hanging to his arm, and talking in a loud voice.

"And this is Tom," the private said, drawing the oldest boy to him. *"He'll* come and see me. *He* knows his poor old pap when he comes home from the war."

The mother heard the pain and reproach in his voice and hastened to apologize.

"You've changed so, Ed. He can't know yeh. This is papa, Teddy; come and kiss him—Tom and Mary do. Come, won't you?" But Teddy still peered through the fence with solemn eyes, well out of reach. He resembled a half-wild kitten that hesitates, studying the tones of one's voice.

"I'll fix him," said the soldier, and sat down to undo his knapsack, out of which he drew three enormous and very red apples. After giving one to each of the older children, he said:

"Now I guess he'll come. Eh, my little man? Now come see your pap."

Teddy crept slowly under the fence, assisted by the overzealous Tommy, and a moment later was kicking and squalling in his father's arms. Then they entered the house, into the sitting room, poor, bare, art-forsaken little room, too, with its rag carpet, its square clock, and its two or three chromos and pictures from *Harper's Weekly* pinned about.

"Emma, I'm all tired out," said Private Smith, as he flung himself down on the carpet as he used to do, while his wife brought a pillow to put under his head, and the children stood about munching their apples.

"Tommy, you run and get me a pan of chips, and Mary, you get the tea-kettle on, and I'll go and make some biscuit."

And the soldier talked. Question after question he poured forth about the crops, the cattle, the renter, the neighbors. He slipped his heavy government brogan shoes off his poor, tired, blistered feet, and lay out with utter, sweet relaxation. He was a free man again, no longer a soldier under a command. At supper he stopped once, listened and smiled. "That's old Spot. I know her voice. I s'pose that's her calf out there in the pen. I can't milk her to-night, though. I'm too tired. But I tell you, I'd like a drink of her milk. What's become of old Rove?"

"He died last winter. Poisoned, I guess." There was a moment of sadness for them all. It was some time before the husband spoke again, in a voice that trembled a little.

"Poor old feller! He'd 'a' known me half a mile away. I expected him to come down the hill to meet me. It 'ud 'a' been more like comin' home if I could 'a' seen him comin' down the road an' waggin' his tail, an' laughin' that way he has. I tell yeh, it kind o' took hold o' me to see the blinds down an' the house shut up."

"But, yeh see, we—we expected you'd write again 'fore you started. And then we thought we'd see you if you *did* come," she hastened to explain.

"Well, I ain't worth a cent on writin'. Besides, it's just as well yeh didn't know when I was comin'. I tell you, it sounds good to hear them chickens out there, an' turkeys, an' the crickets. Do you know they don't have just the same kind o' crickets down South? Who's Sam hired t' help cut yer grain?"

"The Ramsey boys."

"Looks like a good crop; but I'm afraid I won't do much gettin' it cut. This cussed fever an' ague has got me down pretty low. I don't know when I'll get rid of it. I'll bet I've took twenty-five pounds of quinine if I've taken a bit. Gimme another biscuit. I tell yeh, they taste good, Emma. I ain't had anything like it——Say, if you'd 'a' hear'd me braggin' to th' boys about your butter 'n' biscuits I'll bet your ears 'ud 'a' burnt.'

The private's wife colored with pleasure. "Oh, you're always a braggin' about your things. Everybody makes good butter."

"Yes; old lady Snyder, for instance."

"Oh, well, she ain't to be mentioned. She's Dutch."

"Or old Mis' Snively. One more cup o' tea. Mary. That's my girl! I'm feeling better already. I just b'lieve the matter with me is, I'm *starved.*"

This was a delicious hour, one long to be remembered. They were like lovers again. But their tenderness, like that of a typical American family, found utterance in tones, rather than in words. He was praising her when praising her biscuit, and she knew it. They grew soberer when he showed where he had been struck, one ball burning the back of his hand, one cutting away a lock of hair from his temple, and one passing through the calf of his leg. The wife shuddered to think how near she had come to being a soldier's widow. Her waiting no longer seemed hard. This sweet, glorious hour effaced it all.

Then they rose, and all went out into the garden and down to the barn.

He stood beside her while she milked old Spot. They began to plan fields and crops for next year.

His farm was weedy and encumbered, a rascally renter had run away with his machinery (departing between two days), his children needed clothing, the years were coming upon him, he was sick and emaciated, but his heroic soul did not quail. With the same courage with which he had faced his Southern march he entered upon a still more hazardous future.

Oh, that mystic hour! The pale man with big eyes standing there by the well, with his young wife by his side. The vast moon swinging above the eastern peaks, the cattle winding down the pasture slopes with jangling bells, the crickets singing, the stars blooming out sweet and far and serene; the katydids rhythmically calling, the little turkeys crying querulously, as they settled to roost in the poplar tree near the open gate. The voices at the well drop lower, the little ones nestle in their father's arms at last, and Teddy falls alseep there.

The common soldier of the American volunteer army had returned. His war with the South was over, and his fight, his daily running fight with nature and against the injustice of his fellowmen, was begun again.

Reading 40

Gone with the Wind

Margaret Mitchell

No matter how difficult it was for the Union soldier to reach home, he was far more fortunate than his Southern counterpart, for at least the Northerner was returning home victorious. The Confederate veteran had to make his trek home, defeated and frequently without boots. Usually, he walked because many of the Southern railroads had been destroyed during the war. And, when he reached his destination, he often found his home town destroyed by the ravages of war, his farm buildings in a state of collapse or near-collapse, his fields in weeds, his livestock gone or dead, and perhaps even his loved ones missing. This tragedy is seen in this selection.

In that warm summer after peace came, Tara suddenly lost its isolation. And for months thereafter a stream of scarecrows, bearded, ragged, footsore and always hungry, toiled up the red hill to Tara and came to rest on the shady front steps, wanting food and a night's lodging. They were Confederate soldiers walking home. The railroad had carried the remains of Johnston's army from North Carolina to Atlanta and dumped them there, and from Atlanta they began their pilgrimages afoot. When the wave of Johnston's men had passed, the weary veterans from the Army of Virginia arrived and then men from the Western troops, beating their way south toward homes which might not exist and families which might be scattered or dead. Most of them were walking, a few fortunate ones rode bony horses and mules which the terms of the surrender had permitted them to keep, gaunt animals which even an untrained eye could tell would never reach far-away Florida and south Georgia.

Going home! Going home! That was the only thought in the soldiers' minds. Some were sad and silent, others gay and contemptuous of hardships, but the thought that it was all over and they were going home was the one thing that sustained them. Few of them were bitter. They left bitterness to their women and their old people. They had fought a good fight, had been licked and were willing to settle down peaceably to plowing beneath the flag they had fought.

Going home! Going home! They could talk of nothing else, neither battles nor wounds, nor imprisonment nor the future. Later, they would refight battles and tell children and grandchildren of pranks and forays and charges, of hunger, forced marches and wounds, but not now. Some of them lacked an arm or a leg or an eye, many had scars which would ache in rainy weather if they lived for seventy years but these seemed small matters now. Later it would be different.

Old and young, talkative and taciturn, rich planter and sallow Cracker, they all had two things in common, lice and dysentery. The Confederate soldier was so accustomed to his verminous state he did not give it a thought and scratched unconcernedly even in the presence of ladies. As for dysentery —the "bloody flux" as the ladies delicately called it—it seemed to have spared no one from private to general. Four years of half-starvation, four years of rations which were coarse or green or half-putrefied, had done its work with them and every soldier who stopped at Tara was either just recovering or was actively suffering from it.

"Dey ain' a soun' set of bowels in de whole Confedrut ahmy," observed Mammy darkly as she sweated over the fire, brewing a bitter concoction of blackberry roots which had been Ellen's sovereign remedy for such afflictions. "It's mah notion dat 'twarn't de Yankees whut beat our gempmum. 'Twuz dey own innards. Kain no gempmum fight wid his bowels tuhnin' ter water."

One and all, Mammy dosed them, never waiting to ask foolish questions about the state of their organs and, one and all, they drank her doses meekly and with wry faces, remembering, perhaps, other stern black faces in far-off places and other inexorable black hands holding medicine spoons.

In the matter of "Comp'ny" Mammy was equally adamant. No lice-ridden soldier should come into Tara. She marched them behind a clump of thick bushes, relieved them of their uniforms, gave them a basin of water and strong lye soap to wash with and provided them with quilts and blankets to cover their nakedness, while she boiled their clothing in her huge wash pot. It was useless for the girls to argue hotly that such conduct humiliated the soldiers. Mammy replied that the girls would be a sight more humiliated if they found lice upon themselves

When the soldiers began arriving almost daily, Mammy protested against their being allowed to use the bedrooms. Always she feared lest some louse had escaped her. Rather than argue the matter, Scarlett turned the parlor with its deep velvet rug into a dormitory. Mammy cried out equally loudly at the sacrilege of soldiers being permitted to sleep on Miss Ellen's rug but Scarlett was firm. They had to sleep somewhere. And, in the months after the surrender, the deep soft nap began to show signs of wear and finally the heavy warp and woof showed through in spots where heels had worn it and spurs dug carelessly.

Reading 41

Bricks without Straws

Albion Tourgee

With Reconstruction came the desire to assist the newly freed blacks in the South. One of the progressive proposals was free public education for all. In many cases blacks and poor whites went to school for the first time. Despite this and other accomplishments, however, the tasks facing blacks were often beyond their talents because they did not receive the education and other assistance they needed from the federal government to aid their transition from slavery to freedom. Instead, they were expected to "make bricks without straws." Tourgee, an Ohio-born carpetbagger active in North Carolina politics, wrote several novels based upon his experiences in the South.

From *Bricks without Straws* by Albion Tourgee. Published in 1880.

Two days afterward, Mollie Ainslie took the train for the North, accompanied by Lugena and her children. At the same time went Captain Pardee, under instructions from Hesden Le Moyne to verify the will, discover who the testator really was, and then ascertain whether he had any living heirs.

To Mollie Ainslie the departure was a sad farewell to a life which she had entered upon so full of abounding hope and charity, so full of love for God and man, that she could not believe that all her bright hopes had withered and only ashes remained. The way was dark. The path was hedged up. The South was "redeemed."

The poor, ignorant white man had been unable to perceive that liberty for the slave meant elevation to him also. The poor, ignorant colored man had shown himself, as might well have been anticipated, unable to cope with intelligence, wealth, and the subtle power of the best trained political intellects of the nation; and it was not strange. They were all alone, and their allies were either as poor and weak as themselves, or were handicapped with the brand of Northern birth. These were their allies—not from choice, but from necessity. Few, indeed, were there of the highest and the best of those who had fought the nation in war as they had fought against the tide of liberty before the war began—who would accept the terms on which the nation gave re-established and greatly-increased power to the States of the South.

So there were ignorance and poverty and a hated race upon one side, and, upon the other, intelligence, wealth, and pride. The former *outnumbered* the latter; but the latter, as compared with the former, were a Grecian phalanx matched against a scattered horde of Scythian bowmen. The Nation gave the jewel of liberty into the hands of the former, armed them with the weapons of self government, and said: "Ye are many; protect what ye have received." Then it took away its hand, turned away its eyes, closed its ears to every cry of protest or of agony, and said: "We will not aid you nor protect you. Though you are ignorant, from you will we demand the works of wisdom. Though you are weak, great things shall be required at your hands." Like the ancient taskmaster, the Nation said: *"There shall no straw be given you, yet shall ye deliver the tale of bricks."*

But, alas! they were weak and inept. The weapon they had received was two-edged. Sometimes they cut themselves; again they caught it by the blade, and those with whom they fought seized the hilt and made terrible slaughter. Then, too, they were not always wise—which was a sore fault, but not their own. Nor were they aways brave, or true—which was another grievous fault; but was it to be believed that one hour of liberty would efface the scars of generations of slavery? Ah! well might they cry unto the Nation, as did Israel unto Pharaoh: "There is no straw given unto thy servants, and they say to us, 'Make brick': and behold thy servants are beaten; but the fault is in thine own people." They had simply demonstrated that in the years of Grace of the nineteenth century liberty could not be maintained nor prosperity achieved by ignorance and poverty, any more than in the days of Moses adobe bricks could be made without straw. The Nation gave the power of the South into the hands of ignorance and poverty and inexperience, and then demanded of them the fruit of intelligence, the strength of riches, and the skill of experience. It put before a keen-eyed and unscrupulous minority—a minority proud, aggressive, turbulent, arrogant, and scornful of all things save their own will and pleasure —the temptation to enhance their power by seizing that held by the trembling hands of simple-minded and unskilled guardians. What wonder that it was ravished from their care?

Mollie Ainslie thought of these things with some bitterness. She did not doubt the outcome. Her faith in truth and liberty, and her proud confidence in the ultimate destiny of the grand Nation whose past she had worshiped from childhood, were too strong to permit that. She believed that some time in the future light would come out of the darkness; but between then and the present was a great gulf, whose depth of horror no man knew, in which the people to serve whom she had given herself must sink and suffer—she could not tell how long. For them there was no hope.

She did not, indeed, look for a continuance of the horrors which then prevailed. She knew that when the incentive was removed the acts would cease. There would be peace, because there would no longer be any need for violence. But she was sure there would be no real freedom, no equality of right, no certainty of justice. She did not care who ruled, but she knew that this people —she felt almost like calling them *her* people—needed the incentive of liberty, the inspiriting rivalry of open and fair competition, to enable them to rise. Ay, to prevent them from sinking lower and lower. She greatly feared that the words of a journal which gloried in all that had been done toward abbreviating and annulling the powers, rights, and opportunities of the recent slaves might yet become verities if these people were deprived of such incentives. She remembered how deeply-rooted in the Southern mind was the idea that slavery was a social necessity. She did not believe, as so many had insisted, that it was founded merely in greed. She believed that it was with sincere conviction that a leading journal had declared: "The evils of free society are insufferable. Free society must fail and give way to a *class society*—a social system old as the world, universal as man."

She knew that the leader of a would-be nation had declared: "A thousand must die as slaves or paupers in order that one gentleman may live. Yet they are cheap to any nation, even at that price."

So she feared that the victors in the *post-bellum* strife which was raging around her would succeed, for a time at least, in establishing this ideal "class society." While the Nation slumbered in indifference, she feared that these men, still full of the spirit of slavery, in the very name of law and order, under the pretense of decency and justice, would re-bind those whose feet had just begun to tread the path of liberty with shackles only less onerous than those which had been dashed from their limbs by red-handed war. As she thought of these things she read the following words from the pen of one who had carefully watched the process of "redemption," and had noted its results and tendency—not bitterly and angrily, as she had done, but coolly and approvingly:

"We would like to engrave a prophecy on stone, to be read of generations in the future. The Negro, in these [the Southern] States, will be slave again or cease to be. His sole refuge from extinction will be in slavery to the white man."

She remembered to have heard a great man say, on a memorable occasion, that "the forms of law have always been the graves of buried liberties." She feared that, under the "forms" of *subverted* laws, the liberties of a helpless people would indeed be buried. She had little care for the Nation. It was of those she had served and whose future she regarded with such engrossing interest that she thought. She did not dream of remedying the evil. That was beyond her power. She only thought she might save some from its scath. To that she devoted herself.

The day before, she had visited the cemetery where her brother's ashes reposed. She had long ago put a neat monument over his grave, and had herself supplemented the national appropriation for its care. It was a beautiful inclosure, walled with stone, verdant with soft turf, and ornamented with rare shrubbery. Across it ran a little stream, with green banks sloping either way. A single great elm drooped over its bubbling waters. A pleasant drive ran with easy grade and graceful curves down one low hill and up another. The iron gate opened upon a dusty highway. Beside it stood the keeper's neat brick lodge. In front, and a little to the right, lay a sleepy Southern town half hidden in embowering trees. Across the little ravine within the cemetery, upon the level plateau, were the graves, marked, in some cases, by little square white mounuments of polished marble, on which was but the single word, "Unknown." A few bore the names of those who slept below. But on one side there were five long mounds, stretching away, side by side, as wide as the graves were long, and as long as four score graves. Smoothy rounded from end to end, without a break or a sign, they seemed a fit emblem of silence. Where they began, a granite pillar rose high, decked with symbols of glory interspersed with emblems of mourning. Cannon, battered and grim, the worn-out dogs of war, gaped with silent jaws up at the silent sky. No name was carved on base or capital, nor on the marble shield upon the shaft. Only, "Sacred to the memory of the unknown heroes who died——."

How quick the memory fills out the rest! There had been a military prison of the Confederacy just over the hill yonder, where the corn now grew so rank and thick. Twelve thousand men died there and were thrown into those long trenches where are now heaped-up mounds that look like giants' graves—not buried one by one, with coffin, shroud, and funeral rite, but one upon another heaped and piled, until the yawning pit would hold no more. No name was kept, no grave was marked, but in each trench was heaped one undistinguishable mass of dead humanity!

Reading 42

A Fool's Errand

Albion Tourgee

Tourgee was very pessimistic about results of Reconstruction and described the efforts of the North to superimpose its values upon the South as "a fool's errand." Tourgee also stressed the fact that the two sections of the country represented two separate and distinctive societies and suggested that they were going to remain that way indefinitely.

It was shortly after the rupture of his home-life and his departure from Warrington, that Servosse visited, by special invitation, Doctor Enos Martin, the ancient friend who had been at first his instructor, and afterward his revered and trusted counselor. In the years which had elapsed since the Fool had seen him, he had passed from a ripe manhood of surpassing vigor into that riper age which comes without weakness, but which, nevertheless, brings not a little of philosophic calm,—that true "sunset of life which gives mystical lore." It is in those calm years which come before the end, when ambition is dead and aspiration ceases; when the restless clamor of busy life sweeps by unheeded as the turmoil of the crowded thoroughfare by the busy worker; when the judgment acts calmly, unbiased by hope or fear,—it is in these declining years that the best work of the best lives is usually done. The self which makes the balance waver is dead; but the heart, the intellect, the keen sympathy with that world which is fast slipping away, remain, and the ripened energies act without the wastefulness of passion. It was in this calm brightness which precedes the twilight, that Enos Martin sat down to converse with the

From *A Fool's Errand* by Albion Tourgee. Published in 1879.

man, now rugged and mature, whom he had watched while he grew from youth into manhood, and from early manhood to its maturity. A score of years had passed since they had met. To the one, these years had been full of action. He had been in the current, had breasted its bufferings, and been carried away out of the course which he had marked out for himself on life's great chart, by its cross-currents and counter-eddies. He had a scar to show for every struggle. His heart had throbbed in harmony with the great world-pulse in every one of the grand purposes with which it had swelled during those years. The other had watched with keenest apprehension those movements which had veered and whirled about in their turbid currents the life of the other, himself but little moved, but ever seeking to draw what lessons of value he might from such observation, for the instruction and guidance of other young souls who were yet but skirting the shore of the great sea of life.

This constant and observant interest in the great social movements of the world which he overlooked from so serene a height had led him to note with peculiar care the relations of the nation to the recently subjugated portion of the South, and more especially the conditions of the blacks. In so doing, he had been led to consider especially that transition period which comes between Chattelism, or some form of individual subordination and dependence, and absolute individual autonomy. This is known by different names in different lands and ages,—villenage in England, serfdom in Russia. In regard to this, his inquiries had been most profound, and his interest in all those national questions had accordingly been of the liveliest character: hence his keen desire to see his old pupil, and to talk with one in whom he had confidence as an observer, in regard to the phenomena he had witnessed and the conclusions at which he had arrived, and to compare the same, not only with his own more remote observations, but also with the facts of history. They sat together for a long time in the library where the elder had gathered the intellectual wealth of the world and the ages, and renewed the personal knowledge of each other which a score of years had interrupted. The happenings of the tumultuous life, the growth of the quiet one, were both recounted; and then their conversation drifted to that topic which had engrossed so much of the thought of both,— that great world-current of which both lives were but unimportant incidents.

"And so," said the elder gravely, "you think, Colonel Servosse, that what has been termed Reconstruction is a magnificent failure?"

"Undoubtedly," was the reply, "so far as concerns the attainment of the result intended by its projectors, expected by the world, and to be looked for as a logical sequence of the war."

"I do not know that I fully understand your limitation," said Martin doubtfully.

"I mean," said the younger man, "that Reconstruction was a failure so far as it attempted to unify the nation, to make one people in fact of what had been one only in name before the convulsion of civil war. It was a failure, too, so far as it attempted to fix and secure the position and rights of the colored race. They were fixed, it is true, on paper, and security of a certain sort taken to prevent the abrogation of that formal declaration. No guaranty whatever was provided against their practical subversion, which was accomplished with an ease and impunity that amazed those who instituted the movement."

"You must at least admit that the dogma of 'State Rights' was settled by the war and by that system of summary and complete national control over the erring commonwealths which we call Reconstruction," said Martin.

"On the contrary," answered Servosse, "the doctrine of 'State Rights' is altogether unimpaired and untouched by what has occurred, except in one particular; to wit, *the right of peaceable secession.* The war settled that. The Nation asserted its right to defend itself against disruption."

"Did it not also assert its right to re-create, to make over, to reconstruct?" asked the elder man.

"Not at all," was the reply. "Reconstruction was never asserted *as a right,* at least not formally and authoritatively. Some did so affirm; but they were accounted visionaries. The act of reconstruction was *excused* as a necessary sequence of the failure of attempted secession: it was never defended or promulgated as a *right of the nation,* even to *secure its own safety.*"

"Why, then, do you qualify the declaration of failure?" asked Martin. "It seems to me to have been absolute and complete."

"Not at all," answered Servosse with some vehemence." A great deal was gained by it. Suppose a child does wrong a hundred times, is reproved for it each time, and only at the last reproof expresses sorrow, and professes a desire to do better, and the very next day repeats the offense. The parent does not despair, nor count the repentance as nothing gained. On the contrary, a great step has been made: the wrong has been admitted, and is thereafter without excuse. Thenceforward, Nathan-like, the parent can point the offender to his own judgment on his own act. So Reconstruction was a great step in advance, in that it formulated a confession of error. It gave us a construction of 'we the people' in the preamble of our Federal Constitution which gave the lie to that which had formerly prevailed. It recognized and formulated the universality of manhood in governmental power, and, in one phase or another of its development, compelled the formal assent of all sections and parties."

"And is this all that has been gained by all these years of toil and struggle and blood?" asked the old man with a sigh.

"Is it not enough, my friend?" replied the Fool, with a reproachful tone. "Is not almost a century of falsehood and hypocrisy cheaply atoned by a decade of chastisement? The confession of error is the hardest part of repentance, whether in a man or in a nation. It is there the Devil always makes his strongest fight. After that, he has to come down out of the mountain, and fight in the valley. He is wounded, crippled, and easily put to rout."

"You do not regard the struggle between the North and the South as ended, then," said Martin.

"Ended?" ejaculated the Fool sharply. "It is just begun! I do not mean the physical tug of war between definitely defined sections. That is a mere incident of a great underlying struggle,—a conflict which is ever going on between two antagonistic ideas. It was like a stream with here and there an angry rapid, before the war; then, for a time, it was like a foaming cascade; and since then it has been the sullen, dark, but deep and quiet whirlpool, which lies below the fall, full of driftwood and shadows, and angry mutterings, and unseen currents, and hidden forces, whose farther course no one can foretell, only that it must go on.

> "The deepest ice that ever froze
> Can only o'er the river close:
> The living stream lies quick below,
> And flows—and can not cease to flow!"

"Do you mean to say that the old battle between freedom and slavery was not ended by the extinction of slavery?" asked the doctor in surpise.

"I suppose it would be," answered the Fool, with a hint of laughter in his tones, "if slavery *were* extinct. I do not mean to combat the old adage that 'it takes two to make a quarrel;' but that is just where our mistake—the mistake of the North, for the South has not made one in this matter—has been. We have *assumed* that slavery was dead, because we had a Proclamation of Emancipation, a Constitutional Amendment, and 'laws passed in pursuance thereof,' all reciting the fact that involuntary servitude, except for crime, should no more exist. Thereupon, we have thrown up our hats, and crowed lustily for what we had achieved, as we had a good right to do. The Antislavery Society met, and congratulated itself on the accomplishment of its mission, on having no more worlds to conquer, no more oppression to resist, and no more victims to succor. And thereupon, in the odor of its self-laudation, it dissolved its own existence, dying full of good works, and simply for the want of more good works to be done. It was an end that smacks of the millennium; but, unfortunately, it was farcical in the extreme. I don't blame Garrison and Phillips and yourself, and all the others of the old guard of abolitionists. It was natural that you should at least wish to try on your laurels while alive."

"Really, Colonel," said the old doctor laughingly, "you must not think that was our motive."

"Not confessedly, nor consciously of course," said the Fool. "Real motives are rarely formulated. I don't wonder, though, that men who had been in what our modern slang denominates the 'racket' of the antislavery reform should be tired. I fully realize that a life-time of struggle takes away a man's relish for a fight. Old men never become missionaries. Being in a conflict of ideas, they may keep up the fight till the last minute and the last breath. Old men have made good martyrs ever since Polycarp's day; but they don't long for martyrdom, nor advertise for it. If it is just as convenient to avoid it, they prefer to do so; and in this case they certainly deserved a rest, and more honor and glory than they will ever get, alive or dead.

"It was our fault,—the then youngsters who had just come out of the furnace-fire in which the shackles were fused and melted away from the cramped and shriveled limbs. We ought to have seen and known that only the shell was gone. Slavery as a formal state of society was at an end: as a force, a power, a moral element, it was just as active as before. Its conscious evils were obliterated: its unconscious ones existed in the dwarfed and twisted natures which had been subjected for generations to its influences,—master and slave alike. As a form of society, it could be abolished by proclamation and enactment: as a moral entity, it is as indestructible as the souls on which it has left its mark."

"You think the 'irrepressible conflict' is yet confronting us, then?" said Martin.

"Undoubtedly. The North and the South are simply convenient names for two distinct, hostile, and irreconcilable ideas,—two civilizations they are sometimes called, especially at the South. At the North there is somewhat more of intellectual arrogance; and we are apt to speak of the one as civilization, and of the other as a species of barbarism. These two must always be in conflict until the one prevails, and the other falls. To uproot the one, and plant the other in its stead, is not the work of a moment or a day. That was our mistake. We tried to superimpose the civilization, the idea of the North, upon the South at a moment's warning. We presumed, that, by the suppression of rebellion, the Southern white man had become identical with the Caucasian of the North in thought and sentiment; and that the slave, by emancipation, had become a saint and a Solomon at once. So we tried to build up communities there which should be identical in thought, sentiment, growth, and development, with those of the North. It was A Fool's Errand."

DATE DUE

SEP 3 '86			
JAN 26 '87			
FEB 11 88			
AP 26 '94			